To Celine,

Our wonderful French
assistant who was
adored by all.

Best wishes always,
Judy

# WHAT'S SHAKING THE SCHOOL
## A PRINCIPAL'S RETROSPECTIVE

JUDY BERTRAM TOMLINSON

Order this book online at www.trafford.com
or email orders@trafford.com

Most Trafford titles are also available at major online book retailers.

Printed in Victoria, BC, Canada.

ISBN: 978-1-4269-2835-2 (sc)
ISBN: 978-1-4269-2836-9 (hc)

Library of Congress Control Number: 2010902659

*Our mission is to efficiently provide the world's finest, most comprehensive
book publishing service, enabling every author to experience
success. To find out how to publish your book, your way, and have
it available worldwide, visit us online at www.trafford.com*

*Trafford rev. 3/31/10*

 www.trafford.com

**North America & international**
toll-free: 1 888 232 4444 (USA & Canada)
phone: 250 383 6864 ♦ fax: 812 355 4082

*To Gail, who brightened our schools,*

*and*

*to Ivy, Bailey, Mairin, Kai and Dillon,*
*who are working through them.*

# Contents

# FOREWORD

In May of 1990, all applicants for principal positions in the Victoria, British Columbia school district were required to describe, in written form, their vision for a school they might lead in an education system preparing for a new century. I bundled mine with the rest of my vitae and sent it to the selection committee:

*In many ways, school is a doorway to the rest of one's life: how a person views himself and his world, and even the extent of later success, may be shaped by the place we call school. It seems to me that as we move to the Year 2000, our educational system is becoming ready as never before to create programs that open doors for students prepared for a new century. However, programs alone will not be successful without the dynamics of the receptive, enlightened school itself.*

*I believe the administrative pyramid must be inverted and the principal seen as the ultimate helper and facilitator, the person leading change by empowering the collective and individual creativity of the people in that place to flourish. The teaching staff must focus on the individual learner's need to make choices and decisions as he or she moves comfortably through years that should nurture and excite. As a "community of learners," all people in the school setting should feel accepted for who they are and be excited about becoming better.*

Communication must be given a high priority in this school: an excellent network will underlie all the bureaucracy, the formal and informal evaluations, the motivation of all participants and the leadership and decision-making by staff, students and parents. The principal will be seen as the prime articulator of the vision and the school's most receptive listener.

I believe problem solving becomes easier in a school where peer coaching between staff members and between students is an accepted way to encourage success. Cooperative learning strategies will be used inside and outside the classrooms, and evaluation at all levels seen as an ongoing, participative process. An open culture that welcomes constructive input, the school will be proactive in asserting rather than defending its value in the community. Occasional newsletters to neighbors, seniors' teas, evening activities for parents and their children, and neighborhood clean ups are just a few examples of how the community may feel part of its neighborhood school. When problems do occur, this school's participants will be prepared with a basic understanding of conflict management and resolution. Its principal will accept ultimate responsibility for difficult decision-making.

Diversity will be part of the very ethos of this place. Within classes, children may focus on ancestral roots and share family memorabilia. On-going, whole-school activities such as Chinese New Year's cooking, multicultural week awareness, Canadian citizenship ceremonies and First Nations' pageants foster respect for other cultures. Integration of special needs children whenever possible and beneficial, and occasional "family" groupings of children of different ages celebrate differences.

The student should leave this school a successful problem solver and decision maker, a responsible person and a life-long learner. Hopefully, the world will seem one of endless possibilities and continuing self-discovery. The view will be a global one, and the student will be committed to the preservation of individual freedoms and caring for the planet.

As a student looks back upon the years in school, it must be with affection and nostalgia for that safe and stimulating environment *that allowed learning to be a personally meaningful and joyful experience.*

Although my piece reflects the idealism of the inexperienced, I still believe in its substance and direction. Getting to this place I envisioned in the early 1990's, while keeping my focus steady in an unsteady system, was—and is—the thing.

Why write about my professional journey? Why not leave for some place tropical, take up golf and forget it all?

When I retired, I was brimming over with my experiences and I needed some sort of catharsis before I could get on with life. I wanted to make sense of it all, to examine, digest and express those years in our school system and particularly the twelve that I spent as a principal. My daughter Angela had suggested that I keep a journal during that time to help decompress at the end of each day, so I had a good resource to draw upon. People I worked with often suggested I write a book and teachers gave me student work to include in it.

Unless a person has been in the role of a school principal, it is impossible to understand that job completely. I was a principal during a time of tremendous change, a time when the whole curriculum was being examined and affected by the "Year 2000" philosophy. This philosophy proposed that students should work at their own pace, in their own style of learning, in a cooperative rather than a competitive mode. Parents were becoming a force in the school system and so were unions. Students were often in the eye of the storms that gathered and blew around us, and yet just as often they seemed to be forgotten in the overall drama. There were few female principals, so for those of us new to the job *and* female, the challenges were even greater.

"I hope you write a *manual!*" a teacher said when I retired. This book is anything but a manual, nor is it meant to be a tribute to my own work; each principal has his or her own story. What I hope I have done, with candor and caring, is describe the players and the playing fields of our public school system as they affected me personally. I realize that I have, at times, pontificated a little, but only when I felt that something needed emphasis.

A good deal of my story describes the first year I spent as the principal of a Victoria school. However, I write with the hindsight of the twelve years in that role in *two* elementary schools, Margaret Jenkins and Doncaster, as well as teaching and other experiences in many more: I was a student in our district, and a parent. Most names have been changed, and I have compressed a few periods of time. Otherwise, here is what happened in that terribly engaging, frustrating and fulfilling time in my life.

*September, 2009.*

# ACKNOWLEDGEMENTS

Thanks to family and friends who never gave up asking about my book project, even when there were difficult, distracting challenges in my life. Two of the early supporters were my late father, a lifelong learner and my best teacher, and my late husband, Ken, who read some initial drafts and related them to his own teaching experiences. Gail Reed and her husband, Bey, have also been great supporters. Jacquie Van Campen was writing her own book when I began mine, and the initial process was so much fun with her in my life.

Heartfelt thanks to my friend, Mary Lou Gazeley, to my husband, Bob Tomlinson, and to my editor, Kate Wellburn, for creative, technical and moral support. Thanks to my daughter, Angela, for the idea of keeping a journal and for her work on the book's promotion, to her husband, Rajeev, for keeping the computer healthy, to my daughter, Stefany, for a lot of moral support, and to her husband, Jeff,  for perusing the part of the book dealing with the teachers' report card angst and relating to it. And thanks to my sister, Kathy, for her interest in all things we do creatively.

Our former Margaret Jenkins School custodian, John Flegel, kindly allowed his painting of the school to be on this book's cover, and the following helped with the *In Memoriam* page: Melodie Cohen, Cecilia Dishaw, Laureen Evans, Barrie Foster, Len Knoke, Bev Lenihan, Greg O'Connor, Kay Rogers, Doreen Shaughnessy, Connie Simpson and Marilyn Tomlinson. Thank you.

Two school communities were featured in this book: École Margaret Jenkins Elementary (Fairfield) and École Doncaster Elementary (Rowan). Thanks for the memories.

# 1   2001: "OH, PUT A SOCK IN IT!"

The retort hung in the air for awhile, faintly animating the faces at our table.

In the background, the most controversial of school trustees railed on. As educators, we were *failing our clients*. This evening, he charged, we had presented another harebrained scheme to distract attention from the raw truth: teachers were not teaching, principals were not leading, and students were not learning.

It had been a long day for school principals attending that meeting. I, for one, had been at work since 7:30 that morning, and there had been many difficult decisions to consider regarding the best interests of students. Resources were shrinking. Could we double the number of special needs students with one assistant and still be safe? A teacher was going on stress leave and I needed to ensure a good replacement. A child was acting out to the point that his very competent teacher was crumbling. They both needed support. Another child was being violent on the playground and abusive to his mother at home. He needed a psychiatric assessment. And we had a pooper who left interesting messages in a washroom. Just naughty or truly disturbed?

These annual dinner meetings with school trustees were organized as a venue for principals and district staff to talk in small groups around topics of interest. This year's hot item was "reconfiguration," the proposed reorganizing of schools into elementary school (kindergarten to grade five), middle school (grades six to eight), and high school (grades nine to twelve). Elementary schools presently included everyone from kindergarten to grade seven. There were no "middle" schools as such; only a few "junior secondaries" of varying grade groupings. Almost all principals were philosophically supportive of a change they believed would improve the district's graduation rate, and a number of them made excellent presentations during the evening.

By 9:30 p.m., cold sandwiches were turning into an uncomfortable, gaseous lump in my stomach. And a look at the time confirmed my fatigue. I had been working for fourteen hours, if you counted presently holding my facial muscles into their perky and interested position as work. My back ached, and none of my more scintillating colleagues were in the mix at our table.

Finally, the meeting drew to a close. One by one the trustees rose and thanked Victoria's principals for their hard work and enthusiasm regarding the proposed change to the district's organization. They promised to consider our proposal carefully. Then it was the notorious one's turn.

By now we all knew to brace ourselves when he spoke, but on this evening his harangue was particularly offensive. Once again, however, I was proud of my colleagues who could sit, poker-faced, through almost anything and keep their collective cool. The trustee's diatribe reached a crescendo punctuated by short jabs with his forefinger. Suddenly, another voice could be heard, a thin, exasperated but very clear voice wailing, "Oh, put a sock in it!"

Even in my numb condition I realized that someone at my table had succumbed. Here in this auditorium, amongst all the educational leaders of the school district and the trustees who employed them, someone had cracked. My dry, tired eyeballs swept the table sympathetically, searching for someone red in the face, head down, nervously doodling. *Poor devil, no wonder.* Unfortunately for me, another picture presented itself. The half-masted eyeballs of principals, vice principals, district staff and one trustee were looking back at *me* with tired amusement.

Was it a stumble in professional deportment or my younger, less compromised self emerging? Whatever it was, it was rather alarming. And so was the increasing pertinence of some of those emails with "useful work phrases":

- *Well, this day was a total waste of makeup!*
- *Back off! You're standing in my aura!*
- *I'm not tense, I'm just terribly, terribly alert!*
- *You sound reasonable. Time to up my medication!*
- *Don't bother me, I'm living happily ever after.*
- *Therapy is expensive. Popping bubble wrap is cheap. You choose.*

I *had* been hoarding bubble wrap, but there were other signs. I was growing and lightening my hair, and my power dressing was less powerful. I had even responded in very uncharacteristic fashion to some bemused staff members' minor complaints. "Tell it to someone who cares!" had to be an indication that there was more to come, more I might possibly regret. I still cared deeply about all aspects of my work, but I had more to do in my life.

It was time to retire.

## 2   SIZING THEM UP

I have a dear friend in the corporate world who would not have whimpered, "Oh put a sock in it!" and gone quietly into that exhausting night. Oh no. Fully packaged in an Armani suit and fortified with a thermos of something nice (Lapsang Souchong or even a reputable green tea), Mary Lou would have neatly severed the trustee from his train of thought and then derailed the whole off-kilter, offensive harangue. It would have been shredded with precise jabs of fact. And I don't believe she would have raised her voice at all: she would have stood, locked eyes with him, then calmly but forcefully proceeded. When I described my experience to her, the only comparable time she could recollect was when she had to meet with a group of males from an eastern country who did not feel "comfortable" dealing with female executives. A male staff member stood in for a while in his own nifty suit, but the grinding of her teeth became a distraction, and in true Mary Lou fashion, she decided that her firm could do without their business. We were in different worlds.

I crawled into bed that night and lay thinking about my evening. I had been a principal for eleven years and had planned to work a few more. If I retired that June, 2001, there would be many things not wrapped up the way I had hoped. Perhaps that was part of a process of learning to let go: did it really matter if certain things were in place or not? Who would care in a year or two? Why was it that some people could simply detach for a weekend (or a lifetime) without needing to tie up all the loose ends? Principals came in all personalities; I knew that from my earliest days.

When I was a child I did not once announce, "I want to be a principal when I grow up!" A princess, perhaps, or a movie star. I played Jane to my neighborhood buddy's Tarzan and Dale Evans to his Roy Rogers. A principal was not at all how I saw myself.

The principal—or head teacher—of my small primary school was a rather dowdy little lady with bright blue eyes and tight curls close to her head. I knew those curls were always the same, because I counted them every day. Her mouth and nostrils were so tiny that I asked my parents how she could breathe through such small openings in her face. She was strict but kind, and a good basic teacher for my grade one and two years.

Vincent sat in front of me, and he and I regularly received reprimands for chatting during seatwork. He was a very interesting Chinese boy, and the fact that we had finished our work before we started chatting was irrelevant. We had been told: *No talking!* Nevertheless we continued to have our discussions about his passion, tropical fish, and mine, cowboys and cowgirls, resulting in the following comment on one of my first reports: *"Judith does very well in school but she talks too much."*

I did not have grade three, as such. Our teacher was *unsatisfactory*, and by the time my father had seen the principal over his concerns, he was informed that things would not go on as they were. We would have a new teacher after spring break, he was told.

That April, our newly appointed teacher bustled in and told us that she would do her best to make sure that we were "ready for grade four." It was quite a term, catching up. We had spent most of that school year copying printing from the huge slate blackboards that lined the front and side of our room. It took hours, made no sense to us, and was very hard on those with undeveloped small muscles. Another grade three teacher was directing the school's production of *Hansel and Gretel*, and when I was chosen to be

Gretel and went to her room for our first practice, I asked about the strange number configurations on the blackboard. It was long division. That teacher said she was shocked at what we had missed, and so was my father. At the end of the year, we were all passed along to grade four "with reservations," according to our new teacher. I remember being proud of our primary principal for making things they way they should be, and of my father, who always helped to make things right.

I liked it when someone "took the bull by the horns," as my mother put it, and faced up to and righted an unfair or difficult situation. I had tried to do that a number of times myself.

In grade two, for a few days, we had a substitute teacher. The poor woman was not aware of all the details of our routines and must have become tired of being corrected and directed by some of us. When I went home for lunch that day, I announced that my mother would *have* to return to school with me in order to tell this person that a few of us should *not* have to stay in after school. We were only trying to help, and it wasn't *fair!*

My mother was at full term in her second pregnancy and could hardly walk the distance to my school. She did not seem upset with me, however, and waddled into the classroom to the obvious consternation of the lady in question, who, after a rest and a good lunch, may have had second thoughts about remaining after school with a few earnest but annoying youngsters. My mother introduced herself politely and indicated she had heard some of us had to stay in after school.

"Oh, I never said they had to stay *in!*" the teacher responded, one hand flattened to her chest.

I was flabbergasted. "*You did, too!*" I shot at her, comfortably connected to my mother's side and riveted by the realization that adults, this one at least, would lie.

"I *didn't!*" she appealed to my mother, who smiled and told me she would pick me up after school. Mom wore the expression I always enjoyed: a kind of bemusement that made her face brighten. It was the same expression I saw when she told people I could recite the whole of *The Walrus and the Carpenter* at two years old. She also loved to add that my paternal grandmother considered my accomplishment a little alarming. "It isn't *natural*," my grandmother had told her.

"We don't have to stay in!" I informed the others after lunch, just before things were "clarified" for us by our substitute.

That evening, my mother began labor and my sister was born. She always claimed that her excessive walking that day "got things going." And the next morning, when order and sanity was restored with the return of our *proper* educator, I shared graphic details of my mother's beginning labor during "Show And Tell." I was hustled off to my maternal grandparents for two weeks while my mother and baby sister bonded, and although I was well cared for, I believe some of my only-child confidence began to dissolve at that time. I was a little frightened after leaving my mother, weeping, at the hospital, even though my father and grandparents tried to reassure me. Life had some terrible surprises, and although I considered my sister a prize, I thought my classmates should be alerted. Adults could be absent, and then others would not know how to run things. Or worse, they might lie. And there could be awful pain to go through when things had to be sorted out. There were things outside school and family, too, things you saw on the Movie Tone News: tanks and rubble and children crying. The war was over, was it not? Yes, but there was a new one now, which was why we were ducking under our seats during things called "drills."

I had to walk farther for grades four, five and six, to a very old brick school that no longer exists. My principal that first year was an ex-railway engineer in his last year before retirement. That possibly explains a decision he made which amazed, delighted and deeply impressed me with its daring.

"How many of you line up in single file when the bell rings?" he asked us in an autumn assembly.

We looked at each other. Of *course* we lined up, in our classes, single file. In some classes students had a correct *place* within the line, as well. Then we waited while monitors opened the doors and a teacher signaled our line up the steep steps. So we all raised our hands.

"Now I want to ask you another question," he carried on. "When you are out for a walk with your family, how many of you walk single file?"

We laughed hard and waited.

"Here's what I propose," he said. "You know how to walk safely, without getting in other people's way. When the bell goes and you see the doors are open, walk up those stairs carefully and quietly, straight to your classroom. How many of you think you can do that?"

Apparently, we all thought we could and that is what we did, at least for the remainder of that year, until single file was reinstated.

That happened with our next principal. He was tall, young and very much in charge. He liked order, and he was all over that school every day to make sure that things were humming; I know because I saw him in so many places. He was strict but fun, and in grade six we were lucky to have him as our math teacher. He also had a somewhat uncanny ability to cut short the delicious, non-curricular ramblings of the interesting lady who taught us the rest of the curriculum. I remember one fascinating topic cut short as so many were:

"I was in a grocery store on Quadra Street when the A bomb was dropped on Hiroshima. I heard it on the radio, and the owner said, (at this point our principal would stride in looking energetic and on task), *Hello, Mr. Main.* Do you need those marks now? There they are. Class, your papers will be due next Thursday, so you must work very hard to have them completed by that time. Make sure you have your name and the date on them before you give them to me." We would have a nod from our principal and then a quick scan of the room to make sure we looked on task ourselves.

Upon his departure, Mrs. Johnson would direct a frustrated look towards us and explain, "I don't want him to think I'm not teaching what I'm supposed to! Now, where were we?" This last bit would be said after Mr. Main had left the classroom and his footsteps had died away down the hall. He was in charge and was respected by his staff.

Mr. Main personally delivered his grade sixes to Junior High School on a late June day. We were met by that school's principal and a Student Council member. We had a grand tour and we were amazed: we had *lockers* and vast expanses of hallways, an enormous double gymnasium and rooms for woodworking, home economics and typing. There were music rooms, a proper auditorium and a thousand other students taught by a hand-picked staff. We were in awe of this principal, too, and although we whined occasionally because we were not allowed to wear make-up (all the girls in all the other junior high schools could, we had heard), we had a sense, even then, of his gift to his field.

After grade nine, our homeroom class dispersed to different high schools. My high school was very small and disappointing after those junior high years. Some of the staff seemed inordinately uninspired, and the principal was possibly the least inspired of all. He may have been a scholar—he had a worn, slightly befuddled look—but to my knowledge none of us knew where his educational passion lay. "MR. [Principal] LOVES BEER" was regularly painted on that school, a bland but disturbing monthly occurrence for the fellow. Despite the threats, no one was ever caught. According to the older students, it was a tradition, dating back to his first time there.

When this principal announced, in the spring of my grade twelve year, that students interested in writing scholarship exams could pick up application forms in the school office, I presented myself there. I was going to university and knew that any monetary awards would help. Although it was tempting to bypass final exams altogether—my marks would have exempted me—I was enjoying the subject matter of my final year and welcomed delving into it further.

In the office, our top two students had just picked up their forms. They were exceptionally bright young men, and our principal seemed uncharacteristically excited regarding their prospects.

He peered at me over the counter. "Yes, Judy?"

"I'm here to pick up the scholarship application form," I told him.

"You won't get one," he informed me. "You don't have A's in Math. Now those two…" he waved his hand toward the backs of a future NASA scientist and a Rhodes scholar.

"Well, I'm going to try," I said, taking the form that was reluctantly passed over to me.

I worked harder than I ever had in school, aced the exams, and won two scholarships. In retrospect I gave much thought to the pathology of leadership and to this irony: my motivation was at least partly fuelled by his doubt in me.


Principals came in all personalities, I thought as I pulled up my covers, and they could be forces for making things right. They wielded a certain power in my young years that fascinated me, and I never, ever, thought that one of them might need something like bubble wrap. But back then it hadn't been invented, and the job was so much simpler.

I curled into my fetal position and waited for the discomfort from cold sandwiches, coffee and frustration to subside. Mentally, I did my nightly checklist: appointments for the morning, a memo I needed to write, a colleague I needed to phone and a child I needed to see. I was meeting with the staff committee at noon and suspected there was a conflict. What was it? I briefly contemplated examining my leather organizer and then realized I couldn't remember if I had washed my face. I lay a while in a stupor, wondering what to wear in the morning. Then I thought about my career and how it had happened that after teaching for nine years, taking a degree in English literature and raising two daughters, I had chosen that path less taken.

# 3   THE LAUNCHING

I obviously thought I might have something to offer as a principal, but I am not sure if my original drive came from that child who loved to see adults "taking the bull by the horns." I remember dropping my application package in the mail eleven years before, wondering if I was ready.

A mentor had shown me a posting for a school I will call Moonwalk, a small "alternative" school I would not have considered on my own. Although the school had to meet certain curriculum standards, its approach was very different. "Reading and Massage," for example, was among the student combination of choices or "offerings" on a day I visited. Intensive parent involvement was fundamental to its operation and no student was pushed or even prodded, it seemed, into anything unappealing.

I knew there had been some drift away from measurable outcomes there, though many of the students did very well when they joined their "regular" counterparts for secondary education. Some experience in that environment might be rewarding and useful when planning for the more individual approach to student learning in the new Year 2000 curriculum, I thought. I thanked my mentor and read the application carefully. If nothing else, the application process would be interesting.

Moonwalk's principal was happy to show me around the campus, and although he was looking forward to the end of his tenure there, he obviously loved this school. And after he reassured me of Moonwalk's gentle glide to a more central skyscape, I decided to apply.

There were five components to that competition: a meeting with the Student Council, teaching a lesson of my choice, a morning meeting with some staff and parents, an evening meeting with the parents group and a formal interview.

I sat on the floor of the little gymnasium with a dozen students who asked the kind of questions I had anticipated:

"If you were our principal, would you give us candy for prizes?"

"Would we still be able to choose what we *want* to do *when* we want to do it?"

We had a respectful discussion about the need for involvement in decision making (they were all for it), and the responsibilities of adults who were there to help them be the best they could be (some dubiousness regarding the importance of these people to their learning). We discussed who, if anyone, was actually in charge of the school and its accomplishments (much grinning, perhaps their principal, but he was kind of like one of them, too, so they weren't really sure.)

After our meeting I taught an art class to a group who had chosen my offering of oil pastel clowns. We all seemed sorry when this session was over. I went back to my own class in my own school, sincerely impressed with the candor and friendliness of those kids. I didn't mind being called "Judy," and I considered how much fun I might have in such a small, relaxed place.

Early the next morning I entered Moonwalk's staffroom. A group of adults, mostly parents, sat in a circle with coffee mugs and cookies, and the principal asked me to begin by introducing myself. Tell them how you are feeling, he added. I smiled at some rather anxious-looking faces. "Well, I feel great! I enjoyed myself with Moonwalk students yesterday and I love the atmosphere here. It's so warm and friendly."

Somewhere to my left, convulsive sobbing followed a sharp intake of breath. A parent with long, straight hair had fallen onto the shoulder of a woman next to her and a staff member began massaging her back.

"But how do you *feel?*" asked another parent.

"I feel terrific," I said, wide-eyed at the spasms the others did not seem to notice. "Is there something wrong?" My question was ignored, and as the others let the group know how *they* were that morning, I realized that my fit with them was as neat as Mary Poppins at Woodstock. *They* were not feeling terrific; in fact, they claimed to feel apprehensive, fearful, sad, overwhelmed, exhausted, sick and a few more things. Perky was obviously wrong. Being enthusiastic was not too good either, I realized, and wearing a coordinated outfit probably did not help. They were very fond of the man who was their principal and a good match for their philosophy, and they had no intention of letting him go without considerable mourning. At least that was what I assumed was wrong, as they all seemed miserable.

That evening, a crowd of parents was waiting outside Moonwalk. I recognized one among the thirty or so, but no one introduced me.

"I hear the kids like her."

"Yeah, but she is definitely not one of us."

"Don't forget those questions we prepared."

"How could I?"

Finally, after someone arrived with a school key and we were all grouped three or four deep around a large extended table, I was asked to identify myself. Yes, I was there, I said, standing up and nodding. There was no indication of any chairperson and it had already taken an inordinate amount of time to arrange the furniture. I launched into a bit of my work experience as a teacher and a vice principal, ending with my enjoyment of their children the day before.

They began with questions regarding my teaching style, then the motives for my application. Fair enough, I thought. There were things I liked about this place despite the odd morning meeting. I was not going to hold back on expressing *my* ideas for change in their particular realm but, in the event, I did not have time to express them. A peripheral movement caught my eye, and I recognized one of our former trustees waving his arms as if conducting a symphony. Caught by my stare, he lowered them and fired off his own question: "What makes you think you can come into this community and be a good fit?"

It was not an encouraging question, one of those openers that allows time to express oneself, the most common being, "Tell us a little about yourself!" To me his volley sounded sarcastic, and it set off a range of questions for which no answers were expected or given. Finally I was asked if I knew of a certain organization. I did not. It was a group based upon self-expression, I was told. Most of them belonged and shared personal problems and feelings in a trustful atmosphere. Would I join if I were Moonwalk's principal? I certainly would not, I told them, after which someone—the former trustee, I believe—suggested that the meeting come to a close. The attack was over. I mingled over coffee and cookies, smiled and made small talk.

I actually enjoyed the District interview that followed, however. This interview involved trustees, some District staff and some *very* intense parents.

"My son was happy today, because he was allowed to learn to ride his new bike on the playground, instead of going inside and doing schoolwork," one of these Moonwalk parents challenged. "What do you think of *that*?"

"It's interesting you brought that up," I said. "My students didn't want to go outside at all, yesterday. They were so interested in a new project we started, I had to *insist* they get some fresh air! So, in answer to your question, choice and flexibility *are* vital components to a child's learning, and our Year 2000 philosophy is proposing that we include those elements when we teach our curriculum. But I would hope that educators are creating environments in which young people are fully engrossed in their classroom learning experiences. As it is, we have barely enough time to cover all that needs to be done with them."

"You may not be the best match for this school," the chairperson of the Board grinned at the end, "but I certainly hope you will be applying for a regular school soon." A year later, I did.

Maintaining poise under pressure was a strong attribute of mine during most of my career, according to numerous evaluation procedures. This was fortunate, because the interview for the principalship was usually a rigorous ordeal. It required steely nerves and an unshakable, clear and articulated belief in what made a good school. No cracks in one's façade or beliefs could be evident.

In June of 1990, four elementary principal positions in Victoria were advertised province-wide, two for large schools and two for small ones. A female colleague of mine claimed that I was the successful candidate for one of the large schools because I wore red. She also said that I wore a very short red skirt, though I am not sure how that would have affected the female interviewers, and none of my skirts were "very short." Officially, I was told that the reason for my success in that interview was my articulation of a clear and positive vision of school leadership to the trustees, district administrators, teachers, parents and union presidents who filled the board room on that hot June day. The call came the same evening, and I accepted the leadership of Fairfield School, a huge old dual-track (English and French Immersion) school in a rather affluent area of our city.

Immediately after the call, I had two almost simultaneous sensations. Elation was the first, followed by the feeling that I had, symbolically, given birth to thousands of tons of bricks. As it turned out, both sensations were accurate forecasters.

Family, friends and colleagues were excited for me, and my father announced that he had "never kissed a principal before." The staff at my current school, where I had been working as a vice principal, presented me with a burgundy leather desk set, and my husband and I celebrated in Vancouver, taking in *Les Miserables* and shopping for "principal" clothes. Looking broad-shouldered and capable could be a challenge, we thought, when a person is female and five feet one and a half inches tall. I bought two smart suits and a leather organizer.

Nothing could relieve the sensation of that thunderous weight of responsibility, however. Hours after I accepted the position and before it had been officially announced, a prominent district employee phoned to discuss enrolling his daughter there a year earlier than was officially allowed, a spontaneous dilemma for me. Another dilemma: the present principal and vice principal would be leaving before this school year was over; I was therefore expected to be in two places at once.

A few days later, that principal introduced me during an obviously tense Parent Advisory Council meeting as "the winner of the provincial competition for the principalship of this school!" He said a few words and then left the parents to their obvious disagreements. Later, in the privacy of his office, he went over the staff list while I made notes: master teacher/hard worker/not airhead...whole balloon/bewildered/needs encouragement, and so on. In spite of the frosty reception some of his parent group appeared to present to him, he informed me that this was the most wonderful job in the world and that I could keep the office furniture. On the downside, personnel planning for office staff seemed unworkable even with the stars in my eyes. The school secretary was to work half time and an accounting clerk had been hired to do the latter part of the day. Yet another problem, for as anyone in the system knows, a full-time secretary is vital to the good running of a school.

There was more to sort out. Two teachers had to be hired for September, and the neighbors were concerned about the imminent arrival of more portable classrooms that would block their view of the huge, shady trees ringing the grounds. A woman demanding a meeting with the new principal was threatening to throw herself in front of the portables before they could be installed. Five hundred and sixty students were expected to arrive that September to a school with a much smaller capacity, and no plan was in place to organize them on their first school day.

After some negotiating around the impossibility of being in two places at once, I officially arrived at Fairfield on the last Friday in June, the day after the students were dismissed for summer vacation. Teachers I had previously worked with had made a "Welcome Judy!" sign that was taped over the door to my office. I had the keys to the school, boxes that included the burgundy desk set and some small pictures. It was too warm to dress in one of my new suits.

My office was extraordinarily small, with one door to the outer reception area and an opposite door to the staff room. It had huge windows and almost no storage area, an old oak desk which was blocking the door to the staff room, two visitors' chairs, a small table, low shelving under the windows, a small bookcase and a two-drawer filing cabinet. This place could not be considered a comfortable sanctuary. But the view was wonderful, and it was, after all, mine for the duration. I could be close to the staff when they were relaxing in their space or doing preparation in the adjoining workroom, and I thought my physical accessibility would be a good thing. I decided I would have the desk moved away from the staffroom's door.

I was still a bit starry-eyed from the warm welcome and visions of collegiality when I met with the staff committee that afternoon. One teacher had warned me that they were "not as nice as they used to be," and I wondered if this was a sign of the hard-nosed unionism that was beginning to affect the administration of public schools. The group consisted of teachers and support staff and had a constitution similar to other places where I had worked. The atmosphere, however, was as tense as it had seemed at the Parent Advisory Council (PAC) meeting, and it was obvious that they had real concerns about their school and its needs. There was unpleasant history here too, I thought.

The meeting began. The chairperson, a teacher they lauded for seeing them through some difficult times, seemed to enjoy her informal leadership role and offered to remain in her position for the coming year. Much relief was expressed over the notion that they would continue to have a "strong" person chairing their committee.

Luckily for my confidence, I had stupendous naïveté. I wanted the school to be the best it could be for students' learning. I wanted to support the staff, who would help make that happen, and I expected that we would have an exciting, close, collegial atmosphere in which to work. And while all of those good things would come about gradually, I had no idea of the forces that were beginning to work against the notion that good will and hard work would quickly and automatically result in trust. Like many of my colleagues, I had the *theory* to make things work but it would take the *practice* to hone my *sordes*-detecting skills to a fine art.

This meeting with the staff committee, therefore, was my first big test.

After a few questions regarding my general philosophy of leadership, our chairperson came to the point of the meeting. She took a noticeably deep breath and locked eyes with me. I was acutely aware that everyone leaned forward a little at this moment.

"Given the extra staffing which has been allocated to our school," she said, slowly, "what are you planning to do with the *point four*?"

I had studied our allocations carefully. We had a bit of time— the equivalent of 40% of a teacher's time, to be used as we saw fit. We were covered for library and technology (computer education had just begun in the district), but it looked to me as though there was a lack of expertise in music at the intermediate level. Being rather naïve, as I said, it did not occur to me that they might be suspecting a scoop of staffing points to ease the administrative load. An extra "point four" given to a vice principal, for example, would free that person from teaching duties while someone else taught in his classroom. I told them I believed that the hiring of a part-time music teacher for intermediate classes would be necessary in order for me to fulfill program requirements at that level.

There was a perceptible sagging from relief around that table, although I was not sure that the committee Chair was convinced. I didn't dwell on any doubts that beautiful June day, however. Summer was beginning, and I was launched.

"Keep a journal," my elder daughter suggested. "So much will happen, and it's great for relieving stress."

I made one more preparatory purchase.

# 4  SUMMER 1990

Ah, summer: what a concept. When I was a teacher, it had stretched before me as an unbroken time to rest and rejuvenate, but this first year as principal, and for the rest of my career, it would be very different.

A new superintendent from out of the province had been appointed, and her work ethic would amaze us. She scheduled a meeting with each principal in his or her school during July and meetings at Central Office before September. Her memo stated that "shorts are mandatory," and so I wore them, feeling rather foolish sitting in the huge oak chair in my new office with my bare legs dangling in opposition to her panty-hosed, high-heeled lower extremities. I was so caught up in the contrast between the two of us that I had serious trouble articulating my goals for my school. I know I mumbled something about "warming up the atmosphere." She was very kind and encouraging.

The meeting with the Neighbors Against The New Portables was held. Mrs. Grymm, (early seventies and severely bunned, eyes glaring and lips tightly compressed), reiterated her intention to put herself at risk if the proposed portables were hauled onto the school site. Two other women and a gentleman with her accepted tea and cookies and listened politely to the district's facilities' coordinator explain why we could not refuse to register growing numbers of children at their neighborhood school. Mrs.

Grymm kept up a letter-writing campaign all that summer, and on the day in August when the portables were put in place, I half expected the picture of a bloodied, maimed body splashed over the front of our newspaper with a caption reading something like, "PRINCIPAL'S INDIFFERENCE CAUSES GRYMM DEATH."

Of course she was not injured during the installation, but would glower pointedly at my attempts to be friendly if our paths crossed. Three years later, as she walked across our playground, I did have the opportunity to inform her that her "view" would be reinstated. Our enrollment had dropped, and the portables would be removed that summer. "Waste of money," she hissed, eyes squinting against the March wind and shopping bag clutched tightly to her chest. To give her credit, almost seven years after the installation of those portables I knocked on her door in something of a panic. Our kids had seen a badly injured raccoon in her yard, and I had witnessed the poor creature hobble around to the back of her house. When I told her of its plight, I saw the first change in her countenance in all the time we had been acquainted. Her eyes softened and she told me she would phone the SPCA immediately.

Some upbeat things happened that summer. A vice principal colleague was appointed to the school. Greg and I had worked together as administrative assistants and I was delighted to have him as part of the team. He was steady, well organized and had a wicked sense of humor that he used regularly to relieve work-related tension. Together that summer we interviewed three talented young women for the part-time position that was open.

Interviewing potential staff members as a principal was not quite the same as it had been on those committees when I was not ultimately responsible. I had watched people give great interviews then perform disappointingly, and I was convinced candidates had to feel comfortable enough to talk about themselves freely. The questioning techniques needed to be carefully worked out ahead of time. If done well, the unsuitable candidate would sometimes pull out of the competition; listening to his or her own responses to an assignment's requirements was often enough.

Greg and I were well prepared for the three suitable young women we interviewed on one August afternoon. Following a format we used over seven years, he took notes of each response and we had a brief conference after each interview. And when the first two were done, we felt extremely lucky. Either candidate would be an asset to any school, and seniority was not a factor as all were new to the district.

Then we interviewed Laurie. She had an electrically alive yet vulnerable face, a background that more than met our needs, and fresh, fascinating ideas for teaching in that assignment. It all added up: the background, the best letters of reference, and the best responses. The new principal and vice principal of Fairfield congratulated themselves on their thoughtful choice of the best candidate and felt a little smug regarding the process. We were pumped.

Years later, Laurie told me that our custodian had calmed her down as she paced the hall before her interview. "Don't worry," he said, grandly. "I've seen them all come and go. You've got the job."

I had a wonderful encounter with three siblings about ten, eight and six years old.

"Can we meet the new principal? We heard she's here and she's a *girl*!"

"Of course you can," I cried out from my office, eager for the sight of young faces and not waiting for the school secretary's response. Three peach-faced little characters scrambled in, rosy from their summer and freedom. I knew they were bursting with curiosity and the need to be the first to set eyes on me. This story would give them a lot of attention.

"Wow," said the eldest, a girl going into grade four, I suspected. "You really *are* a girl!"

The middle child, a serious but friendly boy, put out his hand. "Welcome to our school," he said politely.

"You look nice," the youngest said, slurping on her thumb.

Could they all be as lovely, I wondered. People who work with children wonder and worry a little about their relationship with a new group of students. As principal in a new school, these relationships would be a vital key to success in the job, as respect for the person and the position is usually reflected in the general respect for the school as a whole and for its expectations.

Bless your dear little hearts, I thought. "You're the first Fairfield students I've met," I told them. "This is very special for me. Thanks for coming inside!"

Staff dribbled in after the middle of August. This was the time for me to visit one-on-one and find out as much as possible about each individual professional persona. Were they confident? Would they need extra support? Most wanted to talk about parents as their June experiences were relived.

"Watch out for Mrs. Standish! She's vicious!"

"Don't meet with Mr. Smith! He wants to run the school!"

"Mr. and Mrs. Taylor will insist their son be put ahead a grade. Don't do it!"

Some very nice parents introduced themselves, including the chairperson of the School Board who had her youngest on her hip. And although they all expressed optimism about the coming school year, I was growing more and more concerned over a number of issues. Our half-time secretary would obviously not be there when I needed her expertise in the afternoons. Teachers seemed vague about first day procedures, and if five hundred and sixty students reported to the gym at the same time, it would be chaotic. Letters were sent out to kindergarten parents, and lists of students with proposed classroom organizations were posted at each entrance. It was not my kind of organization, but it was the best I could do given the circumstances. Next year's school opening would be different.

On the last day in August everything was as ready as I could make it. The unknowns were daunting, but nothing more could be done. The following Tuesday morning I would have the first real sense of my match to this community. I said goodbye to the staff leaving for the Labor Day weekend and locked the door to my pristine office.

# 5   TRAINING GROUNDS

I should be ready, I had thought on that Labor Day weekend before classes were to begin again at Fairfield. I had had good mentors and preparation. After being a classroom teacher for nine years, I had been on administrative teams for seven years in two very different schools. I thought about my beginnings in each of these schools: as an "administrative assistant" in the first, and then as a vice principal in the second.

A teaching vice principal who is new to a school is subject to all the qualms a new teacher faces, and more. Will the students accept the style of teaching? Will the parents be supportive? Will the staff be collegial and will the principal be a transformational leader, one who brings out the leadership in others? The staff sizes up this principal-in-training and makes decisions based on organizational skills, rapport with students and staff, and general affability. Or on other things, depending on the culture of the place.

I was sent to my first administrative position as an "administrative assistant," a kind of educational New Age term for vice principal, except that there were two or three of these people in each school. Given the numbers on those teams, justified by central office as a way to give more teachers experience in administration, some of the "assistants" were affected by the increased amount of competition from their colleagues. They ran themselves ragged while vying very hard to be shortlisted for principalships. Although I was prepared to work hard, I was not, at this point, considering the top job. In this new position of mine there were two other male "admin asses," which was how our mail was addressed to us, and the term fit perfectly. We often pondered the workload we had added to our classroom teaching assignments *and* our decision to take it on in the first place.

The most senior of the three of us looked after some special events, safety patrols and intermediate curriculum. He had put considerable time into the school and was therefore poised, he believed—the teaching staff believed—for a principalship. "George is *so ready*," one of the school's matriarchs would sigh to her other staff members. All their bets were on George, and why not? They felt he was one of them. My other colleague arrived with three years experience in administration and was given the sports program to organize.

*I* was welcomed as a new administrative assistant by one of those matriarchs in the foyer on my first day. She told me that she had been part of its culture from the time the doors first opened. She then excused herself briefly, went into her classroom and returned with a large pile resembling a hotel room's bedding. "This is yours," she said, as she dumped the lot into my quickly outstretched arms. "Table displays need to be coordinated with the seasons. It's been done *so beautifully* by Jane." I staggered from the weight. "Gourds are nice in October," she added, and explained that the bulletin board behind the foyer table should also be decorated with my artwork and, of course, reflect the seasons. "It's important to coordinate the two and change it all monthly," was her parting shot. I shifted the pile onto the foyer's table and went to meet with my principal, thinking that the term "ass" was highly appropriate. I did the part of that decorating job that seemed appropriate to *me*: children's new artwork was displayed monthly, not my own. I also organized special events and looked after supplies, among other things, but I was considered something of a rebel by that staff, and not at all malleable.

"You should have agreed to decorate the foyer," a teacher told me much later. "We like things to stay the same." Our principal, however, liked my approach to the foyer's appearance.

By the time our most senior "ass" had moved along to another assisting position, I was teaching a class with a forty-minute-a-week spare for administration. The latter included looking after the textbooks, school patrols, primary curriculum, special events and much, much more. I was wearing myself out and would probably have given the extras up if I had stopped to take stock of more than the textbooks.

Four years later I had enjoyed some wonderful classes of students and had developed a thicker skin. I was not "one of the primary gals," however, and in my own classroom I adamantly refused to have any of my little boys wear the notorious pink shorts reserved by the others for those boys who forgot their gym strip. The principal, the other new administrative assistant and I developed a friendship despite being considered outsiders, and I came to like many of the other staff. We did not "gel" into that bonding which forms the basis for outstanding school culture, however; our philosophies around children and how they should be worked with in a school were just too different. Our administrative team watched what we said and where we said it, and the classroom provided most of the laughter and excitement for us. Our principal remained an effective leader in the face of all that was negative, and he remained an inspiration for the rest of my career.

By the time I arrived at my next school, the teachers' union had begun to be wary of the numbers of these administrative assistants who were, of course, operating outside their former union as "administrative officers," another term many of us detested. Some of us were chosen to be "vice principals." The size of the administrative teams in our schools began to shrink to what it had always been: a principal and a vice principal in an averaged-sized elementary school, and a principal and several vice principals in the larger secondary schools. I had no intention of applying for a principal position in this role either, but I rather enjoyed organizing school-wide activities, being part of the support team for students and staff, and working on the "whole picture" in addition to my classroom teaching.

During coffee break on a professional development day, this school seemed deserted. I followed the coffee aroma to the staff room, steeling myself a little against possible impending inquisitive stares, forced small talk and the request for some sort of introductory philosophical statement. Sitting in the wrong chair was probably a *faux pas*. I might be landed with more tablecloths and bulletin board decoration, I thought as I made my way through the office. I remembered the young teacher who had returned to my last school after a year's absence. "Same teachers, same chairs," she had said. "Scary." I knew what she meant.

I found the staffroom in the oddest location. It had apparently been the old school's gymnasium at one time.

"Hi!" The principal stood up. "Excuse me, everyone." A group of very animated people settled. "This is Judy Bertram."

"Welcome!"

"You're brave!"

"We're crazy, but you'll love us!"

They all went back to their lively conversations until a woman arrived carrying a covered sterling silver serving dish. The staff quieted themselves in obvious anticipation, watching her set the platter in front of another woman who was waiting with cutlery ready. Ceremoniously, the meal was revealed: a beautifully presented salad, topped with what appeared to be a large dildo.

"I want to thank you all for my birthday luncheon," the recipient said. "I just hope it's all fresh."

A little later that day I recognized a teacher who was making fresh coffee. Mavis had returned to the classroom after many years as a well-respected president of the local teachers' union. "Strong," I remarked on the coffee.

"Keeps us regular," she grinned.

Humor, compassion and a love for children set the tone in that school. I was mooned by the man who taught across the hall, laughed at by the secretary and cajoled into doing weird and wonderful things for third world countries by Mavis and one of her colleagues, Joy. No one could walk those hallways without hearing bursts of laughter or singing. Two teachers taught ukulele and the principal's office was always full of ukes undergoing some stage of repair. The respectful informality of the place brought out the best in the students. It was a school in something of a time warp, "The best kept secret in Victoria," its principal told me.

I learned a lot about gentle leadership from that man who quietly supported his community of teachers and learners. And the staff more than supported me in my role: they encouraged me to go further. Doreen, our "attack" secretary (many items on her desk warned of her wrath—TAKE THIS PEN AND DIE—was one) often said, "I would never work for a *woman,* but I'd work for Judy." My mooning colleague agreed. I was given feedback on small things, such as my voice on the PA system and how I appeared "in charge" while the principal was away. Small things for them, perhaps, but it was incredibly morale boosting for me, because I began to actually see myself in the leadership role, too. Hard work and good organization were not just expected by that staff; they were appreciated. Unconsciously, perhaps, they were guiding me by positive reinforcement, and I felt tremendous gratitude for their support and kindness.

I was as ready as I would ever be, I thought, as I organized myself for the week to come at Fairfield School. It was still too warm for one of those principal suits, so I gave some time to considering my power dressing in the heat.

# STUDENT ENROLLMENT
# INFORMATION FORM

## STUDENT CONTACT INFORMATION

EMERGENCY CONTACT #1:  [Grandmother]
EMERGENCY CONTACT #2:  [Friend]
FAMILY DOCTOR:      [Physician]
FATHER'S BUSINESS: *Lord only knows*
FATHER'S HOME: *Your guess is as good as mine*
MOTHER'S BUSINESS: *Survival*

# 6   EN POINTE

I had not slept, but then what educator has a good sleep Labor Day night? I dressed in my chosen principal clothes, a cream cotton suit with shoulder pads and heels, and hoped I looked the part.

By 7:30 a.m., my little office welcomed me exactly as I had left it. A blank steno pad was ready on a clipboard, just in case I needed to take a few notes. Coffee and tea were already made, thanks to Lynne, a primary teacher who was something of a legend there for doing that and many other extras. She had just started to tell me about her weekend experiences when all three lines on the office phone began ringing at once. I grabbed the nearest phone, the one on my desk.

"Good—did you receive a kindergarten letter? No? School begins next Monday for the kindies."

"Good morn—Are you registered? No? Bring your child to the office at 8:45. Yes, a bell will ring."

"Fairfield School…No, I have no idea which teacher your son will have. Temporary class lists are posted at each entrance, but there may have to be adjustments to the organization."

In my memory, those phones rang all day and were a powerful assault. The secretary and an office assistant handled them after 8:30 that morning so that I could meet briefly with our staff. But that must have been about the time the parent line began forming. It stretched from my office, down a long hallway, down a flight of stairs, all the way to the outside doors of the school. Some were there to register new students, but most wanted to see me.

They had *issues*. An entire grade level of parents needed to express some anxiety. They were concerned about having their children in certain classes, with certain teachers. Like the staff, some wanted to vent about the year—or years—before. There had been bullying on the playground, a lack of Christmas concerts and not enough communication between home and school. Parking was a problem; what would I do about that? And the unleashed dogs on the playground during the long weekend had left calling cards.

My pen took notes for an hour and each parent received roughly the same response. I would be monitoring the situation carefully. I would be visiting classrooms and talking to teachers. I would be on the playground and I would listen to all concerns as they arose. I was sure the children would have a good school year and I was there to help everyone—students, teachers and parents—make this happen.

When the students were dismissed on that first day, we realized the extent of our numbers. Even with the two new portables, we would need to dismantle the computer lab and use it and the music room for classes. The old annex would have to be reopened. A call for more teacher staffing was placed to the assistant superintendent's office, and I turned to tell the secretary that we needed to get a newsletter ready for the next day. Parents needed to know our incredibly high numbers and to expect some reorganizing of their children's classes. Unfortunately, it was noon already, and our secretary had gone home. The poor accounting clerk arrived, knew nothing about the newsletter software, and was unable to answer the questions that kept coming in as the phones kept ringing.

By the time I left for home, the teachers had met with me and looked at our enrollment numbers. Some of the flush of first day excitement had already left tanned cheeks as they contemplated managing huge classes for at least another week. Individual personalities came to the fore.

"Why doesn't the Board plan better?" This was from Miss Jones, a primary teacher proud of her diction.

"I think we should just send the new ones off to another school!" This was offered with a dismissive wave of the hand. Problem solved.

"Get someone from the Board office in here and see how *they* cope! That parent Mrs. Standish is out for blood!"

"How long do you think it will take to get these new teachers in place, Judy?" Ahh, a reasonable voice, I thought. And there had been parents who had peeked into my office and said, "I just want to introduce myself and wish you luck!"

I tidied an office littered with memos and packed the beginnings of a newsletter into my briefcase.

"Well, how was your first day?" my husband asked when I arrived home.

I believe I told him that I really did not know how to describe it.

The second big test for me was to happen the next day: the first formal staff meeting.

By this point in my career, I had attended hundreds of staff meetings. Some were well organized but dry, some dribbled aimlessly on and on, and some were acutely stressful. The ones I remembered most vividly were like the classes I remembered as a student. Something had happened that was unexpected.

As a beginning teacher I remember being thoroughly shocked when a grade one teacher fell fast asleep during a meeting, was prodded awake by a colleague and subsequently chastised by the principal. Another time a union rep, giving an updated report on dental benefits specific to dentures, began to snicker for no apparent reason other than some hidden titillation in his subject matter. As he was usually in full control of himself, this contagious snickering affected some of the rest of us, particularly when it escalated into a rather high-pitched and slightly mad giggle as he plummeted out of control. The more stony-faced our leader became, the more out-of-control the rest of us were, until a break had to be called so that we could all pull ourselves together.

Near the end of one meeting, an informal staff leader stood up to make her pitch for yet another third world situation. Under her guidance we had raised money for many causes in many countries, and our students had learned a lot. We were a little tired on that afternoon, and not as receptive as we might have been. This time, when she proposed that we raise money for tree planting in Ethiopia, a colleague snapped, leaned over to me and whispered, "I don't think trees can *grow* in fucking Ethiopia!" Some of us lost focus and the meeting degenerated into trivia. Once again, another poor principal did not find hilarity acceptable.

I had spent a lot of time thinking about these long, formal monthly meetings. I wanted to make them informative, productive, concise and collegial; they had to cover a tremendous amount without seeming onerous. And with planning and luck, some might contain moments of fun. I wanted to present myself as well organized, personable and in control—of myself, at least.

"Are you nervous?" my vice principal asked, minutes before the staff members were to assemble in the library.

Earlier that day I had heard a negative tone through my office door. It came from the staff committee chairperson, and could have been to do with her views on the world situation, not the way she thought the school was being handled. In any case, the tone reaffirmed what I knew I had to do, and that was to galvanize at least a majority of these people toward a positive year. I had to *appear* to feel positive and strong for everyone, and that included my vice principal.

"No, I feel good!" I replied somewhat idiotically, firmly believing that if I said it, I would believe it.

"That's great," Greg said, probably as nervous as I was.

They looked up at me expectantly. I say "up" rather euphemistically, as some of the seated men's eyes were level with mine, standing. Before we began the business portion of the agenda, I launched into a summary of my teaching background, administrative experience and belief in what makes an outstanding school culture. I talked about teamwork and positive ways to make all our jobs easier and more productive. With considerable emphasis I said, "*Whatever you do, do not let things fester! I am here for you. My phone number is at the top of the agenda. Use it!*" My next bit seemed to bring out some of the galvanizing I was aiming toward. "*Don't spend an evening worrying or wondering, when I may be able to help as a principal, colleague and friend!*"

Sudden thunderous applause took me aback, and at first I did not notice that one of our French Immersion teachers had leapt to his feet, one fist raised in the air. A slim, dark and intense fellow, Jean reminded me at that moment of someone at the barricades in *Les Miserables*. "*Gisela will NOT laminate,*" he roared, dark eyes flashing as the applause died down.

Momentarily rather proud of the response to my initial address, my mind tried frantically to make sense of Jean's mercurial but puzzling reaction. The animated discussion following his dramatic outburst illuminated the issue, scrambled the agenda and took my control of the meeting away. Gisela, a teaching assistant, had been laminating teaching aids in an unventilated room for a long time, and her regular complaints had fallen on deaf ears. Now that Jean had learned that mine would be available at all hours of the day and night, he was moved to seize the moment. "*Don't let things fester,*" I had said. I promised a call to the district's health officer and we settled into a productive and positive meeting.

Greg was speechless later, but gave me a high-five. We were on our way.

The next day the health officer arrived to inspect the room where the laminating had been done. He was new to his job, too, and a very tangible example of responsiveness in action. With a fair amount of drama he declared the workspace unsuitable due to the lack of ventilation. Fans would be installed shortly, we were promised, and they were.

I remember little of the Thursday of that first week, but I know that I was in and out of classrooms, speaking to parents and desperately trying to make sure that the newsletter and other important communication would be ready before the weekend. I was becoming increasing worried about the half-time secretary scenario, and I phoned the personnel administrator in Human

Resources to tell her that the situation was not workable. As good as our secretary was, I needed her full time. I learned that her union had been fuming about the half time, job-share position that had been created at Fairfield, and that it had not sanctioned anything less than full-time.

Friday morning I called an extraordinary meeting of the staff committee and told the group that I was going to have to offer our secretary full time or post the position. There were too many things that needed doing in the afternoons, things that only an experienced secretary could do, and I felt we had to move on the problem quickly. To my relief, they all agreed.

Putting it to our young, enthusiastic secretary was not so easy. She wanted to work half time, but would take the weekend to make her decision. After she left I had to inform the poor accounts clerk that whatever the outcome, *she* would eventually be without a job at our school. She told me she understood my position and seemed almost relieved.

Sometime during that same afternoon a parent asked for a meeting and I invited him into an office already replete with emotion. His daughter was in grade one, he told me, and he and his wife were terribly disappointed in me. Thinking he was going to complain about our weak initial organization or scarce communication, I began an explanation about things over which I had no control for that particular school opening. He raised a hand to stop me. "We heard that you were an advocate for change," he said. "We were told that you believed in the new teaching and learning ideas, the Year 2000 ones." Seeing that I was still having trouble understanding, he shook his head. "You've been here a week," he said sadly, "and my daughter has brought home some of those old fashioned worksheets."

As he stood to go I fought an urge to counter with, "NOT a week! It's been three and three-quarter days!" "Let's stay in touch," I said. He left still shaking his head.

By five-thirty I had loaded weekend work into my briefcase and finished returning phone messages. I had heard from the assistant superintendent that we would be receiving our extra staffing as soon as possible, and, feeling relieved, I took my coffee mug and a bouquet of sagging, congratulatory flowers into the staff room, then went into the washroom. My reflection said it all: I was sagging, too.

I heard my office phone begin to ring as I walked back down the hall.

"Mrs. Bertram? You don't know me. My name is Joan Wright. I have a son in grade four, and I need to meet with you."

"Let's make a time early next week," I said, drawing my organizer to me and wondering if I would ever reach the point when I would be able, in all conscience, to leave a ringing phone and head for home.

"You don't understand. I need to meet with you *now*. This won't wait for next week. I don't have much time."

Had her son taken home worksheets, too? What sort of miracle worker did they think was running this school? "Mrs. Wright—Joan—it's late and I really need to go." To rejuvenate myself in order to handle the likes of you, the new principal of Fairfield thought, ungraciously. "If you'd like to tell me the nature of your concern, I'll make a note of it now and we can deal with it on Monday."

"The nature of it," she repeated. Then, "deal with it." It was as though she was trying to understand my words. "The nature of it?" she asked, more sharply. I could hear her inhale, then her breath sighed, " I have a son, Tim, in grade four. In *your* school. And I'm dying."

"I'm here," I said.

Bulletin: MEET THE TEACHER NIGHT
Wed., Sept 19, 1990 (7:00-8:00 p.m.)

This year, "Meet the Teachers Night" will be a family affair. Come to school with your children and they will lead you to their classrooms and introduce you to the people who work with them. The new Parent Advisory Council will have information for you, and coffee will be provided. Mrs. Bertram, our new principal, is looking forward to meeting as many of you as possible.

P.S. Friday, Sept. 21 is a professional day for the teachers. No students!!

CLASS COLONIST (grade seven)

We Need Columns

If you have <u>anything</u> you would like to put in the paper please contact one of the editors (Brianna, Megan, Jane and Jo). We are in desperit need of anyone who wants to write or submit something thanks!!

If you want to express your idea or say something about one of the stories put it on paper and then give it to Kathy.

The mesapotainiea projects are do on Monday the 25.

News:

- Sarah told me to write this: Matthew is a sweetheart. I didn't say that, she did.

- Kate is feeling sensitive today because somebody was writing notes about her. I don't know who and I don't know why and I don't really care. But whoever did should stop it.

- Well it was supposed to be hat day today. A lot of people forgot but some remembered. Maybe we should try it again and tell those people the day before so they don't forget. You should have seen the teachers, in case you didn't.

- There isn't really much to write about so I'll stop here.

# 7   HATS OFF

"Well! Now I know what principals do," the woman said, her eyebrows raised. We were into the second week of school, with teachers and students miraculously in place. Or so it seemed.

This mother had been in my office for half an hour, trying various approaches. She wanted her child moved to another class and seemed to be unwavering in her resolve. She was well dressed, well spoken and well known to the staff. She had taken time off work to put things right with the new principal, she told me.

The move she demanded for her daughter was not academically sound for the student, according to teachers who had seen me prior to the visit. Nor was the move feasible given the size and makeup of the two classes. I had had an opportunity to do some consultation with the pertinent teachers and, sure enough, Mrs. Donovan was on our case.

Her daughter had a friend in the other class, and besides, Amanda didn't like one of the girls where she was placed, I was informed emphatically. As a grade three student in a split two/three class, her child would feel that she had failed. Well, her mother was going to succeed. Mrs. Donovan wanted her daughter to continue working with Amanda's previous teacher, the teacher who was also teaching her daughter's grade level in a three/four split this year. Her daughter was comfortable with her previous teacher. "The new one is not as nurturing," she added conspiratorially, in lowered voice. I obviously needed to know these things, being new myself.

I pointed out that our students had been in their new classes for one afternoon. As there were other girls in her daughter's group who had just registered at our school, there was a very good chance that she would connect with at least one of them. Her new teacher had already reported that the little girl seemed happy. What I could not express was the rather strong feeling on the part of the teachers involved that as this child was moved along, the mother needed to be moved along as well. As for the nurturing part, both teachers seemed to be warm and caring people, and the vehemence of Amanda's former teacher regarding the need for Mrs. Donovan to helicopter to and hover over another class bordered on alarming. It would be a self-fulfilling prophecy for Mrs. Donovan if her daughter's placement in her new class did not work, but I agreed with the teachers that the child's best placement seemed to be the two/three class.

We went back and forth making the same points until I brought the meeting to a close. "I appreciate your concerns, Mrs. Donovan. However, I am going to keep your daughter where she is because I believe she is well placed. I assure you I will monitor her social and academic progress carefully." I stood to emphasize the closure. I had, in the past, seen that work.

"So you refuse to move her?" Her face was a picture of incredulity.

"That's all I can do," I said, using that expression for the last time.

Shortly after she left my office the same issue was raised by another set of parents who also wanted their daughter to be taught by the same teacher she had the year before. One of the concerns they expressed to me was that the new teacher's classroom contained hardly any primary furniture. Further, it was scantily decorated and therefore not at all welcoming.

After pointing out that the teacher had been appointed the previous Friday, had almost no time to prepare and was expecting the new furniture to be delivered as we spoke, her husband softened. His wife, probably sensing her husband's weakening resolve, tried a different tact. Her daughter felt rejected because some of the students remained with their former teacher. I expressed sympathy, but again pointed to the very short time frame they had allowed for the situation to work.

In what must have been desperation, she went on. She knew the previous principal very well. ("Now there was a mover and shaker!") I did not respond. "I sat on his knee at a party recently," she added, her expression then conveying what seemed an odd mixture of triumph and disbelief at what she had just told me.

With somewhat distracting pictures in my mind (this mother was a good size compared to the previous principal), I told them their daughter would stay where she was. I added that I would look forward to following her progress and I pointed out that a child's attitude could be helped by positive, optimistic parents who were supportive of the school. The father shook my hand and she glowered.

I was already learning that making the final decisions regarding the best interests of a student's learning requires preparation, patience, intuition and even sheer courage. It is likely that most parents will come to respect a principal's judgment over time. In the case of class placements, all sides need to be heard, but the final responsibility rests with the principal.

I was also learning that sometimes parent anger was justified and sometimes it was misplaced. When parents came to rail, my job was to discover the real issue. The toughest part was not getting sidetracked. For example, against my better judgment, I once moved a child only to hear that the mother had complained at the end of the year: he would have been better where he was originally. Her real issue had been her own pride; friends' children had been placed in a class that she perceived as more advanced.

Accusations of racism in school-based decisions over class placements have been rare in my experience, but the few times staff have heard this they have recoiled. Staff members may have issues with some students, but racism is something I have never encountered literally or by innuendo with anyone working in our system. It is a card that is occasionally used, however, by parents.

Two Asian fathers met with me one September, concerned that both of their children were remaining with the same teacher who was also teaching the next grade. It was a racist decision, they told me. These two students were outstanding in every way, and I suspect their teacher wanted to keep them for a second year because she loved having them in her class. When she explained the kind of enrichment she was prepared to offer, the fathers relented. At the end of the year they both made a point of letting me know how pleased they were.

One day shortly after school dismissal, a very distraught Indo-Canadian woman tore into my office. Knowing her to be a beautifully serene, warm and friendly person, I was taken aback by the change in her. She shut my office door and threw herself on a chair, sobbing. According to her, one of our playground supervisors who was also a parent in the school and a particularly gentle soul, had reminded her that she needed to have her dog on a leash when on the playground. Her son was in the same class as the supervisor's.

"This is racism!" she wailed, hand against her forehead, the picture of classic tragedy. "There is racism here! My son won't learn! He needs to be moved to another class!"

I was halfway through my earnest defense of the supervisor, who had politely asked other parents to make sure their dogs were on leashes, too, when her eyes widened and she felt around her forehead. "Oh, my bindi! My bindi's gone!" As we were subsequently crawling over the carpet to find her bindi, she sobbed, "And I just found out I am pregnant!" Not too long after, I saw her in the outer office speaking to our secretary, looking radiant and pointing to her new bindi, a flaming, rocket-shaped adornment that suggested things were going well for her.

That September at Fairfield some parents were testing the waters. What would this new principal "do?" What would the old principal have done in this new situation? In those early days I was, for the most part, meeting with parents who sought me out, although there was one memorable exception.

One of our biggest challenges was to connect with Mrs. Black, the mother of a newly enrolled grade four boy who was drastically underachieving, both academically and socially. At the very least, academic testing needed to be done and learning assistance provided. Corey was from another province and his records had not arrived. His mother would not return our phone calls and we were unable to arrange a meeting with the classroom teacher and other professionals who needed to be involved. Her son could perform basic reading and math, but the gaps in his learning were significant and his self-esteem seemed very low.

Mrs. Black was listed as a single, working mother. I called home and work many times and had no success in reaching her. Notes were sent home and our conscientious counselor did his best to make contact as well. There was no response to our requests for a meeting, although there were some angry letters from her regarding Corey's homework. As a last resort I drafted a letter. The letter laid out what was deemed to be a critical situation in which a school staff was unable to meet the pressing needs of one Corey Black, a boy whose potential seemed to be undermined by a lack of parental support. The letter was sent to Mrs. Black by registered mail.

The next day was Hat Day, a celebration suggested by senior students once the school was up and running. Many of the staff and students wore outlandish headgear and enjoyed the ridiculous appearance of one another. We all felt we could relax, just a little, and the laughter and informality seemed appropriate.

After the assembly, when we all had a good look at each other, students and teachers began streaming back toward their classrooms to begin the academic day. The main hallway was full of bobbing, weird and wonderful hats, and our counselor's stood out, literally, above the others. Being well over six feet, Dick towered above the rest of the crowd. Always elegant, he was particularly resplendent that day in a peach chiffon "bridesmaid style" hat with a wide brim and a long, flowing scarf of the same color.

Later that morning, he described what happened. As he was exchanging banter with passing students, a wild looking woman grabbed his arm and asked if he was in charge of our "looney bin." Noticing the striking similarity to the child we were often discussing, Dick reached out his hand. "Mrs. Black? You must be Mrs. Black! I'm our school counselor, Dick Brown. I know our principal is very anxious to meet you!"

Mrs. Black looked dubiously and dumbfoundedly about her as she was escorted to my office. By this time we had forgotten how we looked and were totally absorbed in the regular demands of a school day. So when our peach-chiffoned school counselor ushered in a woman who looked as though she would have preferred the nearest exit, I saw nothing out of the ordinary and tried to make her feel at home. I leaned forward and smiled.

"Mrs. Bertram," Dick beamed. "Mrs. Black has finally come to meet with us!"

"We are so glad you've come in, Mrs. Black! Please sit down."

Mrs. Black remained standing with her lower jaw slightly slack. After a moment's awkwardness, Dick added, helpfully, "Mrs. Bertram is our principal, Mrs. Black."

Afterwards Dick said that just then he experienced a kind of epiphany; perhaps there was another way to approach Mrs. Black. But it was too late. The woman regarded me intently. I wore slacks, a business jacket, one of my husband's old bow ties and a beanie with a moveable contraption that did interesting things as the office fan blew on it.

"Our principal," Dick repeated, rather lamely.

Mrs. Black's upper lip began to curl as her slack lower jaw snapped shut. "That figures," she said, turning on her heel.

What does a principal do? In this case nothing more, as neither Corey nor his mother returned. The staff and I could only hope that his academic needs were being met and that his mother was involved in his new school.

Our Parent Advisory Council president agreed with me early that fall. An informal open house where students could introduce their parents to their teachers was preferable to the old meeting-in-the-gym kind of evening. Many students introduced their parents to me, as well, on that September evening as I stood outside my office in one of the new principal suits, thoroughly enjoying the positive atmosphere and, admittedly, basking just a little. I had a lot to feel good about, I thought. We had interviewed a couple of excellent candidates for our full time secretary position, and Gail was to start work the beginning of October. She exuded a crisp energy, intelligence and humor, and she had experience beyond our requirements in accounting and office organization. With classes reorganized, teachers were putting their considerable energies into creating learning atmospheres of quality, and the initial concerns over student placements seemed to have died down to a "wait and see" attitude. I was finding a little respite from the reactive mode of the first couple of weeks.

During October I was able to be in classrooms and on the playground more often, and students were beginning to get to know me a little. Our new secretary was eager to organize efficient office procedures and physical space, and a more effective and accommodating work area was drafted and built by district carpenters. I learned how lucky I was in my support team: our vice principal and our new secretary were a perfect match for my style of operating. I felt that the staff and community of students and parents seemed to agree: we were all working hard and having fun doing it. In my memory it was always sunny during that period, and the first gray days did not come until November.

# KID TIMES: HALLOWE'EN (Grade Four)

## An Interview with Mr. Sampson

Hello, my name is Katie Matthews. I interviewed Mr. Sampson and this is what I found out: Mr. Sampson has been here for one year and two months. He teaches a 2/3 split or a primary 3/4. He is not dressing up for Hallowe'en. He likes Hallowe'en, though, because people have to do a trick or treat. Mr. Sampson doesn't mind what grade he teaches because he finds it a challenge to teach all grades. He likes it at our school because the kids are neat. Mr. Sampson doesn't know if he is having a party for his classroom. This is Kids News signing off for now.

## An Interview with Miss. Jones

Q. What kind of costume are you going to wear for Hallowe'en?
A. I am not going to wear anything.
Q. What kind of decorations are you going to make?
A. A cat.
Q. Where are you going to put your decorations?
A. On string in the class.
Q. Are you going to put on a party or have a contest as to whose costume is the best?
A. No treats or candy, games or prizes.
Q. Do you like to dress up?
A. No, I do not like to dress up.
Q. Do you like Hallowe'en?
A. Yes, I like Hallowe'en.

Remembrance Day will be on Monday. Please remember all the dead peoples family's.

CLASSROOM NEWS #3

Dear parents,

Astronomy: We have now put our ecology theme on the back burner until January to allow for the studying of Astronomy. This time of the year is most suitable to observe the sky. Along with learning about the history of this science, the solar system and numerous other elements, we are going to set one evening aside to observe the moon, planets (Saturn most specifically) and constellations.

Mr. George, who has studied Astronomy, will help our class throughout this theme. We would like every student to plan to be back to school on the evening of Monday November 27 at 19h00 until 20h30. If the sky is cloudy our back up dates would be the next day or the following one, November 29.

Students will have made their own Galileo type telescopes and Mr. George will set up his more powerful one.

***Students should dress warmly (hats and gloves). If parents want to stay and observe the stars (little pun!) at work, you are welcome.

[Teacher]

# 8   REPORT CARDS

"It's a typical November day," my husband observed. I poured him a second cup of coffee and we settled at our breakfast table. All the oak leaves had fallen and the predominant color outside our windows was gray. It was raining, hard, drumming on the skylight and bouncing on the deck, a good time to be indoors.

Though retired, I knew what was on the mind of every elementary teacher in our district. "What do you remember most about doing report cards?" I asked him.

Ken's response was immediate. "I'll never forget the time I mixed up the reports and wrote comments on the wrong ones. They'd all been given out when I realized what I'd done, and I had to redo two of them. I was frantic."

Later I took coffee downstairs and pulled out an old file. It was practically falling apart, like many others that held the memories of a long career. Thinking of family, friends and colleagues who were hunkered down at this time of year, I opened the file and spent a long time contemplating the process of student evaluation and reporting.

The mere mention of report cards brings out interesting behaviors in teachers. During the October staff meeting of that first year I was a principal, teachers examined the proposed calendar of events for the rest of the first term. Martha scanned November. Finding the dreaded due date, she sat back in her chair and crossed her arms over her chest. "I can't *possibly* have reports done by then," she announced.

Forgetting that someone usually picked up this refrain, I was concerned for her. "How about a week later?" I asked the staff.

"That's too close to the parent interviews," she protested, her face rosy from the attention.

"Well, we could send them out mid week," I suggested.

"Then we'd have parents wanting to meet with us *before* the interviews." She was on a roll.

"*You* give us a date then," barked one of the men who hated anything that prolonged a staff meeting.

"I guess we *have* to stick with that day," she conceded, dubiously, "but I will probably need more time."

Hers were handed in to me before the due date. They were the first set I received that November and most reporting periods after that time.

Teachers tell of nightmares during this period: awful dreams which involve theft, misplacement, deletion and other scenarios too terrible to contemplate for long when awake. Stories of actual events abound. One teacher did press "delete" on a very old computer and was unable to retrieve weeks of unsaved work. Spouses report perseverating behaviors such as prolonged oven cleaning.

During the first autumn at Fairfield, I walked into a teacher's classroom on the morning of the day our reports were to be sent home. He had an ironing board set up at the back of his class and he was ironing them.

"I was wondering about those," I told him. I had not read nor signed his at this point.

"I always do this," he assured me. His grade fives welcomed me and went on with some seatwork. I assumed they accepted the ironing of their report cards as simply another odd symptom some teachers displayed during this time in the school year.

At the very least, teachers have an abstracted, if not irritable countenance.

"Either he's doing his reports or he's having his period," a Francophone teacher hissed out of the corner of his mouth, smugly regarding a colleague who had slammed his mark book on a table. "Should I tell him I am *fini?*"

As a teacher and as an administrator, I often asked myself the following question: if mark books, records of attitudes and samples of student work are scrupulously kept, why do teachers go through such agony when they have to report on the progress of students they know well? There are many reasons, not the least of which is that this work is done while they are still fulfilling the expectations of a difficult job. And even if a day or two is taken away from school, weekends and evenings are consumed with no respites as the job is tackled. Making sure the "grade" fairly and accurately reflects the term's work takes enormous consideration, especially when these documents receive intense scrutiny at home and may need to be justified later.

Then there is the need to find the *words*. Comments need to be informative but kind, and venting is unacceptable. However, couched too positively, the need for improvement may well be lost in syrup. A few examples from my file reveal this struggle:

- *Mary had a terrific September, a forgettable October and seems to be on track for November.*

- *His project on slime was very popular at the Science Fair, but a disproportionate amount of time was spent cutting letters for the title. As a result, the remainder of the presentation was lacking in polish and scientific depth.*

- *I have made steady progress at deciphering Joe's unique style of cursive writing.*

- *Her allotment of time with me is often spent on disciplinary <u>review</u> rather than academic advancement.*

- *(Science) Although enthusiastic, Georgina has some difficulty calming herself down enough to concentrate on microscopic objects.*

- *Jake gives more enthusiasm and energy in P.E. than in all the other subjects combined.*

- *Jamie is a happy boy who enjoys interacting with others. Sometimes he starts talking about something and it can be difficult to find his "off" button.*

- *Sharon has an engaging smile and a sense of humor that both of us must learn to enjoy at the same time.*

- *Nancy worked very hard on her puppet, but needs to realize that others don't appreciate being continually splattered with her artistic enthusiasms.*

- *He is happy to go to library period, although he spends most of his time attempting to socialize while feigning a reading pose or searching for the elusive but perfect book.*

- *Aaron's ability to camouflage himself effectively in the cloakroom during cleanup time is almost an art form in itself.*

- *Megan is working on the idea that school rules apply to her, too.*

- *Unfortunately, my homework completions sheets and mark sheets are reminiscent of a battle field, pock marked with large zero craters that show Peter having failed to complete a piece of work, or handing it in partially complete or significantly late. Now I know that his broken thumb was a problem, and it made it difficult for him to complete his written work, but a much greater effort is needed to keep up with his basic assignments. The problem may not be as great as it appears if somehow he could overcome the disorganization and chaos that his desk and notebooks get into. Often he just can't find the work that he has done, and he is getting incompletes when he has probably done three quarters of the work. Another reason for Peter not handing in work is, I think, that he is a bit of a perfectionist, and he is never quite satisfied that his work is good enough...*

- *Chantal has a kind heart and is always willing to help others. Often she is so busy helping others she doesn't do what she needs to do to complete a task.*

And finally, possibly conveying pure desperation:

- *Frank enjoys swinging from ropes.*

Often, before the final draft was submitted, a teacher would ask me to read report comments about a child who had been exasperating. Sarcasm is not acceptable, and the following did not go home as it was given to me to proof read. I believe the author had already decided he had gone too far but needed to share his feelings around this difficult child:

FOCUS FOR NEXT TERM: *Angie tries very hard to please, but lacks many primary-level skills and is in a constant state of chaotic disarray. Each lesson change seems to send her into a 10 to 15 minute spin of social calls, scrambling for non-existent supplies while trying to find out from her peers what the latest instructions are. The effect resembles a queer sort of dance, periodically punctuated by fits of laughter, bold yet directionless walking, quizzical facial expressions and random but somehow delightfully regular clockwise pirouettes. When she eventually regains her seat, too much time is spent trying to get others' attention. Perhaps we could discuss Angie's propensity for distractedness at the up-coming parent-teacher interviews.*

During this period many teachers felt the need to give me their own progress reports as they went along:

"Five more to go, Judy! They will be on your desk Monday."

"I'll get them to you by this afternoon!"

"I'm half-way through!"

"Do you want me to bring some to your house on the weekend?"

"I *love* these new reports!"

Judy Bertram Tomlinson

"I *hate* these new reports!"

Report card formats change with the prevailing philosophical and political wind. One teacher, concerned about the additional emphasis on positive reinforcement, sent me a note with some of his reports: *I hope these "can do" statements have not become 'canned doo!' P.S. 12 to go!*

The practice of including the student in the evaluation process was just beginning in my first year as principal. Having students examine their own academic and social skills with the intention of setting viable goals for themselves was, and still is, a valuable skill.

Even at the kindergarten level students dictated their thoughts to their teachers about activities and how they related to them:

FIELD TRIPS: *I enjoyed the Safety Village. I threw up in the apple orchard.*

Other earnest ruminations that I found in my file include the following student comments:

Things I Could Improve On: *I could in prove in Music Theatre, although I feel I tried my hardest.*

Things I Enjoy Or Do Not Enjoy: *Everything, except Music Theatre because I don't think I have to know about Dixie Humingbird to live a good life.*

GOAL: *my Goal is to gat battre at sepaline. My ottre goal is to plae the uke batter.*

PE: *I don't really like pe because theres to much yelling and running that we have to do. Speking of yelling I can't even hear people talking to me. When I'm in a bad mode I relly hate school but when I'm in a good mode I'll just play any game.*

As the report cards piled on my desk that November, the tone in the school lightened and my work on them began. I tried to read them as a concerned parent would. Did I have a clear picture of that term's progress? Were strengths included as well as areas in need of improvement? I read slowly, noting errors or omissions, and added short comments on the students' progress. Finally, finished with each set, I wrote notes to the teachers regarding their work. By the time our vice principal handed in his pile, I was well into my reading and as seriously fixated and abstracted as the teachers had been.

"You're spending an awful lot of time on those," our vice principal observed. "Are you reading every word? I'll do some if you like."

"I think I'll do these myself, Greg," I said. "They're giving me a really good picture of the kids. But thanks."

"Suit yourself. I'm going home to celebrate. I have a cold beer waiting!"

I took home another hundred or so, including his, and thought about his offer. As vice principal I had often read sets of report cards and signed them off. And I knew teachers often thought that principals signed them without actually reading what had been worked over so carefully. Halfway through Greg's reports, I realized that he had set out to test my attention to detail. Among them was one for a student named Ima Hogg. Ima's progress had been carefully evaluated by her teacher, who had written the following comments using the Greater Victoria School District's reporting format:

LANGUAGE ARTS: *Ima continues to root around looking for the right word. She continues to grunt and snort during lessons. Her handwriting continues to be akin to a scratch in the mud.*

MATHEMATICS SKILLS: *Ima can accurately estimate the number of litres per bucket and how those litres can be transferred to a trough (both in liquids and solids).*

PERSONAL PLANNING: *Her desk is like a pig-sty: messy, cluttered, always mud-covered. She continues to squeal when work is assigned. Ima continues to get dirty at recess and lunch on rainy days.*

*FINE ARTS: Clay work was completed with enthusiasm. Good results in finger painting.*

*PHYSICAL EDUCATION: Ima enjoys PE activities but continues to horse around somewhat. She has demonstrated excellent tumbling skills, i.e. side roll, forward roll.*

Principal's Signature: *J. Bertram. In a pig's eye, Ima has reached hog heaven in terms of this school. All the best, Ima, and continue to avoid hot dog days!*

Obviously I signed the report off, giving "Ima" her positive comment and Greg a note thanking him for his hard work. For seven years Greg continued to slip in maverick report cards, each becoming more and more subtle. When he handed them in to me and when I gave them back to him, we were both poker-faced. The only time his fun very nearly backfired was when he caught himself stuffing one of these into a real student's report envelope. The thought of that report going home had us both shuddering for days.

Report cards cause teachers extreme stress, are often redundant by the time they are read at home, are subject to regular changes in format and philosophy, and are costly, as some teachers take time off to complete them. So, the self-evident question is, should teachers and principals continue to take infinite care to see that the best possible evaluation is sent home in those envelopes?

You bet. Parents need to know precisely how their child is progressing in relation to prescribed curriculum, and they need to know that his or her teacher appreciates something positive in the child, even if it is only an enthusiasm for swinging on ropes.

Sometimes sharing that information takes more than a comment on a report card, however. During my teaching years, I remember one parent-teacher interview above all others. It was dark outside by the time I ushered that parent into my classroom for her appointment. Mrs. O'Brien had been early and had waited in the hallway until it was her turn. There was no time for me to grab a cup of tea, I thought somewhat ruefully, as I ushered her in. She was a large, red-haired woman with a red face and hands, and as she settled herself onto a primary chair she sat back, both hands on her thighs, and let out a long sigh. "Shoot," she said, looking past me.

I pulled forward the samples of Michael's work: reading and math exercise books, creative writing, a few written tests and a riotous self portrait with flaming hair and polka dot freckles.

"First of all, Mrs. O'Brien, I want you to know that I really enjoy working with your son. He has a terrific personality."

Mrs. O'Brien waved her hand in front of my face and shook her head. "Michael *O'Brien*," she said tiredly. "You got four Michaels, right?"

"Yes, Michael O'Brien. The only red-headed Michael!" I smiled at her.

"Come on," she persisted. I nodded and she looked at me incredulously. "*My* Michael? He's doing o.k.?"

"Better than that. He's kind of taken off in school!"

"Be damned," she said, still skeptical. Systematically, I began to go through Michael's work. It was a standard routine I used with all the parents and it varied only when emphasis had to be made in one area or another. I was pointing out his considerable improvement in math when something splattered on his multiplication test. I looked up and saw another tear about to fall.

"You like my kid," she whispered, softly.

Had Mrs. O'Brien actually read Michael's report before she came for the interview? I thought I had been clear in my written communication with her. After she left, I pulled out my copy and went over it carefully, trying to read it from her point of view. I decided that Michael's mother may have been overwhelmed by the amount of print on the format of the card, and I wondered if my own written comments could have been more powerful. Possibly she just needed a person to tell her—in the flesh—about her son. However she had regarded her son's report card, I always thought about Mrs. O'Brien when I read teacher reports after that.

In November of my first year at Fairfield, five hundred and sixty reports were going home, one set crisply ironed. Each card had been signed off by the school's new principal, and each one would precipitate some sort of conversation in the homes in that community. Hopefully there would be support and motivation for each student in the coming term. Parent-teacher interviews were scheduled in later that month, some time after the reports had been read and digested.

On the evenings set aside for those interviews, I enjoyed chatting to parents who were waiting outside their children's classrooms. I was learning that every interaction was important for them and myself, and I was receiving feedback about the comments I had written on those reports. The parents seemed upbeat, and by seven o'clock on that second evening I began to really relax. The first academic term was almost over, and the reporting period had been unbelievably smooth.

Shortly after, the custodian tracked me down. "We're flooding," he informed me, rolling his eyes.

I looked at him blankly and then remembered the former principal's warning—a warning I had thought akin to the belief that the school was haunted. "When there's a hard rain, a full moon and a high tide," he told me, "the bottom floor floods." I had laughed. "Honestly."

"Right," I responded to my custodian, "Let's have a look." We walked down the staircase nearest the office and looked up the primary wing. Sure enough, water was seeping in from the outside entrance and had spread halfway down the hall.

"Can't drain it until it gets to *here*." He lifted a large trap door near where we stood. "It's the worst in Fran's room."

We sloshed to that end of the hall and looked inside the classroom. Parents very intent on every word that teacher was saying were huddled around a small table with her. The three of them had their feet up on the rungs of the little chairs they were sitting on, barely avoiding the steadily rising black water. Two other parents were on a couch at the other end of the room, their feet up on a little table in front. I glanced into the other four classrooms on that wing and raced upstairs. I hated to interrupt conferences, but I had no choice.

"Excuse the interruption. We have a flooding problem in the downstairs primary wing. Teachers in that area, please resume your conferences in the library." I turned off the PA system, wondering if they would think to leave a note on their classroom doors regarding the change of location.

In another hour the water from that hallway was pouring into the drain and a wet carpet stench was permeating the lower part of the building. I dared look into the library.

Six sets of teachers and parents were grouped around tables, intent on hearing further about their children's progress. There was an odd sound in there, however, in addition to the soft murmur of voices. It reminded me of fingers lightly tapping on drums before band practice. Then I noticed the buckets.

"Roof's leaking," said our custodian, coming up behind me.

My husband was barely interested in the account of my evening. His last parent/teacher interview had included the student, her parents, four grandparents, three toddlers in a triple carriage affair that contained them momentarily, and a pair of ferrets on a long, retractable but faulty lead.

*December 17, 2002*

*Merry Christmas, Judy! How's your book coming along? I've got a personal story or event, depending on how one sees it, to share with you on your first retired Christmas season.*

*The Pony Express came by the school last week, that's the Canada Post people with their Shetland ponies who go to schools to pick up the Santa letters from the primary kids. I'm sure you've seen them before.*

*Anyway, they all arrived with two ponies and went into the gym. The little kids all came and sat down and I went over to pat the ponies while the loading of the letters was going on. One of the ponies then started to get a very large and obvious erection and the reaction of the kids and some of the staff was immediate. I quickly stepped away and left the Canada Post people to deal with the situation. Of course I've been blamed for all the excitement because I was patting that pony at the erectile moment.*

*I suppose this is one of my highlights so far this year. (I need to get a life!)*

*Feliz Navidad,*

*Vic (your former vice principal, remember?)*

Judy Bertram Tomlinson

Journal Entry: Sunday, December 1, 2002

*Tonight as we sat waiting for the advent service to begin, I reflected on my five months of retirement. As the church filled softly and the choir assembled for the processional, a long-retired teacher colleague sat down beside me. We greeted each other.*

*"Do you miss any of your work?" she asked. She had attended my retirement party in June.*

*"I was ready to move on," I told her. "But now, at this time of year, there are things that I miss about school. The energy and excitement."*

*"You're like me," she said, unbuttoning her coat and folding it beside her. "When it was over, it was over. I never looked back." She settled herself.*

*"Whatever happened to your niece?" I asked. She looked at me, surprised. "She is one I often wonder about," I added. Former students often haunted my thoughts.*

*Maureen had been in my class almost thirty years before. She was a small grade four girl, with large round eyes, curly brown hair and ever-changing expressions. When my teaching partner was even a little impatient with her, those eyes would become overflowing pools in her face. I do not remember hearing any sound of distress from her, but I always remembered her tears. I took the pulse of my class from Maureen, and mostly from those eyes which regularly registered emotional overload. Was I expecting too much? Going too quickly? Explaining clearly enough? Did we all need a good laugh or a good stretch?*

*Maureen was quick to show delight and she had an appreciative sense of humor. She would clasp her hands together in sheer joy when listening to a good book or watching a play. She responded immediately to any kind of positive reinforcement, and I always felt the need to give her lots of it. And yet she was never demanding.*

*Our class was huge. My teaching partner and I registered over sixty children in an "open area" classroom. The school was designated "inner city," which meant that there were many very needy children among them.*

Maureen was always well dressed and had shiny, clean hair. She brought healthy lunches, was always on time and never seemed tired or listless. Her mother attended parent-teacher conferences and showed concern and love for her child. This was a single mother who was working hard to make a living for the two of them, she said, and there was a sadness about her. She was new to Canada and far from her Irish roots. Her daughter always did what was asked of her and responded to her peers and to adults with perfect manners. She was kind and empathetic and the other children liked her; she genuinely celebrated their successes and felt for them if they were troubled. Yet, like her mother, she seemed lonely.

I looked into those eyes for clues. Was her mother sad at home? Was Maureen affected by not having her father living with her? Was she simply an acutely sensitive child? All I knew was that something in me responded to her emotions. They moved away when Maureen finished grade five.

Years later at a house party, the teacher attending this concert had begun to talk about her family and the sister who had left Ireland to have a baby in a new country. It was a stressful and hurtful time for all of them, she said, what with not knowing how her sister and the child were faring. The child, I discovered, was Maureen. "I taught her," I said. "Your niece was a lovely girl." The conversation shifted and there were no more opportunities to question her aunt without seeming to pry. Many more years passed, until we were together at this evening's advent service.

As the lights were dimming and candles were being lit, she whispered, "They live in Calgary. Maureen is finishing a degree in economics. She was living with a young man, the way they do nowadays, but that seems over. She's moved back with her mother to help care for her. Maureen has always been good to my sister, you know. She hasn't been well for years."

"And the family? Did you all reconnect?"

"At one time our mother was going to Canada to find them. At the last minute she told me she just could not go. I came instead, and stayed. I've helped them out, over the years."

*Bless you*, I thought. "*Please tell Maureen I think about her and wish her well,*" I whispered.

The church was dark, now, and the choir's processional had begun the heralding of the start of the Christmas celebrations. As the service went on I became one of the many thinking of the miracle of birth, of family at all stages of life, and of the continued need for peace on a troubled earth. I also thought about the end of my career and the little girl whose eyes still haunted me.

# CLASS COLONIST

Fun Stuff

Our choir is having a dessert auction and concert on the 17th (that's the 17th of December, 1990). For more details, ask Jane or Sara.

I don't know if this is going to happen, but I think it would be fun to have a grade 7 Christmas party. After our super Hallowe'en party I think we should try again.

# 9  CHRISTMAS

As that first term at Fairfield School was drawing to a close there were extraordinary tensions in the world and within the district's teaching ranks. The Gulf War would soon erupt, and the longest job action by our teachers would cripple the school system for weeks and change it forever. Despite the ongoing media coverage, it was impossible to dwell on any of these tensions. It was Christmas at school.

I was, I am, and I always will be politically incorrect about this. We were directed to change "Christmas Holidays" to "Winter Break" on school calendars and memos. We were told that we could not call our concerts "Christmas" concerts. I suppose our acutely consultative and socially aware trustees thought that by renaming our celebrations we would usher in a new era of peace and understanding. What they would have accomplished, if they had been successful in all the name changes they were mandating, would have been the erosion of the culture of the majority of our students. The controversy still goes on, the directives are often happily ignored, and we continue to celebrate Christmas, Hanukah, Chinese New Year and whatever else generates light in the dark part of our year and our selves.

Whatever it is called, there is nothing like the assault on the senses that the month of December brings to elementary schools. Baking seems to be constant, bulletin boards are at their most colorful, and job action notwithstanding, musical practices waft through hallways. Report cards and parent-teacher interviews are over and there is a lightening of the spirits as much pressure is off and holidays are pending.

It was a magical time for me during that first December at Fairfield, and each successive one as well. Unlike classroom teachers whose nerves were often a little ragged from the close proximity to their students, I could roam from class to class and accept sticky treats and pasted cards, encourage art work in progress and marvel over creative writing. I also had time to encourage students in their thinking of others less fortunate. Hampers were organized and donations of food and clothes were accepted in classrooms and at the door on the nights of the concerts. I called the people who did the picking up and studied the pride on the senior students' faces as they helped to load our gifts into waiting vehicles.

Watching those concerts taking shape and giving what support I could was one of the real joys of my job. I saw rehearsals for little classroom presentations and the build-up to big musical productions. I usually knew which students would be careless on the risers, who had stage fright, which elf's hat was not fitting properly and who was not cooperating in the general pulling together. I sometimes knew who would forget their lines and I knew what an otherwise sweet kindergarten teacher had called her little host of angels just before they erupted on stage, halos askew.

For teachers in need of an academic reprieve, the actual preparation for concerts is quite fun. It is the "holding tank" period before and after the few minutes of glory that often has them to their knees. Sometimes frayed nerves were all too obvious.

The year Miss Jones retired she put particular care into her class's Christmas concert presentation. Flashlights were synchronized with military precision and the children's diction was as crisp as hers: *C* is for the *C*hrist child, lying in manger; *H* is for *h*eaven, watching over *H*im. And so on. In the darkened auditorium, we were in awe of the crispness she had drilled into her students for the last concert she would ever do. Unfortunately, poor timing on her part tarnished an otherwise perfect performance. In spite of generous applause, she could be heard saying, as she led the last of her charges away from their audience, *"Thank God that's over!"*

Although Fairfield had some concertless Decembers before I became principal there, parental pressure through a recent accreditation process had resulted in a goal to reinstate them. Carol sing-a-longs in the gym and multicultural craft making in the classrooms were all fine, but Fairfield parents wanted the old-fashioned, class by class performances.

"We *did* make the commitment," our staff committee Chair pointed out.

"How are we going to fit everyone in the gym? Our school's too big now!"

"I'll do 'Six White Boomers'," Peter offered.

"Here we go with the Ho Ho Ho's," a French gentleman said, rolling his eyes.

An old-fashioned Christmas concert that included all the students was announced in the November newsletter. There would be two evenings of concerts so that each student could perform on one night, and primary and intermediate classes would be mixed each night for variety. The band would play at one concert and the strings at the other. Families were limited to two tickets each, but requests could be made for more in case there were any left over.

There were many talented parents at Fairfield, and some became involved in making costumes. One mother made over thirty superb elf costumes for a class of grade six students who were working on a sort of rock 'n roll version of the story of Santa's little helpers. Her son was featured in this production, and she put her considerable skills toward its success.

Another parent professed to know a lot about sound systems and was very concerned about ours. "It carries *very* poorly. I have just the thing for you." The next day he delivered his acoustic marvel. It was so powerful it blew our fuses immediately and I could not use the microphone nor could I see over the top of his contraption without standing on a box that Greg found in some obscure part of the school.

In spite of that setback, things were going swimmingly until the calls began to flood our lines. These were to do with tickets. What about grandparents? Ex-husbands? Nannies? Out-of-town guests? Older siblings and toddlers? There were five hundred and sixty students in our school and the gym should seat a maximum of three hundred and fifty, according to fire regulations.

"You really should be counting all the students performing at any given time *as well as* the audience," one of the parents told me. He was a fireman.

"Right," I said, thinking that if we calculated his way we could possibly accommodate one half parent per child per night.

"Your ticket policy would not hold up in court!" an angry mother told Pauline, our office assistant. Apparently she had two ex-husbands who wanted to see the show.

In addition to working on a presentation, each class decorated a door-sized banner to display in our gym for the big nights, and on the last Monday before the holidays our sporting place was transformed with children's artwork. Chairs were set up, Greg dealt with the fuse problem, stage lighting was organized and a collective deep breath was taken.

On Tuesday morning the dress rehearsal for both concerts took about three hours with a brief recess stretch in the middle. Students were able to see each other perform, and parents unable to attend the Wednesday or Thursday evening concerts were in the audience. Many parents with tickets for those evenings came to the rehearsal as well, as *once was not enough!* I sympathized with the latter, as I had been enjoying the build up for weeks. The staff had prepared concerts with lots of variety, humor, musical finesse and heart.

There were a few moments of near panic. A kindergarten child threw up and a grade six elf rock 'n rolled himself off a riser. The strings took so long to tune themselves that the very excited young audience had trouble refocusing after they had clapped vigorously for the tuning session. Grateful for the end, I thanked everyone in the audience for their patience, reminded them again that this had been a *rehearsal*, and promised that the next two nights would be streamlined and exciting.

"Kind of disorganized," a father said to me as I climbed down from my perch. My face must have carried a distinct message, because he hastily added, "But of course, it was only a *rehearsal*," and slunk out.

That afternoon our custodian put his head into my office. "Bad weather system moving in," he told me.

"How bad?"

"Icy rain forecast. Could be snow. Supposed to go down to minus five tonight. Saying not to drive unless you have to."

I glued myself to the pessimistic weather channel that night and thought of all the work staff, students and parents had done for this concert revival. I thought of all the kids who were excited about performing in their first Christmas concert, and I thought about Mrs. Brownrigg and her elf costumes. I desperately tried to think of anyone who might take on the responsibility of deciding whether to go ahead with the concerts or to cancel them, but no one came to mind. I was it.

There was a snowfall during the night, and as Wednesday dawned grayly my husband told me that the forecast was grim. Apparently there was not enough snow on the roads for good traction; underneath, in most areas, was pure ice. I decided to wait as long as possible to announce a cancellation if that was necessary. Even with extreme winter conditions, Victoria could turn downright balmy within hours.

I called the staff together before any students arrived and told them of my dilemma. Just as I thought, about half thought the concert should go ahead regardless of the weather. I told them I would wait until recess, check the forecast again and make a decision in time for the morning kindergarten classes' departure.

By 10:00 nothing had improved. If anything, things were looking worse. I shut my office door and sat, revisiting my dilemma during the few minutes until recess announcements. I had called a number of other principals, and some schools were canceling, others going ahead with their concerts. The parents I had spoken to that morning were all in favor of things going ahead, but they lived nearby.

By the time I made those announcements I knew what I had to do, and because I believed it was in the best interest of our community I was prepared for the fallout. A newsletter went home with every child, and in it I stated that I was not prepared to put any student, staff member or parent at risk, even for such an important event.

Some parents who could have walked with their children expressed bitter disappointment, others were understanding. "What a hard decision for you, Judy!" one mother said. "It was the right one. If even one student had been hurt…" I hugged her gratefully.

And so the first concert in a very long time at Fairfield school did not come to pass that December. What I did not know then, of course, was that I would experience six years of concerts that were truly memorable: soloists by gifted children, author Eric Wilson narrating our *Scrooge*, funny class performances and beautiful singing before delighted audiences. One night a young violinist played "Ave Maria" so movingly that we all jumped to our feet, many of us wiping away tears. "If I had to die now, I'd die happily," a young father said to me as he led his little daughter away from the school that night. It had been her first concert performance.

I knew nothing of those concerts to come as that term finished with so much disappointment. Staff members were fine; in spite of all the work they had done, many expressed relief at not having to drive in the icy weather. Our students were captivated by the rare snowfall, classroom parties and impending holiday, so the concerts faded in importance. But for Mrs. Brownrigg, a rack of thirty unused elf costumes was a testament to an awful lot of wasted time. I had learned a lot about this complex, demanding and talented community in four months, I thought. Now I needed my two weeks reprieve to digest it all and recoup some energy. I

Judy Bertram Tomlinson

shut the door to my office, feeling the sticky residue from many little hands.

Later, I stood alone on our grounds, marveling at the freshness, the cold and the quiet. It was unusually still. Students, parents and staff had dissolved into their holiday landscape and the sudden void was breathtaking.

January newsletter, 1991

*Dear Parents:*

*Happy New Year! So far January has been a busy and productive month. Our new Primary One students have adjusted well despite large classes. Two new assistants have been employed for an additional two hours each day to help in the two English classes and both of them report that they are thoroughly enjoying themselves. Mrs. Hancock has returned from an Australian summer with new ideas, enthusiasm and an enviable tan!*

*Some interesting projects are underway. The classes of Mr. Belanger and Mr. Drouin are involved in an engineering contest, and Mrs. Bailey and Mr. Frenette are exploring new ways to use the video camera as a teaching device. Our teams are doing well. The Drama Club continues into the new term, folk dancing has begun under the direction of Mrs. Rees, and our peer counselors are discussing the organization of primary noon activities. Staff members are working on plans for Multicultural Week (February 25-28).*

*Looking back over months that have included flooding, blizzards and international crises, I am more convinced than ever of the excellent morale and positive, caring atmosphere of our school.*

*A big welcome to all of our dual entry students who are just beginning their kindergarten year. We have sixteen new kindies in English, and twelve in French.*

*Thanks again to all you parents who do so much to help us!*

*Judy Bertram, Principal*

# CLASS COLONIST

Teachers Report: This week Mr. Smith will share his stories of the grade sevens he teaches. In his own words he said that he thinks that the sevens are having fun this term but a little too much fun. He thinks that right now the sevens are still a little loud and are not learning as they should be. But all in all it is so far a good year. Mr. Smith thinks that soon when the sevens settle down and get down to some serious studying and learning things will be better.

News: What about the snow, and maybe a strike and a war? Some of us are quite hyper, we think, but some just carry on, like: Kate cleans her desk...WOW!...Ben gets magazines from the library... on Debbie's card...Sara has a birthday...and 85 double bubbles... Jess goes out with a fourteen-year-old...that has her name...Jane gives love notes and then gets postal at the writers...Bush takes on Silverchair on Combat eclips...I wonder who will win (hint hint)...Karen got good on the science test...What's with her? Jen and Liz make lipstick!

Journal Entry: Sunday, January 6, 1991

- *My younger daughter is twenty-five today! And she's so far away!*
- *One week on the new diet. Strange eating rice at every meal! This needs to <u>work!</u>*
- *Decided on School Resolutions:*
    1. *More professional and dignified with staff, as opposed to always looking like I am constantly available for personal problems.*
    2. *Have a quiet time to eat lunch.*
    3. *Have some work-free weekends.*
    4. *Always be on top of paperwork.*

*These are important if I am going to survive, I know it!!!!!!!!!!*
*Hard to predict what this new year is going to bring...*

Journal Entry: Monday, January 7, 1991

- *Snow!*
- *Back to school—incredibly hectic! Phones ringing, new registrations, etc.*
- *Thought it might be calm and it WASN'T.*

# 10   NEW YEAR 1991

"Rice and yams and *what else*?" My husband regarded me skeptically.

"Green beans, cooked or tinned pears and peaches. No sugar, caffeine, dairy or wheat. And it's *every* meal." I had been reading from a book on allergies.

"Happy New Year," he whimpered, padding away down the hall.

"It's only for *me*," I shot back, knowing full well the dampening impact my new diet would have on his culinary creations. "Starting tomorrow."

It was an experiment I had to try. Years prior to this decision I had caught a bad flu which left me with aching muscles. The rheumatologist I finally consulted did the mandatory pokes into my suffering soft tissues and concluded that I had a form of fibrositis, probably brought on by the flu and exacerbated by stress.

"Be with you all your life," he informed me clinically. "Some times will be worse than others."

The pain became something I learned to live with, although blow-drying my hair, rolling down the window of my car and putting on a jacket were often excruciating. The previous year this had caused me to think very carefully about applying for a principal position; then I would have times when I would almost forget the condition, usually under a calming summer sun.

It had been at its worst this fall, and when I confided my condition, a staff member loaned me a book expounding the benefits, to some, of a diet that consisted of food few people on the planet cannot eat. The indulgent, rich Christmas was over, a new year and a new term were to begin. I had nothing to lose. If the fibrositis did not improve, I would have to resign.

The following Monday I opened the door to my pristine office at 7:30. I was wearing a January sale special and my new cool, more reserved manner. This dissolved fairly rapidly as a staff member's response to my New Year's greeting indicated distress. His spouse had left him over the holidays and he was beside himself. I gave him a hug and listened to his grief until school affairs took precedence. Areas outside needed sanding before the children arrived and the custodian was going to skate around to test them, he told me; we had the sand. A mother wanted an appointment to discuss sexism in the physical education curriculum and a call came regarding an urgent meeting for principals the following morning. The meeting was going to deal with some much-publicized, proposed budget cutbacks.

By 8:30 most of the staff had exchanged pleasantries and expressed concerns over those cutbacks, possible job action and the impending war in the Gulf. In spite of earlier information meetings, new kindergarten parents were full of questions regarding the Dual Entry program which allowed children turning five to join the classes which had been in progress since September. Nothing, including the weather, felt calm or predictable, and the students, excited by more snow and sensing unrest, seemed unusually agitated.

At 9:30 a student's neediness drew me into the eye of that storm. She was twelve, rather heavy-set and always serious; just then she looked overwhelmed. When I heard her telling our secretary that she was unwell I called her into my office. According to Martha her mother had caused the distress: over the holidays she had told her daughter that there would not be room for her at their house any longer. She would have to return to her foster mother.

"I just *can't* go there! I *hate* it there! What's going to happen to me?" she sobbed.

All other uncertainties were on hold while I listened and then phoned her mother. There had been a misunderstanding, it seemed, and Martha went back to class only a little comforted. I made a note to speak with her teacher.

That week, within the classrooms, students, teachers and support staff carried on with their January curriculum. I had booked all teachers for one-on-one meetings and these were fun, informative, and apparently appreciated by the teachers who were able to express their professional goals and frustrations in an intimate setting. There was confirmation that the French grade sevens would indeed be going to Quebec that spring and there was the ancillary rejoicing and complaining from some parents. I taught some lessons in several classes and hoped for a productive term for our students.

The Primary Teachers January bulletin looked optimistic, but only at first glance:

## HAPPY 1991!

*The Greater Victoria Teachers Association wishes you a productive and fulfilling 1991! Workshops have been designed to provide you with inspiration and assistance in coping with the abundant changes in education, as well as give you a time to relax and socialize with your colleagues.*
*Mark your calendar with these dates:*

- *Jan. 8: Meet with the Minister of Education, S.J. Willis auditorium at 4:00: "Issues of Current Interest in Education"*
- *Feb. 12: Dr. Bob Armstrong, a popular guest speaker. He is a psychologist from Vancouver whose wife is a teacher. The topic, "The Democratic Model"*

- *Mar. 12: Wellness. Teachers need to learn to take care of themselves experiencing stress. Watch for more details.*
- *Apr. 9: Mr. Wyn Davies will bring to us his expertise on the unique topic of Integrating Art and Science.*
- *Apr. 10: A Polaroid Camera Workshop about using the Polaroid camera in the classroom, also by Wyn Davies. Sponsored by the Sooke District.*
- *May 13: A Sharing Session for Early and Late Primary. The topic is to be announced.*
- *June 18: Annual Primary Tea, Celebration and Retirement Party.*

*Your Primary Teachers Association executive is studying the situation of class size at the K, K/1 and 1 level. Our LSA would be able to use the information about class numbers to work toward an improved class size regulation in this district. Please enter your numbers (beside September, 1990 and January, 1991) and return.*

*Thank you for your cooperation!*

On January 16, workshops on the District's "Sierra system," its computer program, began for school administrators. Most of us had limited technology skills and realized that our secretaries would not be crossing picket lines in the event there was a teachers' strike. Our District's "Communication Contingency Plan" memo was specific and simple:

*In the event of the job action by the teachers, it will be necessary to maintain a communication link with the Superintendent's office. This will be done by a modified YELLOW ALERT method.*

*I would suggest that you learn how to access your own or your secretary's Word 11 account to receive your YELLOW ALERT messages.*

*You must access the account and follow the attached procedures to receive any YELLOW ALERT messages. This should be done twice each day: 8:30 a.m. and 3:30 p.m.*

*I would also suggest that you "buddy up" with another school to ensure that you receive the message. (Fifty calls to the Board will not get through). I trust this will be an effective way to communicate, at least one way.*

Following this message was a long and rather daunting list of instructions on accessing our Yellow Alerts.

On the same day that I tackled the Sierra System, the Gulf War began. Somehow the news passed through the school and by late afternoon one teacher was affected to the point of tears. Some of the older students expressed fear to their teachers, and the next day a member of the local police force, making his regular visit, told me that he considered the war to be the beginning of the end of the world. I wondered, when he told me that, if I had succeeded in looking more professional and less open to stream-of-conscious flotsam. My New Year's resolution seemed distant and unattainable at that point.

I had little time to dwell on my own image. In a union newsletter, an executive member expressed frustration at having to serve seventy-two hours notice to the School Board before job action could legally begin. In his diatribe he referred to a book on school leadership unfortunately titled *Atilla To The Rescue* that had been discussed in a principals' meeting with the superintendent. The disgruntled and excited union leader suggested that local teachers "grab your pick and shovel and construct your own Hadrian's Wall." His missive ended, "Oh, for a cauldron of boiling oil!" Obviously, positive district relationships were rapidly dissolving.

A reporter from a local newspaper phoned to ask how the school was coping with the war. Which one? I thought.

I gave the office staff instructions regarding the following letter that was to go home with each student in the city that afternoon.

*January 21, 1991*

*Dear Parents:*

*The Greater Victoria Teachers' Association has given the Victoria School District a 72-hour notice of a possible strike. In the event of job action at our school, the building will remain open during regular hours and school administration will be in attendance. However, please note the following:*

- *there will be no regular instructional program available*
- *all bus transportation will be cancelled*
- *extra-curricular and evening activities will be cancelled during the period, as well as before and after school daycare programs*

*PARENTS ARE THEREFORE ENCOURAGED TO KEEP THEIR CHILDREN AT HOME OR MAKE ALTERNATIVE ARRANGEMENTS FOR THEIR CARE.*

*It is important to keep a close ear to the radio in the morning. You will learn at that time whether our school will be affected. In the meantime, you may want to make plans for the possible care of your children ahead of time.*

*Needless to say, we hope that a strike can be averted. If we can provide any more information, please contact the school or the school board office. Your cooperation and understanding is appreciated.*

*Yours truly,*
*Judy Bertram, School Principal*

On January 22 the Yellow Alert stated, "Negotiations are continuing this evening. Further information to come tomorrow morning. Watch for a Yellow Alert at 9:00." And in my journal that evening I noted that Tel Aviv had been bombed and there were many casualties.

The next morning, the following was pulled from the Sierra System:

## STATUS OF BOARD/GVTA NEGOTIATIONS

As of January 22, 1991 at 7:40 p.m., negotiations with the Greater Victoria Teachers Association have broken off. The GVTA has organized a study session for Friday, January 25, 1991 from 9:00 a.m. to 11:00 a.m. at UVIC Center. All teachers have been requested to attend.

HEREFORE the CONTINGENCY PLAN WILL BE IN EFFECT AS OF 8:00 A.M., JANUARY 25, 1991. PARENTS WILL BE ADVISED THAT, WHILE SCHOOLS ARE OPEN, CHILDREN/ YOUNG PEOPLE SHOULD BE KEPT AT HOME OR MAKE ALTERNATIVE ARRANGEMENTS FOR THEIR CARE.

REGULAR CLASSES WILL CONTINUE AT 1:00 P.M. GVTA ADVISES THAT SCHEDULED SKI TRIPS WILL BE SUPPORTED.

Principals are requested to:
- send letters to parents/guardians home today (Appendix B)
- prepare for the withdrawal of services (Appendix A)
- advise Community School Coordinators (as applicable)
- prepare copies of Principals' Daily Strike Report (Appendix C)

Please ensure that your administration team is familiarized with the details of the Contingency Plan. Secondary schools: You will be advised regarding Provincial Examinations—watch for the Yellow Alert at 1:00 today.


The chairperson of the Board of Trustees sent a letter reiterating the fact that negotiations between the District and the GVTA had broken off. She added, "The Board of Trustees wishes to advise all District Staff of the information which has been provided to the Registrar of the Public Sector Collective Bargaining Disclosure Registry, in compliance with Bill 79, Part 4(2)." The submission contained a summary of "all matters with respect to which agreement has been reached," *and* a summary of "all matters with respect to which no agreement has been reached." It added, "The major areas of disagreement are substantial monetary items which the G.V.S.B. is unwilling and/or unable to meet."

My journal entries for that day and the following two days note that I had meetings with peer counselors and with the primary staff. One grade five boy was causing frustration by repeatedly misplacing his bus pass, and then one recess he became stuck on our roof. I observed a lesson by a grade seven teacher I was evaluating, and he informed me that the "kids were good" because I "was in there." I taught in a grade one class and had concerns about a special needs student that were taken to the school-based team.

Friday I noted that there had not been enough advance notice given for the teachers' "study session," and that it had to be rescheduled for the following Monday. A letter was then sent to parents asking them to disregard the former one, and details of the Monday job action were included. My final entry that day states, *"Gulf War continues—Saddam is polluting the Gulf."*

On the morning of Monday, January 28, the school was devoid of teachers and students. One parent grilled me about the term "study session" and wanted to know why I could not tell him what it was those teachers were *studying.* He knew that

I knew that he knew the answer to his own question. I thought of similar sessions I had attended in the past and did not share my memories.

"You *must* know what they are *studying*," he insisted. "You're the *principal*."

He left, apparently disgusted with my studied neutrality. Perhaps it was lucky for him that he was gone before the teachers returned from their studying. They were sounding militant and the possibility of a strike seemed likely. Later that day at the usual weekly staff committee meeting the chairperson asked me to explain "hiring policies." Greg and I practiced on the Sierra System before we went home and I noted that it was "tricky."

### YELLOW ALERT
January 30, 1991  8:12 AM

RE: GVTA JOB ACTION PLANNED, BEGINNING THURSDAY, JANUARY 31, 1991

MEDIATION TALKS HAVE BROKEN OFF. REGRETFULLY, COMMON GROUND COULD NOT BE REACHED ON SALARIES AND CLASS SIZE.

1. Advise parents/guardians by letter today; use format in Contingency Plan as a guide.
2. Obtain outside keys from staff, other than custodians.
3. Meet with support staff (CUPE 947 and CUPE 382) to advise them of situation, ensuring that they know the Board of Trustees respects their position.
4. Review procedures with Vice Principals re: Picket Lines (BCPVPA Bulletin)

Your ZONE LEADER will be in contact with you today. If there are problems or concerns, please call your Zone Leader directly. If I can be of assistance, please contact me.

THE YELLOW ALERT SCHEDULE WILL CONTINUE UNTIL
FURTHER NOTICE 8:30 and 3:30

People had a slightly wild-eyed look to them as information
and directives sifted down from those in charge of job action.
Each child went home with the following letter.

*Dear Parents,*

*The Greater Victoria Teachers' Association will commence job
action tomorrow, January 31st. Although our building will remain
open during regular hours and school administration will be in
attendance, please note the following:*
- *there will be no regular instructional program
  available.*
- *all bus transportation will be cancelled.*
- *there will be no heat in our building.*
- *extra-curricular and evening activities will be cancelled
  during this period, as well as before and after school
  daycare programs.*

*PARENTS ARE, THEREFORE, ENCOURAGED TO KEEP
THEIR CHILDREN AT HOME OR MAKE ALTERNATIVE
ARRANGEMENTS FOR THEIR CARE.*

*So far, this job action affects tomorrow, January 31st. However, it
is important to keep a close ear to the radio in the morning. You
will learn at that time whether our school will be affected after
tomorrow. In the meantime, you may want to make plans for the
possible care of your children ahead of time.*

*Needless to say, we hope further job action can be averted. If you require any more information, please contact the school board office. Your cooperation and understanding are appreciated.*

*Yours truly,*
*Judy Bertram, School Principal*

By 3:20 we had another Yellow Alert that outlined the need for accurate information regarding any time staff members missed for job action. We were not to allow media into the schools, although reporters might be speaking to people on picket lines. We were informed of our zone contact people, and some February meetings and workshops were cancelled.

Teachers left early that day after handing in their outside keys, and I heard them discussing picket duty and the need for warm clothing. As they left with students and parents, I walked around the playground and waved back to children who were exhibiting Friday exuberance for a Wednesday dismissal. Some were loaded down with homework.

One mother pulled her son's cap down over his ears, circled his scarf one more time around his neck and straightened, facing me. "So, the strike. Explain what it's all about!"

"Class size is an important issue," I said. "We have classes that are far too big to do the job we need to do with our students." Before we were into further discussion I excused myself and went inside to hunker down, if possible. Our school was a political powder keg: one of the negotiators for the union was a teacher on staff and several of the trustees, including the chairperson of the Board, were parents of children attending Fairfield. Negotiations at that time were face-to-face.

*Don't* engage in discussions regarding issues, we had been warned. As arms of the Board in the schools, principals and vice principals were to be seen as opinionless, calm and detached. Judging by the way the staff approached me, I knew I had not succeeded in presenting a detached persona. And further to my New Year's resolutions, the burgundy leather organizer on my desk was stuffed with appointments and notes to myself, overshadowed only by a pile of overdue paperwork that would take weekends to tackle. "*Do the people things first,*" we had been told in our vice principal days. What choice was there?

On the upside, eating blandly for a month had almost cured my fibrositis.

# YELLOW ALERT

DATE:         January 31, 1991   8:39 AM
FROM:         The Superintendent
TO:           ALL SCHOOL PRINCIPALS
RE:           ONGOING COMMUNICATION

Good morning to all. Zone leaders will be visiting each of the schools this morning. If in the meantime you need assistance please call any zone team member who will respond immediately. If I can be of any help please call (the superintendent's number).

Please note that NO MEDIATION is taking place currently. I will provide an update immediately should the situation change.

Your daily strike reports are to be put in the mail and will be recorded and filed once the strike is completed.

Thank you for your cooperation and abundant support.

# 11   STRIKE

The unusually cold and wet Victoria winter continued on that last day of January as Fairfield's two administrative officers marched through the teachers' picket line. "Scabs!" someone yelled, but she was grinning a little. It was 8:00, the pickets had been on duty for over an hour and they looked frozen. *I* looked ridiculous: wool socks, boots, tights, jeans, three layers of sweaters, an old jacket, scarf and toque. All I had to do was to pull in my appendages, I thought, and I could roll past them. So much for pride and power dressing. I told them we would make coffee.

Schools without children are strange, hollow places; without children and staff they are sepulchral. Greg and I had the additional problem of having to open a school with an old manual heating system that required an attending ticket-holding custodian. Our boiler barely groaned and wheezed heat into far-flung classrooms at the best of times; now there was a loud silence from its quarters as we made our way up to the main floor, turning on lights and unlocking doors as we went.

"I wonder how many kids we'll get?" Greg rubbed his forearms. "They'll freeze in here!" Neither of us reiterated our concerns about what we would actually do with them when and if they came in large numbers. It had been a topic of amusement bandied about by staff.

"You can fit three hundred and fifty in the gym," one had mused.

"What sort of film would appeal to all age groups?"

"I think they should have lessons appropriate to their grades and their individual learning styles," one announced, being current with the educational trends. We smiled obligingly and privately wondered.

I reluctantly took off my gloves and began the preparations needed to make a huge pot of coffee. Greg turned the staff room oven up to "high" and opened its door. Eventually some heat could be felt in my own office. Farther away, with the outer office door open, I could clearly see my breath. By the time the first pickets had received coffee and cookies, we had rounded up a couple of area heaters. One was to go near the secretary's desk in order to keep us from freezing as we pulled the Yellow Alerts from the Sierra System. The other would help to keep students a little warmer than they might have been. None showed that day.

As the pickets changed shifts every few hours, we were kept busy carrying all the coffee paraphernalia out and back, cleaning up and starting over again. The phones rang a few times, but on the whole it was eerily quiet. Greg brought a radio into the staff room and we sat close to the open oven, listening to the media's reporting of the strike. Those newscasters, particularly the hosts of open-line shows, were in their element, and from what we heard the public seemed divided in their support or lack of it for this job action. Wherever they stood on the issue, they stood heatedly.

As our routine became streamlined, I began to tackle the backlog of mail on my desk, grateful for something else to accomplish. The pile was interesting. Among the documents regarding the District's budget and the usual items requiring signing authority, were a number of missives expressing frustration. One was from a principal who, like many of us, had reservations about the Dual Entry program. At the top he had put a cartoon of a crossing guard with a sign saying STOP!

*BELIEVE IT OR NOT! THIS IS A TRUE STORY. ARE WE TAKING DUAL-ENTRY A BIT TOO FAR?*

A small four-year-old boy is one of our dual entry students. When he goes for a bowel movement he must be held on the toilet so he won't fall in.

He asks the teacher to "come and hold me while I do pwaps." (plops?) Not only is he young and small but he talks baby-talk which is understandable, because he is.

The kindergarten teacher has asked me if I too would like to take a turn doing "pwaps" duty. I told her I would like to but I am concerned about taking little boys into the bathroom and what that can do to a man's reputation these days.

*PRINCIPAL ON "PWAPS" DUTY*

Another educator was having a problem with some of the Year 2000 ideals:

*YEAR 2000 TRACK MEET GUIDELINES*
*A track meet designed so that no one loses and everyone wins because they do the best they can. (At least we think so, but cannot be sure as we use no system of measuring.)*

- *High jump: There is no bar, as hitting it could produce an attitude of failure.*
- *Sprint: No set distance. Participants may run in any direction they wish, for as far as they wish. We feel this makes for a less stressful event.*
- *Long jump: In the spirit of non-competition, remember this: "It is not how far you jumped, but that you jumped." The tape measure has no gradations.*
- *Ball Throw: Participants place the ball in a spot that makes them feel good. The emphasis is on creativity, not brute force.*
- *Endurance Run: Participants will run until they are tired. There is no set distance as we do not believe in encouraging students to go further than is comfortable for them.*

- *Awards: Everyone will receive a huge trophy with everyone's name on it for each event.*

*In these events, we have attempted to establish a non-competitive, no failure situation. This is to better prepare our young people to be successful in our non-competitive society.*

A former teaching colleague and long-standing union president had forwarded a copy of a letter she had sent to the present executive:

*I cannot believe the vitriolic diatribe in the last GVTA newsletter. I don't mind admitting that I voted with the minority regarding strike—as a pacifist, I am a firm believer that negotiations and mediation are our strengths. However, I do not intend to undermine the majority position.*

*But—when a "cauldron of boiling oil" is prayed for, I am sickened beyond belief.*

*In this time of world turmoil and intense inner anguish for many, surely we, as educators, should set examples of caring, compassion and dignity, not resort to cheap and petty mini-war mongering!*

*If I were a praying person, I would pray only that peace could reign in the heart of the person who penned the violent statements in our Newsletter. I am not amused nor beguiled by such outpourings—only saddened.*

*I trust these statements were not made in a time of thoughtful soul-searching! They do not represent me or my belief systems—I find them personally abhorrent!*

Greg walked in with the coffee tray as I was reading this letter. "How is it out there?" I asked. The shift had changed and his face was an interesting shade of red. Apparently one of the picketers had asked him if we were busy inside, "dreaming up things for the staff to do." His response was vehement, he told me, and went something like, "Not bloody likely!" I thought it was a good thing that he showed them he had spirit and a limited tolerance on that cold January day, when scuds were being launched over the Gulf, when school communities were paralyzed and school teachers, support staff and principals were wondering about coping.

On a happier note, we had each received certificates from our principal mentor in another school. He had thought it wonderful and hilarious that Greg and I would form an administrative team together.

THE PRINCIPAL'S PENCIL AWARD
TO: Mrs. Bertram, Principal, Fairfield School
FOR: Successfully completing her first half-year as principal.
January 24, 1991 Signed, [Mentor]

THE PRINCIPAL'S PENCIL AWARD
TO: Greg O'Connor, Vice Principal, Fairfield School
FOR: I'm sure you can think of something.
January 24, 1991 Signed, [Mentor]

An assistant superintendent dropped in briefly and we completed the daily strike report. Before we left our freezing school, we pulled off the 4:00 Yellow Alert. It stated that, effective at 4:30 that day, access to the computers would require the password "SCUD." The superintendent reported a summary of information about the first day of the strike: Very few students were in attendance, and picket lines were calm and friendly with the exception of one school. Two teachers had reported for work, and feedback from the community was mixed. There was information regarding who was and who was not at the bargaining table. Day One was over and I could not wait to get into a hot bath.

As the strike continued, routines inside and outside Victoria schools became established. Communication improved between principals who did not have a lot of students to attend to, and concerns could be discussed over the phone. The teachers' union headquarters issued motivational bulletins called "Outside Victoria Schools," to pickets regularly. Strike Bulletin #16, for example, reminded members that "Rain falls on your shoulders, not on your hearts!" It gave an informational update, and concluded with a report on the status of negotiations: "Following a lengthy session with the board, the mediator returned to inform us that, despite our best efforts and our expressed willingness to compromise, the Board refused absolutely to move on the remaining issues of class size, salary and benefits." Trustees' phone numbers were listed "if you or any parents wish to know who to call," and teachers were informed about media coverage: "We are buying ads; listen, watch and look for them."

There were other bits of encouragement for the pickets:

- Prince Rupert sends their moral support!
- Quote from a parent phoning in: "I am not happy leaving my children in the care of an administrative officer!"
- It has been reported that bus drivers are waving support and many drivers have honked support along with the appropriate hand gestures.
- It has been reported by our couriers that people seem to be happy on the line!
- One of the superintendent's assistants didn't sleep last night and is supplying pickets with coffee today!
- Tuesday night (8:30) is Comedy Night at the Tally Ho. Apparently teachers-on-strike will be material for at least one comedian.

The strike bulletin on the fifth day must have been reflecting an improvement in the weather, because it was headlined, "Happiness is a sunny day!" The "state of negotiations" reported that "at the negotiating table the Secretary Treasurer told us that the ministry supplies monies for 15 personnel in Curriculum and Instruction. At that time (November) this District had 52 professional personnel in Curriculum and Instruction. Since then the helping teachers have gone back into the classroom (to help pay for an administrative foul-up). This, however, did not help class size."

Pickets were reminded of a coming rally, and one school listed the benefits of picketing. They included quitting smoking, joining a fitness club and losing three pounds. Mission, B.C. teachers apparently empathized with Victoria: "We, too, are aware of the heartbreak of encroaching management." Surrey, also, sent moral support: "Don't give an inch!" The bulletin ended with all the choruses to "Teachers' Lament," to be sung to the tune of "Sixteen Tons."

It was on this day that Greg's own newsletter, "In and Out of a Victoria School," was born. Some examples from one issue follow.

SCHOOL HEADQUARTERS: GENERAL OFFICE
(5 DEGREES)

Ms.[Teacher] *struck a blow for teachers by dancing down the sidewalk with hips swaying, arms waving, and fingers snapping in the air as she listens to the sounds of a Mexican jazz band on the earphones of her Walkman. The neighbors who have seen her feel that teachers definitely need a break from the stress and lock their doors when she strolls by.*

*Parent Questions Librarian: A mother asked one of our teachers what he did at the school. He replied that he was a grade seven teacher. She asked what subjects he taught. He replied that he taught everything. She then asked our librarian what he did at the school. At press time he was still thinking.*

*Crow Attacks Goodies: Several unidentified crows were seen attempting to pilfer some cookies from the tray. After repeated threats from one of our teachers, the crows flew away muttering loudly.*

*Turtle Complains: The turtle living in the brick annex protested loudly during a recent interview. "Not only has my food supply dwindled but my T.V. has gone on the fritz and the repairman won't cross the picket line." Attempts were being made to ease the situation.*

*Inside Administrative Officers Weaken: Inside A.O.'s report muscle stiffening and deterioration due to cold. There is also some concern regarding their states of mind. Children inside complain of A.O.'s squabbling over who gets to read the YELLOW ALERT first.*

*Religion Enters Picture: A.O.'s also suspected of becoming religious….have been seen on knees recently praying that a certain student doesn't show.*

*Flash of Recognition: After picketing for two weeks, [Teacher] has recognized the dark-haired woman he has been holding (gasp!) hands with. It turns out that it's his wife whom he has not seen for three years because of each of them working different shifts.*

*From Your Inside A.O.'S* [Administrative Officers]

Greg dropped copies off on the picket lines, and the pickets loved it. Humor is tricky, though, and was one of the DON'Ts. During job action, and in many other situations school administrators find themselves, they are not, as a rule, to see the funny side if an issue is contentious. At least they are not to *express* it.

During strike action years later, when all schools and central office were connected by an efficient email system, one principal expressed the odd sensation he felt when he looked out the window of his empty school to see cows lined up along the schoolyard fence, staring soberly back at him. As the cows were normally spread across a green pasture, the sight was startling. His subsequent description tickled something scarcely alive in the depths of our psyches after days of quiet and mounds of paperwork. Our bovine jokes and puns seemed, to some of us, to get better and funnier until a stern warning came from a colleague. She reminded us that we were not acting appropriately, the situation was serious, and our correspondence was being monitored.

Something similar must have happened in the superintendent's office, as the Yellow Alert on the second day of the 1991 strike contained the following message regarding the SCUD password:

Note from last night's alert—we aren't too thrilled with "SCUD". Therefore, we've changed it to "PEACE"—however, we won't do that until 1:00 p.m. to make sure everyone gets their morning messages. So here's the message with the correction in it: EFFECTIVE 1:00 P.M. TODAY, ACCESS TO THE VAX COMPUTERS WILL REQUIRE THE PASSWORD "PEACE".

The missile connotation from the Gulf War must have been too controversial, although we rather enjoyed the memos informing us when "a really big one" was due.

There were very few students in Victoria schools, our superintendent went on to report, and the picket lines seemed quiet and friendly. One teacher had reported for work in a school somewhere in our district, and community feedback was still mixed. Concern had been reported over the length of the strike, the unrealistic demands being placed on teachers, especially with the Year 2000 initiatives, how children would make up learning times, and problems regarding daycare. There were no negotiations taking place.

Things were, in fact, very serious. Many teachers felt stretched with large classes and new programs; principals were expected to demonstrate an educational leadership of programs they did not necessarily fully agree with or fully understand, and parents were often confused. New educational jargon was popping up everywhere.

On the second day of the strike, one student attended Fairfield School, but went home at noon. Our pickets seemed cheerful, I recorded in my journal, but the news flying over the airways was depressing. Our principal mentor, who had many students to look after in his school, was wearing down. And many people we spoke with were experiencing a siege mentality.

On Monday, February 4th, it was still very cold. Four students showed up and a primary teacher brought us baked goodies. I noted the following piece of trivia from my stack of correspondence: in his own language, "Sad*dam*" was a compliment; "*Sad*dam" was a young boy who cleans shoes. At 3:30 I attended a principals' meeting and heard more regarding the standoff between the Board and the union. Two items had, in fact, been agreed upon before the strike: an adjustment of class size when the class contained a special needs student, and clarification around teacher participation in extra-curricular activities. The latter was not to be governed by an administrator.

On the fourth day of the strike our pickets seemed more quiet and concerned. Someone voiced a warning: she had heard that classes of seventy students were a possibility. I bit my lip. DON'T respond, I told myself. Don't even change expression. I am not sure that I was successful. The Yellow Alert that afternoon reported a total of seventy-eight students in our schools, and our mentor said that of those, seventeen had been his, and there were more to come. The evening news reported a big rally at the Board Office, with leaders claiming they were out for "however long" it would take. Later in the same hour, the international news segment featured Saddam Hussein rallying his troops.

On Thursday, February 7th I worked on teacher reports and cleaned the office. Our Yellow Alert informed us that the Board and the union bargaining teams had apparently met for "informal" talks, though there were no scheduled negotiations. Parents were apparently expressing concerns about the length of the strike and some felt that children were being used as a political tool. The Board's chairperson had outlined their final contract offer and requested the union confirm its position by 9:00 the next morning. There were now eighty-nine students in our schools,

Judy Bertram Tomlinson

and our mentor reported that not all the students in his school were enjoying *Treasure Island.*

There was no official response to the Board's offer the next day, but the media reported an "overwhelming" rejection of the offer at the previous night's union meeting. There were ninety-two students in the schools, and a copy of the Board's press statement regarding its offer to the union was sent for our perusal:

FROM THE GREATER VICTORIA BOARD OF SCHOOL TRUSTEES TO THE GREATER VICTORIA TEACHERS' ASSOCIATION.

- An increase in salary of 15% over two years
- An increase in professional development funding from $66 per teacher to $106 per teacher per year
- An increase in elementary teacher preparation time from 60 minutes per week to 80 minutes
- Recognition of the support needed for classroom teachers with regard to integration of special students
- Teachers relieved of all supervision duties before school, during recess, at lunch hour and after school.

TOTAL COST INCREASE OVER TWO YEARS: 18%.
TOTAL DOLLAR VALUE OVER TWO YEARS: MORE THAN $11 MILLION.

This final offer was made January 22, 1991. The Greater Victoria Board of School Trustees believes the rejected offer was fair.

A colleague phoned that day, complaining that union members were "pawns of the NDP." When I pointed out that some of the trustees were NDP as well, he cut me off. At the post office later, someone harangued Greg for being connected to the school system.

Monday the impasse continued, and the principals' meeting was depressingly uneventful. I was getting through an amazing amount of paperwork, however, and was feeling on top of the administrivia that had piled up while I was dealing with all those people issues. The teacher evaluation reports I completed confirmed my admiration for some master teachers at the school, and the weather was turning into Victoria's "pre-spring." I had shed at least one layer of clothing and a mountain of paper.

One hundred and six Victoria students were in attendance two days later and our mentor had twenty-one in his school plus a mother who was demanding the right to hold a birthday/Valentine's party in her daughter's classroom. He was beside himself. The Yellow Alert informed us that a new mediator would be involved in negotiations that were to resume shortly. A Five Year Strategic Plan would soon be presented to the Board by central office administrators, and a media blackout was now in effect. Some students were calling the Board Office, wondering when school would resume.

That Thursday was Valentine's Day. We brought donuts out to the pickets and were presented with flowers, chocolates and a lovely card. One comment stated, "Well done, team, you will never be A.O.'s to us!" Negotiations were seriously underway, we were informed, and later we learned that they carried on all night. The next afternoon, our Yellow Alert was positive:

Feb. 15, 2:36 p.m.: We are close to reaching agreement. Details will follow in media. A special Principals' Meeting will be held at 3:30 p.m. on Monday, Feb. 18 in the Board Room. Assuming that school will be back in session on Monday, February 18, principals are to make sure that teachers, students and support staff are welcomed back in a spirit of celebration. Thank you for your support and patience during this process.

On Saturday, a friend and I put up a WELCOME/BIENVENUE bulletin board. And on Monday I walked into a warm school: our boiler was wheezing, the lights were on, and office staff were soon smiling and answering our phones. I heard some teachers express relief and renewed energy for their job. Parents and students seemed happy, although the father who had quizzed me about the study session was still full of curiosity.

"What do you intend to do about all the teaching and learning time they've missed?" he asked, gesturing to students pouring into the school.

"All of us need to do our *best*," I replied rather emphatically, and smiled. He hesitated, probably realizing that my response did not fit his question, grammatically or otherwise. He smiled weakly back at me, however, and left.

A harsh reality would evolve that spring as the ramifications of paying for the new contract hit CUPE workers and teachers alike. And principals who had predicted a problem were yet to experience the loss of the students' teachers on the playgrounds of the District. That morning, however, the mood was celebratory. Fairfield School was in session.

# CLASS COLONIST

We're Baaaaaaaaaaaaaaaack!!! We finally got another newsletter out! There is so much I can write about now.
So much for the Valentines' Dance (duh!) I know it's a while off but how about an Easter party? And an April Fools party? Ok so I'm party crazy but it's a good way to be.

The ski trip was a blast everyone had fun except for the unexpected accident when we were sledding. Gina did go skiing the second day even though she had a bad night. The only problem was that it didn't last longer. (The ski trip) Liz and Jessie are better after colliding with an ice block. Amy got to ski but missed the snowball fight cause she was sick. Poor Amy.

The Science Fair is coming. You better start getting ready because it's on the 10-11 of March. New Girl!!!! Holly is new in our class (double duh)

In The Class: Eric yells insults….the girls cut hair and drool over Brad Pitt….Gina likes horses…Megan swears at computers…. Kevin and Robert play basketball….Tristan flicks things……Mr. G. gets mad whats new……….Nathan streaks his hair…….Steph and Laura are deep in math….Terry dunks a basket but the teams are sluthered by SJD……Matt plays trumpet….Well kinda….Jenny puts on lipstick……Liz does the same while singing of course….. Toby gets glasses…….Sarah plays her gutair and piano too……. Anna survives….Lettie makes faces….Kate is calm.

Judy Bertram Tomlinson

Special needs intake meeting, 1999

*A large group of educators, therapists and advocates were meeting around the Resource Room table on the spring day when Liam was to be introduced to our school. He was registered in the following September's French Immersion kindergarten, and I had my doubts about his suitability for our program. He was described as having profound disabilities: cerebral palsy, potentially fatal tumors, the need for oxygen and a nurse to be with him at all times. He lived across town, far out of our French catchment area. We had a wonderful French kindergarten teacher, but I was concerned about the extra load she would be taking on in addition to the normal challenges of introducing a second language along with the regular kindergarten program.*

*"He's very bright," the special education director had told me after I had voiced some of these concerns. Surely his neighborhood English program would be enough of a challenge to this child and his family? "They feel he needs something more," she added.*

*Our school-based team listened to Liam's therapists and other workers chirp on about his wonderful personality, verbal skills, social adeptness and mental capacity. We posed many questions to them regarding the role of the nurse, his physical limitations, the expectations the teacher might have and concerns his parents might have with him beginning school. They all glowed when they spoke about him, but people who worked with special needs students often presented them this way. It was his mother who was unusual. She radiated happiness when she spoke about her son; she also seemed totally confident in his assimilation into our program and in our positive acceptance of him in it.*

*After considerable discussion, there was a knock. "That must be Liam," a therapist said. The door was opened and a nurse pushed his wheelchair into the room. "This is a huge group," the four-year-old observed, eyes wide as an enormous grin spread easily across his face.*

*The child some of us were seeing for the first time was a small, fair-haired boy who was obviously paralyzed on one side. His head* leaned over on one tiny shoulder and he had tubes in his nostrils. He was obviously very excited.

Our Resource Room teacher welcomed him and introduced each of the school personnel, explaining our individual roles. She asked him if he was looking forward to September and French kindergarten. "Oh, yes!" he beamed. "I already know some French!"

As he demonstrated a few words I could tell that Cecilia, his teacher, was hooked into this child's persona. She was leaning forward, fascinated. "Liam, will you want to ask the other children about themselves?"

"Oh, yes! I can't wait to meet them!" No shyness there. Encouraged, she asked him if he would mind telling the other children about his physical condition. Why was he in a wheelchair? Why did he have a nurse? They would be full of questions and she obviously wanted this out of the way.

"I won't mind telling them I was born like this," he reassured her. "Lots of kids ask me about that." He paused and looked around at our very serious faces. After some silence, he added, "Of course, sometimes I just tell them my parachute wouldn't open. It makes a better story."

For the whole of his kindergarten year, Liam refused to let anyone feel sorry for him. On his own terms, he developed a unique relationship with each of the adults who worked with him. I was the principal and he never let me forget it. "YIKES!" he would warn, if I tried to enter his classroom unobtrusively. "YIKES!" he would shriek if his chair was pushed around a corner and he suddenly saw me. I came to reciprocate this greeting, once to the puzzlement of an assistant superintendent who witnessed a principal and a special needs student barking, "YIKES!" as they passed each other in the hall.

His classmates adored Liam, who announced that he was in love with one of the little girls. Although he was often tired and had to miss school, he was probably the most popular student in that class. When he had to be away on his birthday, Cecilia had the students stand around the office phone, singing "Bonne fête."

*In his adapted program, he did a fine job of kindergarten. He baked cookies, worked at centers, went on field trips and shared family stories. His oral French was good, and as predicted, he shone socially. The Resource Room teacher tested him for giftedness.*

*Liam died a year after that. At the memorial service, his nurse told us how hard it was for him to miss school as his condition worsened. On one of his more difficult days, she pushed his chair through a park near his home. He was lethargic and very quiet, she told us.*

*Suddenly, he was more alert. "Listen, Jenny!" he demanded. She strained to hear any sound at all. There was a distant swish of cars on a road barely visible. "No, not that! LISTEN!"*

*His nurse described hearing what she thought was someone chopping wood, a bird calling and what might have been a plane in the distance. And then suddenly she knew, because she, too, could hear the very faint sound. It was unlike any other. She looked down at her small charge. His face had gained color and his eyes were shining.*

*"Can you hear it, Jen? It's the most wonderful sound in the world! It's the sound of children at recess!"*

# 12 I KNOW I CAN BE EARRITATING

Young people wonder a lot and expect the adults in their lives to make things clear and all right for them. After the 1991 strike Fairfield students wondered, probed, tested us and generally reacted to that upset in their school lives. They tried to make sense of things: in this case, what seemed to be the loss of a comfortable predictability their school adults had previously shown. We worked hard at re-establishing the order and trust they needed.

Young investigative reporters at the grade two level summarized some staff interviews that answered their own important questions:

*I interview with the principal. She was a teacher then a vice principal then a principal. She said talking on the announcements is not her favorite thing. She loves kids.*

*This is the vice principal. His grade 6s get out at 3:00. He likes different persons. He helps Mrs. Bertram.*

*This is Mrs. Reed. She is the secretary. We learned that she likes accounting. We learned that she likes kids. We learned that she likes helping people. We learned that she likes the principal.*

Fortunately, young people are not shy about letting adults in authority know when they have started to doubt their accustomed order. After teaching a library session to a class of kindergarten students for the first time, I had five minutes to spare. Thinking they might enjoy seeing the top floor of their three-storied school, and knowing their teacher had more prep time coming to her, I led my small charges up the stairs. It was obviously not the way back to their downstairs classroom and my explanation had been ineffectual. From somewhere near the end of the line an alarmed voice warned, *"She doesn't know where she's going!"* And she's attempting to give the impression of running this school, I thought.

I found another of these kindies looking at me intently one day during a story. "Are you trying to look strict, wearing a man's jacket?" she asked. So much for my Jones New York power dressing.

When they are first enrolled, young students seem to regard new adults in their lives as people to be appealed to or to be avoided. A new grade one child was crying loudly on his first day and an assistant had taken him out of the classroom, trying to calm him down. "What is upsetting you so much?" I asked him, having rushed to the racket.

"I don't want *that one,*" he sobbed. Pointing to the poor teacher who was trying to salvage some sort of ambience with her new class, he bellowed, "TOO MUCH MAKE-UP!"

Appeals for my help in restoring order or making something happen often indicated that something more was going on than the students might have expressed. Sometimes teacher reluctance was an issue:

*Dear Judy Bertram,*
*Smith's grade 7 class is trying to get a dance going and your support is needed.*

Having a substitute teacher who does things differently can cause great anxiety.

*The following Students do not agree with the way Mrs. Jacks
disiplins + teaches the way we mean are the following:*
1. *Going threw desks if she finds one peace of paper
   ripped.*
2. *Or washing faces.*
3. *Play gym in skirt and high heals*

One group of boys had had enough by the time this was placed
on my desk:

*PASN (People Against Sharp Nails)*
*This is a petishtion against all the unnecessary blodeshed cosed by
girls nails. Help!*

Another group was also expressing a need for order and justice:

*Mrs. Bertram,*
*Brent, Tyler have had some problems in the class concerning Adam,
Jacob, Andrew. They have been taking things out of Brent's bag
without permision and took a Twinky through it on the cloak room
roof and it fell on Tyler's Trumpet case and smushed on the side of
the case. (Div.5)*

Comments about staff were sometimes very dramatic,
and often very specific. The following concerned playground
supervisors who replaced teachers after the 1991 job action:

*Duties cut down your self esteem and make you feel small. They
don't care if you do a nice thing but if you do something bad they're
right on your ----. I find they make me and my hopes smaller by
the day.*
*FROM MANY UNHAPPY STUDENTS.*

Then there were teachers breaking the rules:

*Mrs. Bertram,*

*Miss Jones was setting a bad example by j-walking. Please speak to Sean, Jeff, and/or Erica. You know where we are. Thank you.*

I was not the only one considered to be a prime helper. One afternoon a tiny, excited boy ran into the office. Out of breath, he looked at me and decided that Greg would be a better candidate for the task at hand. Full of the seriousness of his mission, he drew himself up to his full height and gasped, "We need the *bearded* one!"

Students often feel they have to be completely honest, in spite of parents who may "bend" the truth a little:

*Peter lost the sheet for the lunchin but he will be going.*
*[Parent's Signature, sort of]*
*P.S. My mom told me to forge this because she had to leave.*

Most students are earnest, helpful young people who love nothing more than being part of the organization and the orderly running of a school. In senior years, many elementary students take on monitoring younger students while they eat their lunch. This is not an easy job, as one girl described in her note:

*I will be on leave of absence for today and tomorrow. Because I find lunch monitoring stresses me out. It is not really the kids fault. But its been every recess for almost two weeks now. I never see my friends in another class. (Recess is the only time I can see them.) I'm sorry but I'm in grade six not grade one. I will find a suitable replacement for those two days. If when I return and find it too stressful still, I will resign and find a new person. I'm not quitting now. I hope you understand.*

Answering phones in the office during the noon period is one of the best jobs, because it puts students in the hub of the action:

bloody noses, chats with the principal, relaying and/or being privy to important messages. I always stressed that if calls were from central office, I should be paged. Sometimes they could not reach me.

Date: Sept 4
Time: 12:32
To: Mrs. Bertram
From: Suzanne, Human Resources
Tel No: 123-4567
MESSAGE: CALL THE BORED OFFICE!

Date: Jan 11
Time: 12:45
To: Mrs. Bertram
From: Super Attendance Office
Tel No: 123-4567
MESSAGE: CALL RAY!

Students wonder how far they can push the limits that have been set for them. And adults are expected to be calm, fair problem solvers at all times. Often little recalcitrants feel badly after the fact, or at least profess to, as in the apology written to our band teacher: "I know I can be earritating!" And after pinning a note that stated, "SUGGESTION: FIRE MR. S" on a bulletin board, I received the following from its author:

*Dear Mrs. Bertram,*
  *I am writing to tell you that I apologized to Mr. S. I should not have writen what I did. I did it because he does not lestin to me. I relize that it hurt his felings. I hope you don't hate me for doing this.*

The call of the lawn sprinklers is an ongoing problem on hot days in the spring, and every year it overrides whatever warnings are futilely and routinely announced.

*Dear Mrs. Bertram, we are sorry we did not lisson to the onosment. We did not follow the rules, and we ran thrugh the sprinklers. Next time we will lisson.*

A yearly invitation for notoriety is the all-school photograph. Hundreds of students are lumped together by classes, with staff on the periphery and one poor photographer on the school roof imploring order through a loudspeaker.

*Dear Mrs. Bertram,*
*I am sorry for stiking my tong out at the camera and putting my hands in front of my face where they were not wanted. Please forgive me. Now that I think about it that was very rude.*

At Fairfield we designed a "discipline contract." Our objective was to encourage students to analyze what they had done and to make plans for improving their behavior. This contract was signed by the student, myself or Greg, the parent and the teacher. One of our first penitents accomplished his contract with only a little prodding:

1. WHAT I DID THAT CAUSED ME TO BE HERE NOW: *A small prank that be came a very large prank which I helped in putting stickers with bad stuff on which I did put some bad stickers on other people and tried it on Miss Jones twice and did not suceed.*
2. MY PROBLEM IS: *that should not of continued what someone else started.*
3. WHAT I CAN DO AND WILL DO TOMORROW TO IMPROVE: *will not start any pranks or countinue any pranks and will write a sorry letter to Miss J.*

I supervised the writing of many such contracts and used the time to try to connect with kids needing in-depth discussion around their behavior. There were many revelations during those times and often outside problems were manifesting themselves within the school. When not being worn down by repeated offences as the supervisors outside or the teachers in their classes often were, I could approach the objects of their ire objectively.

"He's *not* cute!" I would be warned by primary teachers, concerned I might be disarmed. I often was. One little blonde boy looked positively angelic as he sat outside my office door that February. He also had an engaging lisp. I asked him why he had been sent to the office.

"I lied to my teacher," he told me.

"What did you tell her?" I asked, ready for anything.

"I told her the lunch monitorth were forth feeding me," he said. I checked on his story; they had told him he should eat his apple rather than throw it away. At such times I had to walk away until I could project a stern principal countenance.

My own ongoing quest to find ways to bring out the best in students who were not exactly lovable sometimes backfired. Our patient, kindly secretary returned to her desk after lunch one day to find that two of our truly tough girls, given the chance to show responsibility as office monitors, had jimmied her locks with paper clips. She let it rip and the girls received a well-deserved tongue-lashing. It was some time before I suggested character building at her desk again.

I did keep trying in other ways. Sometimes the operations were strictly covert, for obvious reasons. In order to draw one group of troubled boys off our playground and into the gym without anyone being aware of what could be regarded as preferential treatment, I regularly announced a meeting of "Boys' Ballet." My tough little crew had decided that this was the best possible name for their gym time: no kid in their right mind would show up except them. My morning announcements of activities included Boys' Ballet on those designated days and went over the heads of staff and students alike, except for the dozen or so characters operating underground with me. "It's boys' *ballet*," I would emphasize to any other fellows who had actually caught the gist of something happening in our gym and thought they might take part. Horrified, they would vanish to the outdoors. As one muscular little rotter worked off steam with a basketball, he told me he would never put down ballet again. Some supervisors commented on improved playground behavior and wondered where some of our "troublemakers" were.

Three of the calm, fair problem solvers on staff at Fairfield ran a program promoting social skills and conflict resolution. Our vice principal, counselor and a classroom teacher worked hard on this very successful venture which was advertised in the school newsletter:

*Fairfield Staff recently staged primary and intermediate assemblies to highlight the first of three skills to help children avoid, or cope constructively, with conflict situations. The foundation of all communication, problem solving and conflict resolution skills is empathy. It consists of the following components:*

- *identifying feelings (disappointed: frustrated: elated: confused...)*
- *predicting how other people feel (reading non-verbal behaviour, body language, facial expressions)*
- *showing others they care.*

*This then is where we are beginning our efforts at fostering mutual understanding and sensitivity to others.*

*In addition, we are offering an eight step approach to deal with conflict. These 8 steps are itemized on posters throughout the school. As well, each student received a bookmark reinforcing the 8 steps. You'll find them on the next calendar. Talk to your child about their preferred ways of dealing with conflict using these items as a point of discussion. Second Step, used in many schools throughout our district and province, is the source of our program. It is a social skills training curriculum focusing on empathy, impulse control and anger management. We will formally address all three of these over the school year, laying the groundwork for a continuous reinforcement of these skills over time.*

*Our slogan for this term is: DON'T PUT UP WITH PUT DOWNS! Look for impulse control and anger management in newsletters to come.*

Signs reflecting these themes were mounted around the school and staff members reported seeing students reminding each other of some of the helpful hints: "Stop, Tristan! Think!"

One day shortly after dismissal, the normally calm and exceedingly patient teacher on the committee asked to see me. His face was uncharacteristically flushed and he was upset. "I've done something awful," he began. While teaching a science class for a colleague, his lesson had been continuously disrupted by one of our most difficult grade fives. He had tried everything he could think of to keep things moving along, and then had snapped. "OUT!" he had commanded, pointing to the door with one hand and bashing his opposite elbow, hard, against the old slate blackboard. The student had left and the board had crumbled.

It took me some time to stop laughing. The poor fellow offered to pay for the board and then, characteristically, waited for me to explain myself. "Oh, Calvin," I gasped when I could, "it's Anger Management Month!" Just outside the office, one of our signs advised us all:

ARE YOU ANGRY? STOP. TAKE A DEEP BREATH. THINK.

I was not immune to having my own buttons pushed. After a particularly long and difficult day, a student burst into my office with an expensive toy and announced, imperiously, that he needed new batteries. "So do I!" I snarled.

Occasionally, our attempts to work hard at being patient, firm but forgiving role models were recognized by students.

Dear Mrs. Birtram,
I would like to thank-you for going out of your way to make sure I get ontrack once again. I am quite glad that you are principal this year. I'm sure that another principal would suspend. (Either in-school or even out of school.) I, myself, think that out-of-school suspensions are absurd! To us kids it's more like a reward than a

*punishment. But back on the 'mail train' I want to tell you that when I enter grade 8, I'm going to miss you.*

*Sincerally, Matt*

From the earliest school years, students wonder about their bodies. *"I'm* ready to fertilize!" one kindergarten boy announced proudly toward the end of the fish tank and duck hatching part of his curriculum.

A grade one boy briefly flashed his small member around during story time, distracting some of his classmates. The brevity of its moment in the proverbial sun probably took his breath away. Treating his behavior the same as if he had brought a toy to class, his teacher told him to *"Put that thing away!"* and carried on with *Charlie And The Chocolate Factory.*

During a curriculum fair someone pointed out an interesting cereal box contribution. In amongst the other imaginative creations was "Sexy Cereal. Eat it and you will feel sexy." The pragmatic teacher had decided that making an issue of that grade three student's obvious testing of limits would be a mistake. Besides, the term "sexy" is flashed at youngsters ad nauseum.

I wasn't so pragmatic myself, at first, when I found a huge penis attached to a stegosaurus in my class's plastercine display. But that was easily remedied by a pinch when no one was looking.

The grade five "maturation" classes were given by public health nurses who did a remarkable job of handling excited, shy, nervous and sometimes rather frightened students. I often helped with the girls' classes; some had already begun to have periods. Regardless of their stage of development, by that age girls and boys have heard rumors and facts. Their knowledge is often a muddle of childish nonsense and adult attitudes.

The end of the boys' and girls' sessions always involved allowing the students to write any question on a slip of paper and hand it in to the nurse. She answered as many as time allowed with as much information as she felt appropriate. One complete set contains the obvious, the surprising and the poignant wonderings of this age:

- *How many eggs are there in the overy?*
- *Why do boys have a penus?*
- *What is addalesence?*
- *How do you know when you're pregnant.*
- *Are you saposed to make noises when you have sex.*
- *How big is a normal size for your pennis?*
- *Does it hurt when your brest grows?*
- *What color is our sperms?*
- *Does it hurt to stick a tampax up your virginia?*
- *When youre nervous does your penice get bigger?*
- *How do you know when to have sex.*
- *When <u>boys</u> have a period what happens?*
- *Why are wet dreams called dreams?*
- *Why do man masterdat?*
- *Does it hurt to have sex?*
- *Can your penis brake.*
- *Why do they call sex (The Birds and the bees)?*
- *Why does your penis harden?*
- *Why do you have a pleasurable feeling and what does it feel like.*
- *What if your sister knows what sex is and wants to try it and asks your brother to try it with him?*
- *Can your eyes get bigger when you grow up?*
- *What happens when men and women have surgury and they cut the tubes that carry eggs and sperms.*
- *Why does your penise get bigger?*
- *What makes us feel horny.*
- *Why do people have sex?*
- *Why do girls have eggs and boys have spurms and why do spurms come out of a penus.*
- *Why do you get hair in places and not in other places?*
- *Why do you get cramps when you're going threw puberty?*
- *Why do you get boner?*

- *Can identical twins get stuck together?*
- *When do you get pubic hairs?*
- *How many times could you have sex.*
- *When do you have twins etc. and do you get bigger than usaul.*
- *Why dose you dick get hard.*
- *How do you have sex?*
- *What happens if an egg comes out each overy and they both get ferdalized.*
- *How do I get aids?*
- *When do you need to youes a kodom*
- *When do boys get sperms?*
- *How do you know that your body is normal or not normal?*
- *Whens the usual age you go into puberty?*
- *Why do boys and girls have to change?*
- *Why does everything change?*
- *Why?*

After those sessions we would sometimes experience a period of snickering, quickly nipped in the bud by classroom teachers. For the most part I believe these students were relieved to hear some simple facts from a medical professional. Each year they seemed to take in what they needed to know and then go on with the business of being children, as much as the media allowed for that.

A year later, in grade six, students with parent permission were inoculated against Hepatitis B. A team of nurses administered three injections over the ten months school was in session. This was organized with precision. Class lists were provided, candies readied for a sugar fix, stuffed animals were in the room for hugs and consent forms were made ready by class. How traumatic can a small injection be? For some reason, for some children, *very*. Nurses experienced fainting, crying, shivering and even biting. Most cuddled a stuffed animal during the shot, sucked a candy afterwards and wobbled back to class, often letting the uninitiated know there was "nothing to it."

Grade sevens who eyed the sixes on their way to the nurse would offer support from their smug vantage point:

"It *really* hurts!"

"Don't worry. You won't die. Not quite."

"I still have the scar!"

It is unclear why some students react so strongly to what would be an unpleasant but manageable necessity at another age. Possibly some are intensely worried about how they will react in front of their peers. Certainly some of these sixes were much more fragile if they knew ahead of time when their shots would be.

Near the end of our grade sevens' elementary experience, I regularly booked a trained public health person to teach "Sex Ed." I had known a few grade seven teachers who were brave enough to tackle this on their own, and during one of my vice principal years I found one of these in a state of near panic one morning just before class. He was setting out the plastic model of a uterus in preparation for his morning class and frantically trying to figure out where to attach the fetus models that were at different stages of development. Not being in his state of stress but imagining his students pouring in and the guffaws beginning, I did manage to find the small, magnetized color-coded spots. The truth is that most teachers would rather be unemployed than teach Sex Ed to a class he or she has come to know well. And so a person trained in this field was paid to spend a few hours with students who were fascinated, repelled, amused and alarmed, and who tried to look "cool" and "mature" the whole time. We knew it was vital for them to acquire certain information at that stage. They often reacted, briefly and inappropriately, and then settled down for the year-end celebrations that launched them formally into a world away from childhood.

Students also try to make sense of where they are in time. While looking at library books, some primary students told me that the world was in black and white until color was "invented." And for many students, including these grade three children, researching and then expressing a summarized account of an historical figure is a monumental task, even when spelling is not at issue.

## RATTENBURY

*Rattenbury built and lived in the Glenlion Norfok House. He had an affer with another woman but his wife didn't even like rattenbury. The children cared for their mother but when Rattenbury asked them to stop playing the peanio they just played louder. Finally they got devorced and Rattenbury moved to England because the people didn't respeced him any more. Rattenbury had a nick name it was Ratz. Rattenbury had marred his feoncea and she was about as old as the choffer. Later on in there life Rattenbury's wife had an affer with the choffer. The choffer and Rattenbury's wife wanted Rattenbury out of there life so one night Rattenbury was killed. The police came and talked with them, they were no help. The police acused the choffer with murder and jail for life. The wife felt bad because both of them she couldn't be with. She felt so bad that she committed suisid.*

## WHO IS WILLIAM SHAKESPEARE?

*William Shakespeare did something called playwrighting. It means he wrote plays. William Shakespeare was born around the 1560's in Stradford-Upon-Avon near a busy market place. When William turned six or seven he was sent to Gramer School. He worked his hardest. School began at early dawn and lasted till late afternoon when light was nearly gone. When William was sixteen he met a pretty girl Anne Hathaway. A few weeks later Anne and William got maried. Things could not stay the same for this family for Anne soon had a child Susana was her name. A few weeks later Anne had twins. William was exstatic they were pressios as could be. Soon William went to London where his fortiojn could be made though he missed his wife and kids the trip just could not be delaghed. The black Plage hit London bringing many people grief. Things were going well until one stormy eve young Hannah died a tragic loss his family left to grieve. He went back to his quiet home with his vivid lines of thought. His 52ⁿᵈ birthday is recorded as his last. So he lived for 52 years.*

Another grade three student was puzzled after watching a television program on which the actors in the film "Titanic" were interviewed. "How could they be on that show?" he asked me the next day while taking out a book on the subject. "They *drowned!*"

After the strike students returned to Fairfield a little wary and a little difficult. They wondered about us, their educators, and they wondered how things might have changed. Ten years later, on the morning of September 11, 2001, I stood outside the main entrance of another school and greeted students. Many had watched the morning news and were agitated.

"What do you think will happen *now?*"

"Will a plane hit our school?"

"Will they find us at home?"

"Are *you* scared, Mrs. Bertram?"

Our staff had met and decided on our strategy: if the students wanted to discuss their feelings they would allow time for that. If not, teachers would carry on as if it were an ordinary sort of day. I believe these students arrived into an atmosphere where they felt safe, with adults they trusted. Some classes had discussions and some wrote about that awful event. And although none of us could make sense of events that morning, we adults were, to them, secure, stable and predictable.

Student trust in the power of authority figures was brought home to me during a real earthquake six months after 9-11. Parts of our school shook dramatically, including the office area. In case anyone doubted what was happening, I grabbed the P.A. mike and gave the command, "Earthquake procedure! Earthquake procedure!" Debriefing later, we found out that a number of students at different grade levels had argued with their teachers over the *validity* of that quake. They maintained steadfastly that

I could make the school shake for the purpose of an earthquake drill. As one boy put it, "She has a *program!*"

I could not explain why things had to change in their bodies, nor why anyone would commit a terrorist atrocity. I could not make sense of the world for the little girl who apologized for her dizziness as she told me that a family member had hit her so hard on the top of her head that she had a headache and needed to go home. I could not make sense of things for all the students who waited with me for social services to pick them up so they could be placed into emergency foster care. I could not explain why a child was not popular, nor why a parent did not attend a concert. I could not take home with me those students who did not want to leave the security and predictability of the adults who worked so hard with them at school.

But I could make the school shake.

# CLASS COLONIST

Hi. This is going to be a pretty short paper because there are very few of us working on it. There will be a lot of sections missing.

The French grade 7's are planning an Easter dance. That's for all of us, in case you didn't figure it out. Now all we have to do is find another holiday to have a dance for. Maybe Victoria Day? Or Mothers Day? Maybe not. We might have to invite our mothers! (duh)

Mr. Duval has us working again! French! This time we don't have to write our own plays though. The plays will be performed in a few weeks.

One life in school: Jan likes volleyball, basketball, badminton, all track and field events and horse back riding (of coarse). She wanted to do the Class Colonist because she wanted one like we get every day at home. She's going to dye her hair Auburn. She loves rainbows, Simon, and navy blue, sunshine yellow and forest green.

Dear Miss Jones,

Jason has a doctor's appointment at 3:30, Tuesday 31<sup>st</sup>. I figure the law of averages being what it is, that's the day he'll get a detention for tunneling under the school. Would it be possible to delay any detentions, or send work home so he won't be late or miss this appointment.

Thank you


Dear Mrs. Bing,

Jonathan <u>refused</u> to do his homework last night. As punishment, <u>he has to do his homework with you, at recess.</u>

On another note, he has had his reading books in his bag for days. He keeps "forgetting" to hand them in. He can read them very well now. Please, as his teacher, insist that he hands them in.

I have heard that he is throwing his apples away periodically. I would appreciate it if you would look into this and if it is true do a lesson on waste.

Thank you.

Richard, 1984

Richard was a small, elfin grade two boy with huge eyes and slightly protruding teeth. His mother fretted anxiously over those teeth and the mouth guard he wore on the playground to protect them; she could imagine him being knocked over by more robust and rough children. There was also concern about meeting Richard's needs intellectually: he was an amazingly gifted student in a class with many bright two's and three's.

As an extension to their usual reader story work, this group loved to critique the often shallow and dull writing in their texts. Adjectives and adverbs would be added irreverently; stories would be changed to have improbable but more exciting endings. Taking that considerably further, a play evolved as the result of a group brainstorming that took place over a few days, and Richard contributed enthusiastically. The dialogue was witty, rather subtle for their ages and often hilarious; the performance in front of the school was well received. On impulse, I showed the class's script to the drama teacher of a local secondary school. She read it to one of her own classes, and her students decided to stage it and invite some local elementary classes including the authors.

I warned my little thespians that the high school's version of "Rabbit Stew" might seem considerably different from their own version. I secretly worried that they might be let down and told them that they were not, under any circumstances, to do their usual "critiquing" until we were back in our own classroom. They agreed. As one of them put it, teenagers were a different breed. Those bigger kids would probably not take their play as seriously as it should be taken.

A bus delivered us to the old and impressive secondary school auditorium. Our two rows of dutiful children sat among those from other schools and clapped politely at the slapstick performance. It was clever and colorful, designed to appeal to primary children. When it was over, the bus took us back to our school and my students trailed mutely behind me as we filed into the building, up to the second floor and into our room.

Richard was right behind me as I led them into the classroom. "All right, Mrs. Bertram," he said with a tone of pained restraint, "we've been very polite for a very long time. Now let's rip it to shreds!" And they did, very cleverly and very thoroughly, with him leading.

Two years later Richard was killed by an underage driver as he rode his bike toward home after watching a school game. My first reaction was to the terrible waste of such a creative, promising mind: projecting Richard as an adult had fascinated me. Cancer researcher? Environmental scientist? Playwright? I thought of his sense of humor and his need to express himself precisely. I thought of his dear and wise little face, and mourned with many others in that school community.

# 13   THE MOST POWERFUL THING

After the strike we worked on our relationships with the parents as well. Like their children, many were uncertain about what to expect when school resumed. Would teachers feel the same? Some parents were a little resentful. Many were tentative but eager to reestablish positive routines. They wanted to trust us again; it was like another beginning.

Most parents who bring their children to school for the first time are entrusting the most precious part of their lives to adults they do not know at all. They hope their children will be loved, cared for, stimulated and educated. They expect them to be *happy* at school, and they expect school personnel to be experts in stimulating and educating them. What else are all those degrees and years of experience for? They know there may be blips on the horizon; they were students themselves. But happiness for their offspring is mandated.

As school years go by, the expectation of having their child loved usually gives way to hoping they are liked and then, sometimes, put up with. It is the public system, after all!

Most parents experience some early let down. Little flaws emerge. In this new environment Johnny may never stop talking, and Mary may be as mute as a post. Or Mary may be unbelievably messy in all her seatwork and Johnny a perfectionist who accomplishes very little and cannot take suggestions for improvement. The perfectly behaved child at school may begin acting out at home.

Worst of all, behaviors may begin reflecting a less than perfect home environment. "I'll break his bloody head!" coming from a sweet looking, well-dressed little girl at a play center may be an indication that things are a tad volatile at home. Further, calling the teacher "Mrs. Poop" may suggest that a child's parents have demonstrated some lack of respect for the school. Or not. Perhaps television shows are not all that well monitored, or an older sibling or friends have been an influence. The child may have just heard a name on the playground. Whatever the reason for a youngster's questionable behavior, the parents are usually horrified.

Many parents feel hurt when the first reporting session includes areas for improvement or even average assessments. The "satisfactory," if that is the current term, has to be explained. No, she does not need a tutor or Learning Assistance. Yes, reading to her at night is good. No, hours of homework in grade one are *not*. And even with the "perfect" child, the teacher seldom gets off lightly if there is a "B" among those "A"s. Lucky are those children who have parents concerned about their progress, however, and lucky are those parents whose only concern is in the fine tuning of their child at school. For those are the parents who do not have to wonder about the assimilation of a child with special needs.

Most parents are naturally flummoxed when social problems occur and their child is on the "outs" with all or most of his or her peers. Often these situations are no-win for all concerned, because issues from the home or the community are brought into the school in the attitudes of the children. Obvious, overt bullying is often more easily addressed than the more subtle, exclusionary or quietly mean behaviors which cause heartache to the student victim, the victim's parents and the perpetrators' parents, as well. Too often parents of otherwise lovely children, high academic achievers and teacher pleasers, will not accept that their son or daughter has a mean streak that needs work.

One mother was very upset when her daughter was the brunt of some nastiness. After much questioning and discussion with a large group of her peers, it turned out that three were at fault in the eyes of all the others. They admitted they had been unkind and wrote letters of apology after the usual admonitions from their teacher and their principal. It should have ended there. The father of one of these girls was furious, however. *His* daughter would not behave that way and she was recanting her earlier "confession." The teacher and I knew of another piece of evidence: this girl had written a nasty note about the victim that could not be shared with the father. The families were friends, a mother had found the note among her daughter's things, and we could not speak of its existence. So a pound of flesh was taken, in a lose-lose for everyone. The child knew she had lied to her father. He thought he had saved face for his daughter but had to have known there was more to it. The bullied girl had no real closure because of the dishonesty, and the teacher and the principal had an insight into the parent that he would probably have rather avoided.

What would be a better way to handle hearing that the apple of one's eye had acted unkindly and was in a group with students who were behaving poorly? Rather than becoming defensive, how about letting your daughter know how much you despise such actions? Never mind "lawyering" the principal or the teacher. As another father said to me, "I would want to know if my child was bullying or even if she was just hanging out with kids who were."

One boy was regularly in some sort of trouble and I often tried to track his father down at his government job. More often than not he was unavailable, and I would have to leave a message. This was infinitely preferable to calling his mother, whose language was loud, colorful, and punctuated by a slammed phone. Sometimes I would wait for an hour or so before hearing back from that father, and it was always interesting.

"Hello, Judy. I'm sitting here with the premier. I hope all is well." Well, no, it *wasn't*. James had sworn at our first aid person and threatened to have her fired if she did not get him an aspirin immediately.

"The premier and I were just talking about schools. What can I do for you?" You can come and take your son home. He has just thrown raw eggs at passing cars.

The proximity to the premier did not do a thing for me, nor did it seem to make any difference to his son. I never heard dismay or disappointment from that father, only frustration and annoyance because of the disruption and inconvenience to his day.

One morning the father of a kindergarten boy, child in tow, tore into my office. He was hyperventilating with emotion, his eyes were bulging and his face was red.

"Not only has Joey's teacher been giving out condoms to the kids in his class, he's blown some up in front of them!"

My own eyes bulged back and I thought of the teacher in question: quiet, patient and rather shy.

"They must be balloons," I responded hopefully. He reached into his pocket and flung the offending object on the table between us. It looked like no balloon I had ever seen.

"Mr. McDougall will have an explanation," I assured him, and paged the teacher to the office.

Jim shuffled into the room, surprised to see one of his students there with his father. "Jim," I said, "Did you give these out to the students?" I pointed to the article in question, for some reason hesitating to pick it up.

He nodded. "They're great balloons. Really strong. What's the matter?"

"*The problem is that these are condoms, not balloons,*" the father barked.

"That's...." Poor Jim was lost for words, or else he thought better of finishing his sentence. I asked him if he still had the package. He did, he assured me, and left to retrieve it.

"I *know* this is a misunderstanding. Mr. McDougall would never, consciously, do anything like you are suggesting." The father still looked wild, and grabbed the offending object from his son who had begun to try to blow it up.

Jim returned with the bag that still contained some items. He did not explain where he had purchased them, but they came in all colors and were, in fact, labeled 'Party Balloons.'

"I really am sorry," the father apologized after close scrutiny of the bag. "It's just that…it looked like…well don't you think…?" He gave each of us a desperately appealing look to which neither Jim nor I responded. "I'm sorry," he repeated. Jim picked up his bag of treats and left.

"It's always a good idea to talk to the teacher first, by yourself," I told the father as he left with a little boy who must have wondered what all the fuss was about.

One mother was in a fury over her son's science project, which was due to the teacher the next day. She phoned me after she realized that her son had to do all the work on it at home. Guidelines had been given, the school library was available, but class time was not being freed up. Her son had obviously waited too long to let her know when the work had to be finished. "I assumed the project was being *monitored*," she rasped, "only to find out that he has to do this volcano thing *on his own!*" I pointed out that there was another week until the Science Fair, and that she could help him to find some information and make a model. Having lived through her predicament, I knew my suggestion was lame. "Yeah, make a model. What do you think I've been doing all afternoon? My volcano looks like a *breast!*" she wailed.

Sometimes when I expected the worst, I was surprised.

I was concerned about reactions one day while phoning parents on behalf of a teacher-on-call. She had endured a terrible day that climaxed when a number of students scribbled felt pen all over their faces. Armed with soap and a wet sponge, she had wiped each face clean as she lectured them about the chemicals in the ink. Only after she had dismissed the class did she panic, thinking that her scrubbing was probably not acceptable. Every parent was understanding, however, and intended to pursue the matter further at home. "Hell, Mrs. Bertram," said one father, "I would have knocked their blocks off!"

Judy Bertram Tomlinson

When the school—and home—saw "eye to eye," it was always refreshing:

*Dear Mrs. Bertram,*

*So…Tracy has been leaving the schoolgrounds to buy junk food, has she? She's been rude to the supervisors, has she? And lied to you as well?*

*She will be getting up earlier every morning from now on so that I, her mother, can supervise her making her lunch before she leaves for school. She will not be going to the store because she won't have spending money for some time.*

*Her letters of apology are attached. And the bag she's given you is full of the junk food she bought yesterday.*

*Enjoy.*

Then there was the time the motorcycle gang roared into Fairfield. The leader of the group, incarcerated a while for a violent crime, was a concerned parent. His son had been in an altercation with a boy two years older, and, recently released from prison, this father was going to "take things up" with the principal.

We had heard rumors of some sort of imminent visit by him and his gang and sure enough, shortly after 1:00 p.m. one day, I could hear what sounded like a combination of grunts, hard heels on linoleum and rattling chains. Even if I had been deaf I would have suspected they had arrived: I could smell leather.

"You the principal?" a gravelly voice asked Pauline, our office assistant.

With her broad shoulders and significant height, he could be forgiven for making the assumption. "In there," she pointed quickly, to my small but besuited self.

"You must be Mr. Christie!" I smiled, wobbily. After all, he had phoned regularly from prison. We had had short exchanges, because someone always yelled at him to "Get the fuck off the phone!" Apparently he did not have phoning privileges at that time.

This dad was clad entirely in skin-tight leather. Chains looped over his black second skin like metal cobwebs. His hair was long, greasy and curly, and he had a beard to match. His eyes were a deep brown and surprisingly warm, and seeing me reach out my hand, albeit tentatively, he grinned widely. His teeth were a shocking yellow and his skin was cratered.

"Leave us alone!" he ordered his mates who were, according to Pauline later, "perspiring like crazy" in their leather. It was hot.

We spent about fifteen minutes going over the facts of the case. His son did tend to antagonize other students sometimes (wide grin, "chip off the old block," etc.). However, the older boy had called him names and pushed him onto the concrete, repeatedly. That boy had been suspended. Both were going to have some anger management sessions with our counselor.

Mr. Christie liked what he heard. He stood and hitched up some leather at his waist. "Principals weren't like you when I was in school," he snorted, looking intently at me. "Don't put up with any smart stuff from my son, will ya? Hey, let me know if ya need me." We shook hands again before he left. And as the clanking, stomping and grunting retreated, I realized with amazement that he had handled his son's altercation better than the older boy's father, who was a lawyer.

The smell of leather still lingered when our custodian raced in, wild-eyed. "Did you *SEE* that lot? They *burned rubber* leaving the grounds. You should *DO* something," he told me.

"And I suppose you told them to slow down," I sniped, post-event stress buckling my knees.

There are many versions of this story told by the staff who worked at Fairfield. What is irrefutable is that when the gang asked where the principal's office was, the male teachers who were in the hallway simply pointed in my direction and seemed to flatten themselves against the wall.

"Nice of your father to pay me a visit," I said to his son the next day. He already knew that his father and I were on the same team.

Judy Bertram Tomlinson

Having school and home on the same team is powerful, but I knew this was often not easy or even possible.

My younger daughter was not as robust or as school successful as her older sister in her early grades. She missed considerable time due to her asthma and schoolwork was often a chore to be finished so that she could get on with her real interests, among them creating art that was amazing.

During a parent-teacher interview in a particularly unmotivated year, the stack of Stefany's work samples was topped by a spelling test. She had received a perfect score and, as always, her printing looked perfect. There was an "A" in black ink at the top of the list, but a red circle around something toward the side.

"I let that go, that time," her teacher said. Her tone was teacher-to-teacher; "we" knew we should not let students get away with undirected performance of any kind.

I leaned forward and squinted, hard. A small, exquisite flower had been drawn there, a gift on the otherwise perfectly sterile, perfectly acceptable primary seatwork sample.

I said nothing and the "interview" was finished.

"She would have meant that as a *gift*," I told my principal, back at my inner city school. This extraordinary leader gave us all the time we needed—when he had it.

Mr. Campbell shook his head. "Amazing, isn't it? We deal with such huge issues, every day..." his voice trailed off. He was probably thinking of our latest one: a boy had poured lighter fluid on a younger student and tried to set him on fire.

"I didn't *say* anything," I pressed.

"Put how you feel in a letter," he advised as our secretary signaled that he was needed elsewhere.

I could not find the words. At least I could not find words that would alter the fact that this person, presently teaching my daughter, considered the miniscule flower offering a kind of graffiti on foolscap. Then I thought, maybe that *was* what Stefany intended. Mar the monotony, but do it cleverly. And maybe her teacher was clever enough to recognize it. The fact was, I did not trust my own feelings on paper for that woman's perusal and possible sharing. However I put it, it would sound trite. Yet it was profound, this anger I directed toward myself for my silence during a fifteen-minute opportunity to discuss my child.

I knew then and knew even more clearly as principal, that having a parent and the school staff on the same team is just about the most powerful thing that can happen for a child academically, socially and emotionally. This does not mean that a parent should hesitate to raise a concern or accept less than what is mandated: the child's welfare is, after all, their primary job. But Johnny and Mary may not be "happy" all the time and there are some lessons to be learned at school that are not all academic. When the adults pull in the same direction, however, almost anything is possible.

Fairfield's parents were an incredibly talented lot. Artists, writers, musicians, doctors, educators, social workers, lawyers, conservationists, architects and many other vocations were represented in the Parent Advisory Council. This PAC met again soon after school was in session in February of that first year.

In typically creative fashion, they brainstormed what was to be a kind of celebration of all the extras that were offered at their school by the staff. These included clubs, sports, outings and student leadership activities. One woman offered to put it all together in the form of a large poster that would be mounted on the bulletin board outside the office.

"Most of us don't realize all the hard work these teachers put into this place," a parent said. "It's a way to highlight what they do."

And so, shortly after the strike by the District's teachers, our parents diagramed, in a prominent and detailed display, our staff's extra-curricular offerings. They were proud of their school and ready to be an important part of it.

## THE CLASS COLONIST

Come Home, Mr. G, Come Home!!!!!!!!!!!!!

Poor Mr. Gallagher he's sick and the rest of us are miserable. Mr. Gallagher is a fair and good teacher and we really wish he would come back, and we can't believe the teacher he got to replace him. It's not as if Mr. Blumenkopf is a bad teacher or anything he's just a bit harsh and of course he's not Mr. G!!!!!

Mr. G had better be better soon. I sure hope it's nothing serious because if he's not back this year, he won't know what happened to us!!

*Dear Judy,*

*PLEASE block out my picture in that school photo! I DO NOT wish to have ME UP looking like that! (White out will do!)*

*Signed,*
[A Concerned Teacher]


*Judy,*

*Mrs. Smith is a bomb ready to go off! Please see me!*

*Signed,*
[Another Concerned Teacher]

Journal Entry: May 2003

*Tracking local newspaper articles that have something to do with education will be interesting at this time of year! As teachers prepare for classes that may be reconfigured during September due to enrollment variations, they are bombarded with the annual media blitz:*

- May 16: Liberals miscue on Teachers' College
- May 25: Failing grade—educator attacks miserly Canadians for neglecting public schooling
- July 15: Supreme Court ruling fires anxiety over risky field trips BCTF files challenge on Bill 51
- July 16: It's time to scrap failing schools
- July 17: Parents head to court over school closures
- Aug. 14: Easing your child's move to a new school
- Aug. 19: Schools battle opens in court
- Aug. 21: Reading wars ("Debate still rages over the best way to teach reading")
- Aug. 23: Parents bow to ruling that school closures stand
- Aug. 26: Future in fine arts for closing elementary school
- Aug. 27: Report cards revamped ("Standard format on the way to improve clarity" "Sugar-coated report cards for students are on the way out") Minister of Education says letter grades for primary students may be considered
- Aug. 30: Education minister's musing on letter grades startles teachers
- Sept. 3: Schools specialize to gain enrollment
- Sept. 14: Single sex classes creating a stir
- Sept. 14: Education minister deserves failing grade
- Sept. 17: Teaching Profession Act complaint process sparks fear

- Sept. 20: Nailed: Unsafe grounds for children. School play areas closed
- Sept. 28: Parents vow to keep up push for seismic safety
- Sept. 30: British Columbia schools to boost fitness training—to be assessed, just like three R's
- Oct. 1: Playground searches turn up plenty of hazardous metal
- Oct. 2: Grade four pupils show decline in reading levels, but are up in math
- Oct. 4: "If we want our children to be more literate, they need grammar, spelling and composition"
- Oct. 5: Minister of Education "motivated by different interests than those of individual teachers"
- Oct. 12: School computers get short shrift

# 14   A FAIR AND GOOD TEACHER

"We *do* have a problem," the staff committee Chair announced. We were hunched around a primary-sized table on metal chairs that sent shocks of distracting cold up through our nether regions. "*Quite* a problem," she emphasized, watching us shuffle.

The committee members stilled themselves and made a conscious effort to be focused and interested. It was freezing in that little room on the ground floor of the school. We waited.

"Well?" Julia snapped. "Out with it then." It was obvious our Brit had things to attend to in her classroom, and wanted to be back to them in short order. She was not one to waste time cheerfully, if that was what we were doing.

"There are *concerns*," our Chair said, eyeing me carefully. "A lot of them." She withdrew a number of slips of paper from her staff committee envelope. "People are *uncomfortable*," she went on. "The teachers are *very* uncomfortable." Another pause.

"Spit it out!" our librarian insisted with uncharacteristic staccato precision. We all sat up a little.

"The concerns are about that thing the parents put up," our Chair said, putting us out of our misery. "The one that lets everyone know what jobs we do. The extras. It's not acceptable."

"You mean the big poster by the front office?" Jean asked. "What's wrong with it?"

Judy Bertram Tomlinson

"Depends what the purpose is. Why did they put that up there?"

"I suppose some people might feel it was a way to get people to do even more than they do now," our student assistant representative offered.

I could see their point. By itemizing and advertising the extra-curricular work done by the teaching staff, parents could see the fine work that was being done by many. With color-coded clarity, they could also see where there were gaps in activities or sponsors.

"Did they talk to you about doing this, Judy?" Our committee Chair's eyes had narrowed on her new principal.

Oh, they had talked all right. And been terribly excited, some of them, with this "salute" to their teachers. By the time the discussion had come up that evening at the parent meeting, it had been very late. Who would have thought those parents could have mustered this so quickly, before an explanation could have relieved some anxiety? I knew this was a time when teachers were cautioned to be wary of principals *and* parents. Without checks and balances, the former could be egotistical autocrats; the latter might be out to control professional prerogatives.

There had been some comic relief. Earlier that day I had opened a note from a teacher friend in another school. He asked if I had seen the circulating chain letter that was attached:

### School Improvement Chain Letter

*Simply send a copy of this letter to six (6) other schools that are tired of their principals. Then bundle up your principal and send him/her to the school at the top of the list. Add the name of your school to the bottom of the list.*

*In one week you will receive 16,436 principals. One of them should be dandy. Believe this...one school broke the chain and got its own principal back.*

Bundle me, I thought. I could not possibly intercept every missive, however glaring in size and ramifications, that parents might put forward. Not up to the job, are you, a small voice insinuated itself. Seven months prior I was a vice principal teaching in a classroom and relying on my *own* principal to clarify and uphold the boundaries as well as the bonds between parents and school personnel. The problem was that these boundaries were being drawn so emphatically, the path toward a good relationship between these groups was not only murky, it was difficult to find at all.

I rearranged my coffee mug, pen and paper. I knew three things for sure:

1.  I could not have stopped the parents' initiative without damaging relations between them and their teachers and between them and their new principal.
2.  In spite of the good will of the parents and the justified concerns of the teachers, there was an element of power-struggling going on that would hardly be resolved with this one issue.
3.  I had to make it right.

"This is entirely my fault," I told the staff committee. "I didn't foresee your feelings and I should have. But those parents were thinking about the great place we have here and were into celebrating it, not pointing out flaws. I'll explain their intent to the whole staff tomorrow, and I'll bring up your concerns to the parents." They seemed satisfied, and there were no other issues that day. We scrambled gratefully back to the other demands on our time.

Instead of responding to the pile of pink phone slips that had accumulated during my absence, I looked out my office window. It was gray and wet outside, and beginning to grow dark. February blossoms were just beginning to show on a few of the old trees on our playground. Over half of a school year had passed and there had been no reprieve from the testing of what I stood for and how I handled direction or pressure from people not responsible, as I was, for the overall interests of a good school. I was a new principal in a new era in education and I wondered how long it would take until I had the trust of the teachers as a whole.

So much seemed to be about trust, yet consultation over every minutiae of business would have us debating *ad nauseum*. Not that the poster could be considered miniscule in size or impact, I thought wryly. The word "trust" had been bandied about all throughout the strike period, and that evening I took out my old *Collins* and, out of curiosity, made some notes in my journal:

Trust
1. reliance on and confidence in the truth, worth, reliability. *Teachers are being bombarded with school issues. Who are they supposed to believe when government, school boards and union leaders are conflicted?*
2. the obligation of someone in a responsible position: a position of trust. *There was a time when school administrators and teachers were in an "association" together, and the term "union" was frowned upon. Leaders of these formal associations were usually well spoken, diplomatic individuals who garnered respect from trustees and the public in general. We always felt proud of our profession when they spoke for us. Unfortunately, those "obligations" haven't always been upheld the way they should be by people in different positions in our system!*
3. to consign for care: the child was trusted to my care. *Parents want to trust the system to do the utmost for their children; the trustees appoint principals to run schools to do just that.*
4. to allow (someone to do something) with confidence in his or her good sense or honesty. *Teachers expect the parents to let them do their job without interference; they are wary of allowing their administrators the freedom to do the same.*

The dictionary origin of "trust" was most fascinating to me: from Old Norse *traust*, related to Old High German *Trost*, solace.

Solace? We all needed that: trust, solace, a calm resting place where we drew energy from each other's ongoing goodwill.

In spite of the prevailing political winds, I still felt enthusiastic about my role as supporter to these people so vital to student success. I set about doing everything I could to help and encourage them, and I thought I knew what to do. I knew teaching as both an art and a science and I had been doing it for some time. I had found myself in some situations where I had excellent support, and others where support was lacking. I knew that teachers could close their doors and do classroom jobs in adverse school climates, but I also knew that when a collective, positive spirit was lacking there was a drain on everyone's energy. It would take all of us to make it work, and all of us had to feel supported.

Experience had also taught me that making it work was not about homogenizing the group. Diversity in a teaching staff is good for students and for the school as a whole. Ideally, there are some young teachers with energy and fresh ideas, and senior ones to mentor them. Most elementary schools have more women than men; a mix of sexes is good for the obvious reasons of role modeling and simple staff interactions. Teachers approach their students' curriculum differently, and diversity here, too, can contribute to learning experiences. One teacher may have a great sense of humor or fascinating project work that motivates students, the next be more reserved, a master at teaching skills and superbly organized.

Extreme differences may cause staff dissention, however. If someone is perceived to be doing as little as possible there is often resentment. Many staffs have teachers thought to be prima donnas, male or female, whose programs within their classroom or outside of it are given a lot of attention. When a teacher is seen to dominate in meetings, the staff room and anywhere else because of a need to be noticed, the rank and file sluggers become tired of it. Some remain quietly enduring; others confront. Depending upon how these extremes are handled, they can affect the climate occasionally or permeate and color it severely.

Judy Bertram Tomlinson

In the early sixties, which is as far back as my own professional experience goes, very young teachers were appointed to classes in British Columbia after two years of teacher training—or a Bachelor of Arts with no training—to fill the urgent need of districts experiencing an acute shortage. These teachers went back to university later to finish degrees or acquire formal training, but initially they faced their classes knowing that they were appreciated and, by virtue of their profession, respected. Everyone I knew at that time in the profession was excited about their work and saw education as a lifetime vocation.

Today, graduate teachers with five or more years of university and the same stars in their eyes enter our school system believing that they are truly blessed to have chosen a field in which they can make a difference with young people. They begin as teachers-on-call. This tenuous school-to-school and day-to-day work often lasts for years and they encounter situations a novice teacher could not have imagined decades ago. Sadly, many drop out after the prolonged wait for a class of their own, a class like the ones teachers acquired automatically in the past.

In that early time at Fairfield, a young Francophone teacher left a note on my desk at the end of a difficult day, a note which impressed me with its optimism. It was flu season, and he had been assigned to an English class:

*Believe me or do not believe me, I would love to work in your school. I spent time today in the class of Mme Smith. During the storytime Candice got sicked and vomitted on the floor.*

*I told them my rule: "Have a good behavior or the Hell will fall on your head."*

*I was surprise how much they worked well, cooperative. I had a good afternoon with them, much than expected.*

*Jake tried to make the clown between 2-2:30. I made him pick up all the garbage on the floor, he did not like to pick up with his hand an ugly slice of salami...his career as a clown was short.*

*All of them were "goodies," no "baddies."*

*Excuse my English. I hope this is to your entire satisfaction. Please consider me for your school. Thank you.*

There were other issues as teachers matured on the job. Some continued to find their profession exciting and rewarding. They often attended to and became leaders in professional development, self-starters who were open to new ideas and were not afraid of change. These types usually welcomed monitoring their younger colleagues and sharing their expertise with the rest of the staff. In the other extreme, some slid into a grade level comfortable for them, organized a good program and wondered why it was not all that effective decades later. Without trying new things occasionally, those teachers could become afraid of any change that seemed to threaten their status quo. Couched in comments such as "We don't have the textbooks," "It won't work," or "Imagine trying that with *my* class," their mantra clearly defined their fear. Sadly, some became more entrenched as the years went by and were often a drain on the collective spirit of the whole. Or they might have remained good solid staff members, teachers liked by students who were never inspired by them. Principals often spent a lot of time mulling over people in that latter category.

It is well to remember, when sharing stories with old classmates, that there is a unique rhythm in the life of most teachers. These are people who have lived by the school calendar since they were four or five, many with no years of reprieve except a slight variation of their timetables in university. Eccentricities might therefore be expected if not always understood. "Don't *ever* interrupt me when I'm talking to myself!" was a serious admonition, for example, not jest. And, "Alfie made a mistake on the parking lot!" meant that a primary teacher's little dog had relieved himself there.

Teachers—classroom artists and scientists—have personality traits that may craze and/or endear those who work with them. Precision in the classroom may be replaced by startlingly vague and disorganized behavior outside of it. When one of those dears told me that she was "thinking fuzzily because of the fresh paint,"

I did not tell her how common this was when the walls were dry. Three calls came in one morning for another person while she was teaching: her china order was in at the Bay, a video was overdue and a grocery clerk wanted to talk to her about her order for Swedish goat cheese. She was not consciously abusing the school's communication system; she just let the outside world swirl around at will. Representative of this type is the following:

*Judy,*
*I will be having five families for a student-led conference on Wednesday, from 5:00 to 6:00 p.m. I don't know if you need to know this. Please let me know if you do.*

There were many more things I did not need to know over the years:

- "Do we have a staff meeting? I have a piano lesson!"
- "I have just had my first hot flush. I wanted to experience it, so I was late for the meeting."
- "I'll have to leave early. My husband's testosterone level is low. We're getting it checked."
- "That student shouldn't be in my class! The holes in my ear lobes have grown over due to stress."
- "I shouldn't be docked a sick day. I'm working at home!"

*Judy,*
*I'm not well, so I've booked at T.O.C. for Thursday, Friday, Monday and Tuesday.*

*Judy,*
*Please book a T.O.C. for me. I will be attending workshops on Monday, Tuesday and Wednesday morning. (see attached information.) On Wednesday afternoon I will take a sick leave because I will have a loss of voice.*

Obviously, the Teacher's Collective Agreement made it difficult to question the validity of leave requests. The response to one leave request was sent to one of our teachers and copied to me:

*I am in receipt of your letter dated ------, in which you request three days compassionate leave of absence to visit your ailing father in --------, Alberta and ---------, Ontario. Please be advised that I am granting you three days Emergency Leave of Absence with pay... Teacher-On-Call costs to be borne by the District, in accordance with Clause 34.3 (a) (I) of the Teachers' Collective Agreement. I do hope that you have a nice visit with your father in ---------- and -----------.*

The above was signed by a person of some responsibility at central office, who was likely overworked.

As in any organization, there are self-absorbed individuals. And dealing with the parents of difficult children did not always bring out the best in these people. In one long meeting with the father of a very needy boy, the administrative team, the counselor, a social worker and the teacher drew up a contract that looked promising. We were all going to plug into the situation to help. The child had lost his mother, was depressed and was acting out. After much discussion, the father softened in his attitude to the teacher, of whom he had been critical, and thanked her and the rest of the professionals for the time spent to help his son. He told us that our collective work toward building his son's self-esteem would bring about positive change. The word "positive" must have triggered a negative memory for our teacher. She suddenly changed her demeanor and let us all know that "We have to be careful with his *positive* reinforcement; I shook this boy's hand

and needed three chiropractic appointments!" We were back to square one.

At Fairfield, forgetfulness and sloppiness with paperwork was often forgiven by the very people who had to pick up the pieces, simply because they respected and cared about the teacher responsible. Office staff proofed and typed report cards for a talented fellow who was always respectful and kind to *them*, and they regularly took calls regarding his lost property. "Did we participate in a track meet yesterday? We're trying to trace the owner of a knapsack." The owner was our teacher. "Did we have a student named -------living on --------? We have found some keys in the pocket of a jacket in our store." The latter call came in after six days, during which an army of staff had scoured the school. Mothers made lunches for this teacher when they found out he had often forgotten his, and students helped to keep him organized. One day I stopped two boys running down a hall. "We have to hurry, Mrs. Bertram! Our teacher doesn't have his clothes and he's sent us to find them!" I nodded as though their mission was completely normal and reminded them to walk in the hallway.

Teachers are artists, scientists and often characters. For me, as principal, the best times I shared with them occurred both inside and outside their classrooms. During that first year at Fairfield and until I retired, I was invited to potlatches, classroom drama presentations, chocolate finger painting, big buddy groupings, reading centers, math contests, science activities and celebrations of all kinds organized and run by people with amazing, motivating talent. And in one-on-one sessions, we conferenced and explored their work together.

Everyone who works in the public school system is affected by the media, but teachers are probably affected the most. The confrontational relationship between union leaders and the Ministry of Education regularly makes headlines, and everyone who has attended school has opinions. The rhetoric espoused by union leaders and the patronizing language of the government and its Ministry of Education may not only alarm teachers but do real damage to morale. Problems may be unresolved because of the confrontational stance of each.

During that first year I marveled at our teachers' ability to get down to business despite the media frenzy which carried on long after our students were back in their classes following the strike. And even as I contemplated my frustrations during that wet February dusk (*could* the pyramid of my theoretical studies be inverted or was I naïve enough to believe that could happen?) I knew I was lucky to have a teaching staff as diverse as the one at Fairfield. The vice principal, counselor, librarian and eight of the twenty-one teachers were male. French Immersion teachers accounted for almost half of the staff, and of these, four were Francophone and one was from Paris. On the English track, we had three teachers from Britain, one from the States and a special needs teacher from Australia. They ranged in age from mid-twenties to late fifties, from beginning their careers to near retirement. Most were mid-career and most liked each other, although there were some colorful exceptions.

As a novice principal, I wanted the parents to appreciate this talented group as a whole, and I wanted the teachers to be more open to the concept of community. So I did what I had promised both groups, explaining, in separate meetings, the parent motives for and the teacher concerns over the controversial poster that advertised extra-curricular activities and their sponsors. In each meeting, the parents and the teachers nodded and smiled. Mission accomplished, I thought. Later, I heard differently.

"Teachers don't seem to appreciate…"

"These parents are getting a foot in the door…"

First rule, I told myself: *never, ever,* feel smug. This will be ongoing, this building of trust. Kind of like breathing.

# CLASS COLONIST

Well we did the Funky Friend People thing. I don't think it worked too well because a lot of people didn't get letters. A lot of people also told who they were. But that's old news.

Yesterday we had what you might call an ALL STAR GAME. Three classes came to watch. It was a pretty good show. Denise went from Mr. Smith to Mrs. Smith and George was selling gum for $200.

Easter Dance (party). Talk to Jen if you have any ideas. There is a possibility that we might have it outside. Help is wanted because it is a big job. And when the weather gets better, we could possibly have a beach party. We can hope it will be sunny.

Memo
To:      Judy
From:   Your custodian
Re:      Those balls
The teetar balls have been constantly abused, so they will be put away for a week by myself. Cheers.


Memo
To:      Judy
From:   Your custodian
Re:      Your note about the boxes
Those packages weren't labeled incorrectly, like you thought. They just had the wrong things in them! Cheers.


IT'S FUN DAY!!!!
MAY GOD HAVE MERCY ON YOUR SOULS!
(note to evening custodian from daytime custodian over Open House activity due to begin at 5:30)


Dear parents,
Thanks to everyone who helped to see our students out safely during last week's storm. Dismissal was made more difficult due to the tree that was blocking the Fairfield entrance.
Judy Bertram, Principal

Memo
To:      All Custodians
From:    Supervisor of Operations
Re:      Custodians Meeting

Please be advised that there will be a custodian's meeting held in the S.J. Willis Auditorium tomorrow, from 9:00 to 12:00 noon. This meeting will be to analyze your role as Custodian in these trying times. Please be there.

Please fill in the order form below and bring with you to the meeting.

I require ___ cases of toilet paper and ___ cases of paper towel for the next school year.

• I would like my order delivered in 2 lots; Sept. and Feb.
• I would like my full order delivered in September.

Custodian: _____
School: _____

# 15  SUPPORT

"Well," said Joan, as she sat down for the support staff meeting. "I've had *quite* a morning with Brian! He has been too naughty for words!"

This grade two boy was mentally challenged, plump and full of mischief. We loved Joan's stories about her work with this student and were prepared to offer advice and support. Everyone loved Brian, and we waited for the story we knew would follow. In spite of herself, she could always see the humor in the episodes with her little charge. She was a perfect special student assistant for him, I thought.

"No, this time it really *is* too much!" she protested to our grinning, expectant faces. "And you may as well know, Judy, that I was in the boys' washroom, in case of any complaints." She obviously was reading my expression when she added, "There could be some!"

"What happened?" I asked, probably a little too eagerly.

"Do you know, he ran into the boys' washroom after saying, 'Have to go, Joan!' Well, that was fine, except that it was taking forever and I finally called, 'Brian, are you in there?' Of course that was a silly question, because I *knew* the answer and I could hear a lot of laughing going on, including him. He sounded sort of hysterical, actually. I guess it was because he was getting a lot of attention. So I reminded *whoever* was in there that the bell had gone and everyone needed to get to their classes. Four older boys came out and did they look sheepish! One of them told me that Brian had taken all his clothes off and was dancing around starkers. I told them they shouldn't have laughed at him, because that makes him worse!"

We all tried to stifle ourselves.

"I said, 'Brian come out here this minute!' And do you know what *he* said?"

We shook our heads.

"He said, 'Don't have to, Joan!' I said, 'Brian, did you take all your clothes off?' All I could hear was a *snicker*!"

A few of those were suppressed around our table.

"I said, 'I'm coming in to get you, Brian!' I was so mad by this time. Then this impish face came around the corner of the door, and said, 'Can't come in, Joan!' Well, I said that I would if he didn't come out *that minute*! And I told him that his teacher would be very cross if he were late. He disappeared at that point, and shouted, 'Can't come into the BOYS washroom, Joan. You're a GIRL!'"

Apparently our fifty-five year old girl marched into the forbidden territory at that point and tucked him quickly into his scattered clothing. "I suppose he didn't get his stickers this morning?" I asked.

We moved along to the formal items on our meeting agenda. The CUPE support staff had monthly meetings the day after the teachers met with me. The support staff had an open invitation to attend the after-school meetings with the teachers on Wednesdays, but preferred the after-recess time on Thursdays when teachers released them and grade sevens took over the office. All could attend this meeting, unless there was a serious problem with a student.

These meetings were relaxed and productive from the beginning. Support staff members were not under the same degree of political pressure as teachers were at that time, and although we went over the Wednesday teachers' agenda carefully, Thursday's meeting always zeroed in on their specific needs. They seemed to trust that all items relevant to them would be discussed at their own meeting, and they had a complete summary as Gail, our secretary, took minutes at both.

Our support staff members were a competent, caring and fun group, and they were usually well appreciated by the teaching staff. Occasionally and understandably, however, there were tensions, often due to a lack of understanding of negotiated contract items or of the full responsibilities of a job description.

*Dear* [Superintendent],

*Sometime in November our school was invited to take part in a tree decorating contest in Market Square in Victoria. The contest was organized by Market Square and the emphasis was put on decorating trees using solely recycled material. Our school entered six classes in the contest and it represented the largest individual school participation. This high level of participating classes also mirrors the total commitment of our school towards recycling.*

*All the materials used to decorate the trees were provided free of charge by an organization named Imagination Market. The trees were also given free of charge by a local nursery. Therefore, the total cost to the school for the project was $0. Where else can you find in these hard times a project involving close to 150 students for that kind of money? Nowhere!*

*One of the major benefits of our participation was that we were getting six beautiful trees to enhance the school grounds. The culmination of our project was to be the planting of the trees on the school grounds in early January. Our jubilation turned rather quickly to frustration when our custodian started to make decisions without consulting us. He, in fact, interfered with the outcome of our educational objectives.*

*Before leaving for the Christmas Holidays we received verbal approval from our principal Judy Bertram to go ahead with the* planting of the trees on the school grounds by our students. In early January the custodian was approached to check with him for possible problems with drains, underground wires, etc. He was also informed of our plans to plant the trees with the children on Friday, January 10th. Without any consultation or discussion with us, the driving force of the project, he went ahead and ordered a team of maintenance men to finish <u>our project</u>. The role of our students went from full participation, hands-on activities, to let's sit and watch and do very little.

On January 9 and 10, our vice principal and later our principal were informed about the problem and we expressed our frustration about the aggressive way in which our custodian was conducting his unilateral decision making exercises. It quickly became obvious to us that his thinking had prevalence over our educational goals.

Friday the 10th around noon our principal contacted the director of maintenance. It was agreed that maintenance personnel were to dig the holes, prepare the soil, fill the holes again and that the head gardener was going to come to school on Monday morning and talk to the students before they would plant the trees themselves. We agreed and were under the impression that we did our fair share of compromising. Friday, the students were informed about Monday morning activities and they were asked to bring some shovels to redig the holes.

Monday morning came and yes you guessed it, another crew from maintenance was at work. Helpers were redigging our holes, wheel barrows were zigzagging the field, trucks were ferrying our trees to their final destination, mud was flying and by recess we informed the head gardener that the students were not going to take part in an activity that had been taken away from them.

We feel that the actions of our custodian were unnecessary and that they interfered directly with our pedagogical activities. The least he could have done was to inform us of his intentions and consult

Judy Bertram Tomlinson

with us. *We also feel that his actions were very costly considering all the manpower and equipment he unnecessarily mobilized for a project that was supposed to cost nothing...*

*We hope that in light of the Year 2000 objectives and the hard financial times facing our district similar projects involving students will no longer be undermined by Union objectives.*

*Yours truly,*
[Four Intermediate Teachers: three French Immersion, one English]
*c.c.*[Principal, Custodian, Staff Committee, Head of Maintenance, GVTA Chairperson]

MEMO
To:     Greg
From:  Judy
I have a copy of the teachers' letter to the superintendent regarding the tree-planting fiasco. Please give me your notes regarding the timeline. Thanks.

THE PINE TREE INCIDENT (Greg's Report)

Jan. 9: Two teachers approach me at 8:30 re: conflict with custodian. They want kids to dig holes. Bill says union contract doesn't allow this. I say I'll discuss with him after recess and get back.

Jan. 9: I speak to Bill re: trees. He says CUPE must dig holes but kids can plant and fill in.

Jan. 9: I speak to teachers about Bill's comments at 12:00. I say it is in Regulations. They say they can live with it.

Jan. 9: They return at 12:30. Say they want to see Reg. in writing. I show them Reg. 3521.2. They go away chagrined.

Jan. 9: Unsatisfied with me they speak to J. Bertram at 3:30 – she phones director of maintenance and receives assurance that CUPE will dig holes, kids will re-dig, plant and cover. The teachers want this done on Mon. instead of Fri.

Jan. 10: Custodian and CUPE foreman arrive and ask what's going on. I repeat arrangement. They go away happy, dig holes and lightly refill.

Jan. 13: Gardeners and crew arrive, re-dig holes, plant trees (no student involvement.) Teachers vow to write letters – very upset.


MEMO
To:      [Involved Teachers, Custodian]
From:  Judy
Re:      Tree-planting
Please meet with me at 3:30 tomorrow regarding this issue. I will be in contact with the Grounds Department before then.


*Dear* [Superintendent ],

*Regarding our letter of January 15:*

*We believed at that time that our custodian interfered with a compromise regarding the student involvement of the planting of trees on our school grounds.*

*We have since had a meeting with Mrs. Bertram and him, at which time he explained his involvement, which appears to have been to try to assist the involved teachers, rather than hinder their project.*

*We understand his position better and wish to apologize.*

*Sincerely,*
[Four Teachers]

In the best school cultures, in the best of times, the give and take involved in meeting the needs of children tends to blur the perimeters of job descriptions to some extent. Regardless of how strictly he or she may adhere to a job description, the custodian who works hard at keeping a school clean and safe is highly prized by the staff and is, hopefully, given regular feedback for a fine job. Work with the administration includes meetings around the overall safety as well as cleanliness of the school. How safe is the playground apparatus? Are the tiles on the roof loosening? Are the air filters clean? What about dive-bombing crows and weakening tree limbs? There's a child on the roof! What about union job descriptions and emergency situations? The afternoon of the hurricane comes to mind whenever we have an extremely violent windstorm in Victoria.

On that day the winds had steadily increased in velocity until mid-afternoon, when large branches whipped past our second floor Fairfield windows. The light outside had become an odd, metallic color; there was a high whine in the air and heavy thumps and rattles as the old building withstood the record-breaking force. I listened to the weather report and warned the staff to keep classes indoors. When the dismissal bell rang, primary students were to remain in their classes until collected by parents.

Twenty minutes before students would normally be dismissed, a woman came into the school and told us that she had heard a loud cracking noise in one of the trees on Fairfield Road. Greg and our custodian raced out with bright orange cones from our gym, intending to warn people away from the tree and away from the primary area underneath where dozens of parents congregated each day to pick up their children. As they left two things happened: another person called the school from across the street to tell us that she could see a huge part of the tree was beginning to give way, and our power went out. Thinking mayhem, Pauline, Gail and I raced from classroom to classroom, letting people know that the Fairfield exit was to be avoided.

Outside, Bill and Greg were risking their lives. Just as the cones were placed to circle off the area round the entrance, they heard a sickening crack. As Greg recalls,

*I didn't even look up and yelled, "Run!" as both of us went flying to the street. A heavy thud hit behind us. We had been spared, or so I thought, until I realized both of us were wrapped in black wire which the tree had brought down. I said, "Bill, we're dead!" expecting both of us to be electrocuted at any moment. We pulled the wires off and nothing happened. In the driving rainstorm we thought we were goners. But as it turned out on our side of the street were the cablevision and telephone lines while the power lines were on the other side.*

The force of the tree crumbled the concrete bicycle rack, crushed the chain link fence and cracked the sidewalk area usually packed with people. Parents eventually arrived, many held up because of downed branches on the roads, and calmly picked their children up from school. Everyone marveled at the size of the downed tree and the damage it had done; few knew what our two staff members had survived. The press was not made aware of what could have been the major news event of Victoria's hurricane.

Although vice principals are sometimes involved in outlandishly hair-raising adventures, the day to day work of the custodian seldom includes excitement, let alone feats of bravery. In fact, there are some interesting examples of district custodians fending off boredom by making their own excitement. One was reported to be feeding leftovers from student lunches to the area's crows, resulting in birds that were looking like stealth bombers and becoming belligerent. Another was said to get through a novel a day. Our talented Fairfield custodian used his artistic flair to paint the whole of the huge old boiler room, floor and all. The boiler became a submarine surrounded by a whimsical underwater seascape, and was toured by students as awed as if they were in a foreign art gallery. With increasing cutbacks in budgets, however, the custodian's daily routine became a race against the clock and there was no longer time to kill when a work run was finished.

There are other unsung heroes among school support staff. Those special student assistants, like Joan, who help to make integration happen effectively for all concerned are particularly appreciated by teachers who may feel overwhelmed by the range of special needs in a class. This assistant must understand the particular needs of the designated student, bond with the child, fit into the dynamics of the class and help the child fit in. He or she must understand the curriculum, be able to help interpret it for the child and have a good working relationship with a range of teachers who may or may not welcome their presence, let alone their input. Their daily jobs may range from wiping a bottom to exercising highly refined diplomatic skills.

One Resource Room assistant who worked in our school turned children on to math as late as grade seven. Kay could obtain nitty gritty information we sometimes needed to help students at an age when they did not "share" with adults. A supervision assistant who worked only an hour a day could diffuse trouble just by her warm and friendly presence. She owned a collection of unusual, funky watches, and wore them in order to begin conversations with the lonely, the troubled, and the angry. A young assistant was determined to see a boy succeed in spite of family dysfunction in the extreme. Up late at night, this student had a rude awakening many mornings when he and the rest of his family were called in time to get ready for school. Library assistants helped to excite children about books, and clerical staff played a major role in setting tone and organizing major events. Our office assistant, Pauline, always stood at the entrance to the gym on the nights of the Christmas concerts at Fairfield. She knew how many tickets each family had purchased and was determined to see each member perched on a chair in a fair and equitable manner. Her good size made it impossible to squeeze around her or see over her, a fact that gave some of us no end of pleasure and a few members of our community some chagrin.

Elementary school secretaries are probably the most underpaid people in our school support system. They are also the most multi-tasked. At any one time they may be collecting money, answering a phone, placating a child, giving someone a Band aid and accepting a new registration while their principal hovers with work that needs immediate attention. They must be skilled in accounting, word processing, and dealing with people; they must have extraordinary patience when whatever they begin is invariably interrupted again and again. They need to be quick, cheerful and have superb organizational skills with a good sense of humor when it all goes awry. Perhaps most importantly, they need to have a high level of integrity and discretion. When even one of these skills or personal attributes is lacking, the effect upon the school can be momentous.

When Gail, our new Fairfield secretary, was hired that first October, she immediately set about creating an organized, efficient workspace. Within weeks we had carpenters measuring and plans drawn up for the transformation of the outer office. Over the nine years I worked with her in two schools, her support for staffs and students was unflagging, even when she was coping with personal tragedy. I was able to trust her implicitly, whether with a deadline that needed to be met or information that could not be shared at a given time. As secretaries are privy to most things that happen in a school due to their proximity to the principal's work, their trust is one of the principal's greatest assets. And if, in addition, the secretary has a welcoming personality and a good sense of humor, the school community and its principal are lucky indeed.

In a former school where I had worked, a Learning Assistance teacher dealt daily with a boy who constantly tested his teachers. On one particular day, this child had been doing word puzzles on the carpet in her room, and when the bell went at noon he was reminded to pick up all the pieces before he left.

"*Why* do I have to?" he asked. "I want my lunch *now!*"

Judy Bertram Tomlinson

Joy was in no mood to quibble. "You have to," she told him, "because I'm the boss of the world!"

Jason let nothing slide by him. "Oh no you're not! God is!" This was just the sort of bantering he loved.

His teacher knew she was in for it. "Well, I guess I'm the next boss, and you *do* have to clean up and clean up right now!"

On a roll, he countered, "No you're not! Mother Mary is!"

"Well, then, I must be next," Joy said, a bit wearily.

"Oh no you're *not*, either," he said triumphantly. "Mrs. Shaughnessy is!"

With Jason's invocation of our powerfully competent secretary, the teacher knew she had lost. They picked up the pieces together.

# THE TOP 11 CORNY THINGS IN THE CLASS:

11.  our sub.............

10.  suspensions.........

9.  flirting..........Amy!!!!!!!!!!

8.  Andrew's column.............

7.  Devin's attitude..............

6.  Lettie's taste in guys...............

5.  Jess's dreams...................

4.  Greek gods.........(get some clothes)......

3.  getting only one week for spring break.....(what's up with that?)

2.  the tribal dance

1.  Jason singing the reading rainbow song.................

This corny thing brought to you by Liz for the Class Colonist

Science Fair!

The Science Fair is coming!! All the science projects I've seen so far are good like Jenni's and Liz's on makeup. Ang and Kaytie's on germs on money was really good but kind of freaky when you thought about it. Nat's, Matt's and Ross's is cool but SPEAK UP! Martha's and Andrea's was cool but that's probably mostly the cat (just kidding). Good luck everyone!

Stuff: St. Patrick's Day is coming...try to remember to wear green! Put green food dye in your cereal, and everything turns green! ENJOY! This friendly tip to get you to wake up on St. Patrick's Day!

# 16    ON THE VERGE

Journal Entries, 1991

*Feb. 19: Tim drew a picture of his face to show how he would feel if his mom died. I followed Sally around...kid's going to drive some staff over the edge! The media coverage on the buildup to war is non-stop.*

*Feb. 20: Secondary principals worried about proposed contract. Great staff meetings...we're on track. Sally going to special class—poor little mite, she was the first kid to say, "Welcome to Fairfield!"*

*Feb. 21: Support staff still fuming about the strike...heard someone from teachers' union had said that school administrators weren't necessary. Apparently person was royally told off. Dealt with little grade five thugs. Blossoms on Japanese cherries just visible—yellow and pink—but not out. Spring is on the verge, and so is the ground war.*

*Feb. 23: Ground war began, in spite of USSR trying to help.*

*Feb. 26: Superintendent here—nice chat. Child asked if she was the person who picked up the garbage.*

*Feb. 27: Teacher expressed concern about kids not being supervised by them when the new contract takes effect. "How that's being done is NOT our concern!" was response from one of her colleagues.*

*Mar. 1: (PRO-D) snowing lightly but blossoms popping. Worked on paperwork and had some good visits with staff in building who weren't attending district workshops.*

*Mar. 4: Tim away. His mother's not doing well. Principals' meeting with superintendent. Projection figures given out and we were asked to do a number. Some people quite upset about it.*

I sat in one of my principal suits and regarded my elementary and secondary colleagues carefully. The few of us who were new to our positions looked the least affected by the recent job action; possibly we were so intent on our daily navigating around the trees that the future of the forest was lost on us. Besides, some reactions were coming from experience or knowledge we did not possess.

The unthinkable had been announced in that principals' meeting. Our superintendent had told us there was a deficit of 1.6 million dollars in revenue at a time when our district needed every cent it could muster. The enrollment figure used for budget planning was 22,470 students, while the actual district enrollment confirmed by the Ministry was 22,162. There was a shortfall of 308 students. With each student generating $5,260, we were in serious shape.

The superintendent offered a number of reasons for the crisis. Some part-time students involved in adult education courses had been counted as full-time equivalents. Some special education students were not counted at all in the final enrollment, and there was confusion in the actual reporting of students enrolled in Native Education programs. Some Ministry procedures were unclear; school secretaries were encountering problems with the technological part of the system's input and the volume

Judy Bertram Tomlinson

demands of doing this at the same time as school opening was overwhelming for them. Added to the problems with accuracy at the school level was the lack of district office coordination and individual department complications.

The superintendent stressed that no one person could be held totally responsible for the problems that caused the deficit, and that there was no evidence to suggest negligence on anyone's part. However, she did say that there had been "some initial denial of the problem at the district office and school levels." Privately, I wondered if she regretted taking on a district so fraught with turmoil in her first year.

She concluded with the organizational changes necessary to ensure that problems with projected figures did not happen again. Coordination of the enrollment data, which included the collection, reporting and verification of actual enrollments would be established within the office of the District Vice Principal, who was directly accountable to her. All departments involved with those processes would develop a collective set of procedures under his direction.

The school-based responsibilities were clear. Each principal was to ensure that the Student Information System records were kept updated and current, and that proper procedures were in place for the collection of accurate data according to established timelines. A procedure was to be established for internal verification of the data prior to its communication to the District Vice Principal, and administrators and secretaries were to be "enabled" to participate in district workshops involving the technology of the SIS.

Most principals were far from computer literate in the spring of 1991, and in most cases their secretaries had a head start out of necessity. This may have been part of the reason for the extreme reaction to the report we had received, or perhaps it was that it came to us at a time when many were already feeling the effects of testy school communities, union muscle flexing and concerns around the new contract.

Whatever the primary reason, elementary principals let it all hang out during a meeting the following day. The restraint exhibited in the formal meeting with central office staff and secondary administrators was gone. There was a great deal of talk from experienced principals regarding possible heart attacks and other stress-induced illnesses. And the following week, in another grim meeting that zeroed in on proposed district cutbacks, some administrators railed at the teachers' union president who had been sitting in on meetings not labeled "in camera."

Life within the school carried on with the usual commitments, successes and upsets. I noted that the staff committee meeting on the eleventh was "great" and that we planned the next staff meeting to include a discussion about the district's proposals for cutbacks. That subsequent meeting I described as "heavy." I met with teachers regarding their individual evaluations and observed that they were wearing their reporting period expressions. A few grade sevens were involved in some rather obscene computer use, and the whole school was hopping with preparations for the upcoming Science Fair. On Saturday, March 16th, I wrote that I had a bad cold but went into the unheated school to read report cards. Foolishly, I did this again on the Sunday, with the result that I was worse by Monday.

On my journal page on Monday, March 18, I let myself relax and ponder a little.

*I'm home sick. Feel weak, cold, etc. Need a few days to recoup. Reading reports. Most are so good—talented people! Am sitting in our little sunroom with the sun pouring in and the doors open. Feels wonderful. Daffs are up. Just over two years since mom died; she loved this time of year! The new roof will take half my salary this year. Oh well! I am a middle-aged lady with a wonderful but demanding job sitting in the sun hoping the wrinkles don't spread too quickly.*

*1:00—Greg just phoned. Tim's mother died today. She was the first parent I spent a lot of time with at Fairfield. Poor little guy. I'm going in to work tomorrow.*

It felt good to be back, cold or not, and I continued to go over report cards between other jobs.

For four hours the next day, district principals and vice principals met again for more consultation regarding cuts to the school system. Our newsletter went out with a typo that read, HAVE A LONELY SPRING BREAK! and a union member reported to our teaching staff that the superintendent and assistant superintendent had given him inside information: Learning Assistance would be cut out completely the following year. I contacted our assistant superintendent and he assured me that nothing of the sort had been said nor would it happen. When I informed the teachers of my conversation I suspected they wondered whom to believe. But the information was crucial to the two women doing that job, one in English and the other in French. If they were to transfer to a classroom position, their timeline for doing so was short.

The celebration of the life of the lovely young mother who had met with me in September was held that Friday afternoon in a church not far from the school. Afterwards, the attending staff walked the few blocks to a stately old home owned by another Fairfield parent and close friend of the grieving family. It was a time out of time, as these events often are. I remember drinking in the beauty of the spring day, swallowing a lot of emotion and thinking that my job would require courage if I were to tackle some of the things that needed to be done in the face of the intense unionism that was emerging. And I remember thinking how paltry my concerns were in the face of this death.

Talk at the reception centered on the woman who had died: she had been an exceptional mother and community volunteer. There was also some discussion among educators about our district's budget problems and about a high school boy who, along with two friends, was being charged with killing his mother and grandmother. One of his former principals described him as an exemplary student. There were concerns about a little boy who had disappeared from an elementary playground that weekend. Greg and I talked a little about our year thus far, and I remember thinking how strange it was that we were sitting in the living room of that beautiful old Rockland house with parents and staff around us: a still frame in that reeling year.

The following Saturday I talked to the new teacher who had been appointed to relieve the kindergarten class size, and on Sunday I wrote that I went into school to tackle the "paper mountain."

Monday morning I stood by our gym entrance and watched science projects being lugged into the school by proud students and by proud but sometimes frustrated-looking parents. The volcano "breast" creator was one of those, although she smiled when she rolled her eyes at me. Once again our gym was being transformed as hundreds of colorful backboards were set up with researched topics including environmental issues, taste experiments, cleaning products' effectiveness, animal behaviors and plant growth. This time, the build-up came to fruition.

The science fair was incredibly well organized by the teachers. There was a day to set up with time for the intermediate students to view each other's work and make presentations. This was followed by an evening for the public to attend and interact with the students, time the following morning for primary students to tour, and a final assembly of the young scientists for a formal, overall assessment and some individual recognition of outstanding work.

I knew there was ongoing controversy about projects done at home when parent help was often significant. One of our Fairfield teachers reported overhearing two parents from his son's school discuss the issue: "What mark did *you* get on *your* project?" was followed by a heated debate. Then there was the issue of pressure on those students who had no one with the time, energy or will to help them, and pressure on parents for the same reasons.

Issues aside, I tasted, peered into microscopes, listened to sound tracks and smelled things (*it's called oleFACtory, Mrs. Bertram!*). And in between periods of delving into project work I stood near our stage and took it all in: the color, the extent of community involvement, the parent, student and teacher interaction and the students' apparent excitement and pride.

Judy Bertram Tomlinson

"Great school you have here," a father said as he scooped up a toddler who was grabbing green slime from an unattended project. I grabbed another who was about to taste something from the *oleFACtory* exhibit, much to the delight of the pair of boys who had worked on that venture.

"You haven't seen *mine*, Mrs. Bertram! First you have to tell me the year you were born…" There has to be art as well as science here, I thought, following her through the crowd and contemplating to which decade I would assign myself.

"*This term needs to be over!*" enunciated Georgina Jones after school on our last day.

"I'm exhausted!"

"Never mind, we've gained a lot!"

"Who's going to the pub?"

"Those bears are a *riot*, Susan!"

"We need more than a week to recover!" I agreed with those sentiments and did not intend to stay late.

Miss Jones was outside her classroom door talking seriously with a parent when I left the office and stopped in front of the "bear" display board. Grade one bears lumbered, careened, danced and leered from that board. As there were no lines on the paper to guide any of it, the children's printing of their poetry tended to lumber and careen as well, and the overall effect was so joyous I made a mental note to copy a few when I returned.

There was a bear who lived in Palm Springs
Who ate all the berries and onion rings
And he ate so much
He could not touch
The floor, so he ran out of Palm Springs.

There was a rich bear from France
Who always loved to dance
He had a good job
At the Oak Bay Lodge
And decided not to go back to France.

*There was a cool bear in a cave*
*Who always used to shave*
*He tripped on a rake*
*And made a mistake*
*So went home very bare to his cave.*

"Don't stay too late, Judy!"
"Have a good holiday!"
"Come to the pub!"

I chatted with the teachers who were leaving and noticed Georgina Jones and her parent continuing their chat. They were at the far end of the hall from me, silhouetted against a huge window that let in the beckoning spring sunshine. I turned back to the board:

*There was a Kodiak bear from Mazda*
*Who had lots and lots of asthma.*
*He took some pills*
*And didn't feel ill*
*That puffing bear from Mazda.*

*There was a bear who had golden hair*
*And he never wore any underwear.*
*So he was arrested by a man*
*Who said, "You mustn't think you can*
*Run around without your undies, bear!"*

I looked down the hall again, hoping for our teacher's sake that she was going to get away shortly. She was spending spring break in Mexico, and had a flight to catch. Did she need some help? I was not sure if joining them would be a helpful thing to do, and went on reading.

*There was a panda bear from a parking lot*
*Who danced and danced until he thought*
*He was a big pig*
*Dressed up in a wig,*
*That dizzy oinking bear from the lot!*

"Bye!"

When I turned, the parent had obviously begun to walk down the steps, because only Georgina Jones was visible. She was still silhouetted against the window, but with a difference. *She was in the air,* all of her, literally, one hand still raised in an "*au revoir*" to the parent. I watched as she neatly clicked her heels together, emitted a very clear, "*Yes,*" landed, and turned to her classroom to shut the door and leave for her vacation.

Grinning, I picked up my briefcase and left for mine.

# 17   PAPER MOUNTAIN

"Above all else, remember: do the *people* things first. The paper can wait."

The well-seasoned and confident secondary principal had smiled at us as he had finished his workshop for vice principals; he was ready for lunch. Great advice, I thought it made sense.

By the spring of my first year as principal I understood why paper was an issue, and nine years later, when the district's schools were all connected by computer technology, it remained an issue. There were often hard copies sent to schools as well as emails, and if not, well, you could not take an email to a staff meeting without printing it.

Most of the time there was no choice between people and paper. The people were living, breathing, emoting beings. If they were female and adult they could follow me into the washroom with their concerns and requests. They riveted the senses of sight, hearing and smell, while paper relied on sight only, and the inclination to read what was on it.

That is not to say that paper did not have power. For one thing, in spite of determined efforts on weekends to discover the tops of desks and tables, it *accumulated* and *proliferated*, kind of like a genome, sometimes with breathtaking speed. People tended to do that only in really adverse circumstances, and then they usually had paper with them, too.

Judy Bertram Tomlinson

Paper was silent, but it had powerful effects. Its piling up was insidious, even when contained in hopeful folders labeled, DO OR DIE, URGENT, READ NOW, READ, DON'T IGNORE!, and MISCELLANEOUS AND SUMMER. These folders were simply pathetic attempts to avoid the round file sitting on the floor, which was where much of the paper mountain went in the end when no one was around and I was clear headed and bold enough to let go of it forever. My secret and unspoken wish was that it would mulch itself into something useful. But it never did. Nasty but pertinent little bits of information would insist on remaining pristine under piles of trivia that office staff thought I should see in spite of protestations to the contrary.

Paper had the power to discombobulate my sense of order and efficiency. I found it difficult to think clearly and feel calm when piles were growing on chairs. One shuffle so that a visitor could sit down in my office and the whole organization of some important endeavor could be derailed. My weekend or "holiday" forays cleared my head, however. Paper and paperwork attended to, I would clean the newly emerged surfaces and feel clear enough to tackle real problems. A few fresh flowers on my desk, a good night's sleep and Monday morning looked hopeful. The printed words themselves, of course, had the real power. And they could be on the most insignificant looking missive:

THE OFFICE OF THE ASSISTANT SUPERINTENDENT
TO:     Judy Bertram, Principal
FROM: [Assistant Superintendent]
I received your memo respecting needs for the office area and I recognize these needs. Unfortunately your list is an amalgam of equipment (P.A. System), and capital or maintenance items (shelving, etc.) Please develop a plan for the area and submit it when submissions for inclusion in our next capital budget proposal are requested. Please note that equipment is not to be included in this proposal.

This memo, received early in that first year, told me to learn more about budget processes immediately, something that had not been emphasized by principal mentors or district staff. The memo did not explain that equipment items could be purchased through school funds (if there were any left over from the year before), nor that the maintenance requests needed to be applied for on a specific form. Develop a plan? We thought we had done that. When would submissions for the next capital budget proposal be requested? Next week? Next year? "You two are *rookies!*" that assistant superintendent laughed, referring to the work Greg and I had done.

Even as a rookie, I did occasionally try to assert some pressure on paper:

DATE: October 1, 1990
TO:     Assistant Supervisor of Operations
FROM: Judy Bertram, principal
As per your memo, we are in real need of five replacement venetian blinds in rooms 3 and 7 here. These blinds are THIRTY YEARS OLD and have deteriorated badly. Thanks!!!!!!!!!

Going through Paper Mountain, I learned that administrators needing to vent or simply needing a little humor reveal their various levels of stress, perhaps unconsciously, through their approaches to communication.

TO:     All Elementary Principals
FROM: Director of Special Education
RE:     Special Education Eats Crow
Please disregard Student Assistant allocation sheet sent out. Also, disregard layoff timelines. There are errors. Students who appear as Low Incidence are not. There will be the same allocation of assistant time for all Low Incidence students as last year. We will send out new sheets for allocation. Consultation will follow.

### URGENT: RELATIONSHIP SOUGHT!!!

Principal struggling with development of plans for organization of students into classes seeks (needs) to consult with colleague(s) having similar struggles, or, even better, answers. Triflers need not apply. Only those prepared to grapple seriously and immediately with possibilities will be considered. Reply to this principal in plain brown envelope, or call my school but leave only discreet messages.

MEMO
TO:      Human Resources
FROM: Judy Bertram, principal
[Supervision Assistant] presently sits with [Special Needs Student] while [Special Student Assistant] has her lunch. [Student] needs ten more minutes to eat, and [Supervision Assistant] has to be outside on supervision by 12:20. We have .02 not used in our supervision time. May we please add .14 from our special needs allocation, converted to supervision time (.02+.14=.16). This will allow [Special Student Assistant] to eat from 11:50 - 12:20, and the student will have ten more minutes to eat. Please excuse the extremely complicated nature of this memo, and congratulate yourself if you understand it. Thank you.

*Dear Principal or P.E. Coordinator:*

*Our school has become quite concerned over the amount of dirt that can accumulate on the gym floor during the winter months. This causes some considerable damage to the varnished surface as the students exercise on it. I am writing to ask for your help and guidance.*

1. *Do you have any specific policies or procedures that help you to keep the gym floor clean?*
2. *Do you have any policies for the whole school?*

*Please reply in the space below and return to me at my school as soon as possible. Thanks.*

*Signed,* [Vice Principal]


Fairfield's School solution to gym floor maintenance:

*Students take P.E. in the nude. Those with dirty feet are excluded.*
*Signed,* [Vice Principal]


Humor, even the gentle tongue-in-cheek kind, often needed to be avoided when corresponding with Central Office in busy times. I was well aware of this, but occasionally indulged myself. In the following example, a child in a class at maximum size was causing the system's alarm bells to go off. The contract with the teachers' union stipulated *twenty-two* students as the maximum allowable for that primary class. Late in the year, this child was given a behavior designation, which meant that she was now in the "special needs" category. This class's maximum number, then, should have been twenty-one. If it had been late September, the school might have been rearranged to accommodate the contract's demands. In this case it was March, the other classes were full, the child had been settled for over six months, and there did not seem to be any alternative but to keep her there. Nor should any other have been considered. I ignored the initial mail around this for some time, and when I finally dealt with it, my "solution" caused quite a fuss.

INFORMATION TECHNOLOGY AND PLANNING
TO:     Judy Bertram, Principal
FROM: [Secretary]
RE:     Class Size Violations
We are in the process of preparing Elementary Assistance numbers and first need to rectify identified class size violations.

Could you please:
1.  Examine the attached sheet which targets the source of the class size violation
2.  Make the necessary adjustments (i.e. move students to available classes)
3.  Let me know what adjustments you have made by writing your changes on the attached sheet and faxing it back to me as quickly as possible

Thank you for your patience and help. As soon as all schools have corrected their violations, numbers will be forwarded to Financial Services for purposes of calculating assistance numbers.

Ah, yes. Deep down in Paper Mountain I unearthed the grid for our school. Twenty divisions or classes were listed, with a "no" beside every one except division eleven, which had a "yes," being, as it was, IN VIOLATION. Ridiculous, I thought. Under no circumstances could anyone suggest that a student be uprooted this late in the school year. Tongue-in-cheek, I sent a response:

*Our division eleven has one child who was designated Severe Behavior a couple of months ago, but at this time we do not have space in another grade two class. We are wondering about the possibility of another school somewhere? = : )*

The response came quickly, and in spite of the many times I had been privy to principals complaining about how unfair this dramatic move would be to students and staff alike, I had never had to organize anything like it myself. I could not believe what I was reading.

*Good morning Judy:*
*Janet just handed me some responses to the Elementary Class Size violations that were sent out last week and I just read your note explaining that you have a Severe Behavior student in Grade*

*2 for whom you don't have space. You were wondering about the possibility of another school.*

*I am new to this process but it was mentioned to me that in the past, schools with violations that could not be resolved internally, typically contacted other schools to see if space was available.*

*So you have that option I believe, but could you contact [Assistant Superintendent]—you may already have done so—to keep that person in the loop on this? We are trying to get assistance numbers to Financial Services asap so that schools can receive funds but I cannot do this until all violations are resolved. I understand your situation. Please keep me posted.*

Adrenaline pounding, I emailed back.

*[Secretary], the response was meant to be humorous. We would never condone moving a child at this time in the school year. The "problem" is resolved, however, as a student is moving away from that class to another district this coming Friday. Thanks for your help.*

I felt better after I read her reply, at least for a few seconds:

*OH…sorry…I did not know this (I mean the humor part)…sorry, with all this rain I must be a little humor challenged (smile)…so… THANKS for letting me know. I will get assistance numbers to Financial Services as soon as schools have responded.*

Her email had been copied to someone under the superintendent who then sent a note back to let me know that the union had "agreed to allow the violation for the time being." I believe my teeth were grinding when I responded,

*Believe me, this was all an attempt on my part to be humorous! We would never-ever- seriously consider moving this child to another school!!!!!!!!!!!*

The last email I received was in response to the above:

*Okay, we are all a little tense up here, good to hear that there's no problem.*

Words could relieve stress, however, and laughter was better than pills. During those early times I found the following letter from Greg in my piles of paper after a very difficult scenario. Obviously neither his letter nor my response was ever sent to anyone. The composition was the release.

 

TO:O.C. Ohyl
RE: Your letter of November 21.

You're right. Herbie has not been involved in three fights this year. Smacking one child on the back of the head, throwing another into a drinking fountain and body-slamming a third into a wall does not constitute fighting in any way, shape or form.

In fact, "fighting" is defined in Webster's Seventh New Collegiate Dictionary as follows:

*Fight: to strive to overcome a person by blows; to contend in physical combat or battle.*

Obviously by punching, throwing or body-slamming, Herbie's actions do not fit this definition.

But during my perusal of dictionary definitions, I also looked up the term "bully". This is defined as: *a blustering, brow-beating fellow, esp. one who is habitually cruel to others weaker than himself.*

Mrs. Bertram and I were indeed remiss in our statements in which we accused Herbie of fighting. Fighting was not what Herbie was doing. The correct term appears to be bullying.

While further scanning the dictionary I came upon the word "sphincter". Sphincter as defined in aforementioned dictionary is *an annular muscle surrounding and able to contract or close a body opening.*

I also looked up the word "hole". One definition is: *an opening into or through a thing*.

Since you, as a builder, have a lot to do with contracts and contracting as is defined in the word "sphincter" and since you have provided us with an "opening" into the meaning of the word "fighting", I do believe you truly fit the meaning of the term "sphincter hole".

Since we now know unequivocally and fiducially what you are, Mrs. Bertram and I are somewhat relieved in our ability to wipe the slate clean and begin a truly enemic relationship for the excremental months of the school year.

Therefore, in conclusion, I hope to see you twice more this year (i.e. bi-anally) at our student-led conferences and Knowledge Fair.

Suppositorily yours, [Vice Principal]


TO:     O.C. Ohyl
FROM: Judy Bertram, Principal
RE:     Fairfield Discipline Policy

Slipping into my administrative role is a delight on these occasions. As we slide along the school year, it is with increasing pleasure that the well-oiled machinery of the Fairfield administrative team spews out its updated Discipline Policy for your perusal.

Trusting that none of this will stick in your craw, and that the enemic relationship my esteemed colleague refers to will result in a truly kakathic experience for you.

Yours smoothly and regularly,
Judy Bertram, Principal

There were times, over the years, when I was stubborn about issues and therefore did not reduce Paper Mountain as quickly as I might have. One of these involved a break-in at Fairfield by two boys from a neighboring school. They triggered an alarm by breaking a window and then, while trashing a primary classroom, they were caught red-handed. The police escorted them away in front of numerous people on that Sunday afternoon, and our custodian was called in to clean up on overtime wages. Each month when the bill for the damages arrived, I would not pay it. We knew that one of the boys was the son of a prominent man in Victoria. Was that the reason no one would insist the boys' families pay the bill? And why hadn't those parents marched their sons into our school to apologize? I repeatedly refused to pay the damages from our school budget and finally the bills stopped coming.

Another, lighter example cluttered Paper Mountain for some time. This following one sent to me, however, had closure:

FROM: Supervisor of Operations
RE:       Invoice #3369
We are in danger of losing police support which will result in many extra costs. Please be more careful with your security checks.

TO:      Supervisor of Operations
FROM: Judy Bertram, principal
RE:       Invoice #3369
Please explain the comment "please be more careful with your security checks." We have a faulty alarm system that has activated three times so far this year. One time the fire alarm was triggered by municipal workers doing drainage checks on hydrants. The other two times remain a mystery to the people who investigated. Specific to the incident in question (at 1:30 a.m. on Dec. 21), the problem was apparently a fault in the center stairwell, second floor, motion-detector alarm. My concern is that we will have to keep paying for a faulty system. Please advise. Thanks.

*Dear* [Supervisor of Operations],

*I was called out by A.D.T. on December 21 at 1:30 a.m. for an alarm. It was a fault in the center stairwell, second floor, motion detector alarm.*
*(During the holidays) I was approved by yourself to come out and check the heating system here as a heat call out. Could* [Accountant] *please add 4 hours straight time and 3 hours straight time to my banked overtime. Thank you.*
INVOICE NO. 3369
Call Out:$23.02 (hourly wage) x 4 (time) = $92.00
[Fairfield Custodian]


DATE:  January 13
TO:     Judy Bertram, principal
FROM: Supervisor, Operations Department
RE:     INVOICE #3369
Invoice #3369 refers to the daycare annex and you should only have been copied. It's their bill. I apologize for unnecessarily raising your blood pressure. Please be advised that your school is scheduled for an alarm upgrade which should eliminate the concerns raised. Again, sorry for any inconvenience caused. All the best in the coming year.


Precise and clear communication was not always easy, and occasionally appropriate words were elusive. For example, one year we had a problem in the computer lab when the balls from the bottom of the computer mice kept disappearing. The week this began to happen, we had an exterminator in the school due to the discovery of mice droppings near a teacher's seed art.

I had a problem. The first part of the problem was that I found the juxtaposition of the two events hilarious and my humor on the subject was widely frowned upon. The second part of the problem was that the head of the technology committee was insisting, understandably, that I copy a memo to teachers and announce the theft to the students. I spent considerable time trying to craft a suitable description of the situation.

1.  It has come to our attention that the mice in the computer room are missing their balls.
2.  Four lab mice have had their balls stolen.
3.  The mice in the lab do not work properly without their balls.
4.  If anyone knows anything about the theft of the mice balls from the computer lab, please see Mrs. McLean or myself. This is important. The mice do not operate effectively without them!

The final announcement and memo were so vague they scarcely registered: "Something has been stolen from the computer lab. Please see Mrs. McLean or myself if you know anything about this." By the end of the following week the droppings had disappeared, but it was a very long time before our lab mice remained intact.

Precision was not always sought after, it would seem. Some of the early union missives I found in Paper Mountain were interesting. Under the heading, "Preparation Time—An End To the Confusion?" an executive member wrote to his brothers and sisters, *A principal told a teacher of Special Education that a supervisor at the Board told the principal that the Board lawyers told the Board official that teachers of Special Education are not entitled to preparation time—does all this sound familiar?*

Another picked up on the numbers of acronyms being added to our vocabulary in that time of massive change:

*What Does It Mean?*
*Every day we seem to pick up a new acronym. How many do you know? The answers follow. Good luck!*

*DCC, EHB, SIP, DLT, PSA, WCB, LOA, ERI, LSA, SIF, SUB, TOC, EAP, BLT, HAND*

*What's Shaking The School*

*Answers: District Consultative Committee, Extended Health Benefits, Salary Indemnity Plan, or….District Leadership Team, Provincial Specialist Assn, Workman's Compensation Board, Leave of Absence, Early Retirement Incentive, Local Specialist Assn, Salary Indemnity Fund, Supplemental Unemployment Benefit, Teacher on Call, Employee Assistance Plan, Bacon Lettuce and Tomato, Have a Nice Day!*

Delving down, it was not unusual for me to find odd, and often inexplicable memos:

TO:     All Schools
FROM: Coordinator—Administrative Services
RE:     Steroids
If anyone approaches your school to speak on the issue of steroid use, please contact me immediately. Thank you.

TO:     Elementary Principals
FROM: Curriculum & Instruction
RE:     AIDS Kit  *Urgent*
Recently an AIDS Kit produced by the federal government was delivered to elementary schools (one or two schools may not have received these). This kit is NOT appropriate for elementary use and I ask that you return it to me immediately.

*Sixteenth Annual Short Course for Principals and Vice Principals*

*The Short Course is to be held at the UBC Campus from July 12 to 16th. There are two changes to the course this year. 1) It is possible for people to participate on a non-residential basis, and 2) there is a reduction in fees to $730 (residential) and $570 (non-residential). The Course will focus on matters of significance both to newly-appointed administrative officers and to those who feel they would like a refresher course. The program is designed to help creative leadership ideas emerge. The title for this year's course is NUTS, BOLTS AND THE MAGIC PROPELLER.*

A copy of the registration form could be obtained from the superintendent's office and applications had to be signed by the superintendent and submitted before April 30. I did not attend that workshop but I still wonder about the "magic propeller." Was it the opposite of the "principal" pills some put under their tongues when faced with the unfaceable? We had so much adrenaline pumping so much of the time that a propeller would have put us in orbit.

TO:     All Principals
FROM: Central Office
RE:     Human Remains: Bones and Soft Tissue
A reporter has contacted the District to determine if any of our schools are in possession of human bones. Upon making a few phone calls I have discovered that we do in fact have some! Educationally, I can't think of any justification that would require our schools to have real human bone and tissue when replicas could serve as learning resources. Our Superintendent has asked me to survey the schools and produce an inventory. Once completed, the materials will be donated to institutions that have legitimate needs. Please complete the attachment and return to us by Friday, February 17. We need ALL schools to respond, so if you have nothing to report please sign the form below and merely indicate "NIL". Thank you for your cooperation in this matter.

School Name: *Fairfield*
(Vice) principal's signature: *Greg O'Connor*
Please list materials (Real human bone, tissues, etc.)*NIL*

My personal favorite came from a principal during a particularly stressful time in an extraordinarily stressful year. Principals were scrambling to figure out ways to make their school organizations work for the following September when a principal sent this out to all of us:

*I have no idea how to buy lima beans (dry and ready to paste on paper in order to create density representations for gas/liquid/solid.) Where can I get a gross of these beans?*

Our office assistant's favorite was the phone message she took from my husband during the first fall of his retirement:

Telephone Message
FROM: *Ken B.*
RE: *your lunch*
MESSAGE: *You should heat the peanut sauce so that you can dip your little things into it.*

Paper ebbed and flowed with words that clarified, confused, demanded, beseeched, galvanized, bored, threatened, calmed, impressed and titillated. Words came and went via memos, letters, newsletters, advertisements, phone messages, pack ups, agendas and, finally, email. They were posted everywhere, and sometimes they conveyed more than intended, as in the case of the sign mischievously posted on the Learning Assistance room's door: SCHOOL SUX!

Our office assistant, Pauline, was a diligent proof reader of words that were to convey messages to the school community and her hard work often made my own easier. A former primary teacher, she did not approve of two entries among the "bio's" in the grade seven yearbook she was expected to reproduce. These pieces reflected the attention-getting behaviors their authors had exhibited for months. I agreed the originals were unsuitable as mementos of a Fairfield grade seven year, a keepsake to be treasured by many of those classmates. We knew the students would not receive their books until they were leaving us on their last day of elementary school, so we edited, just a little:

Original:
*Molly was a strange person, as we all noticed. She had days when she went into seizures and slammed into walls, it was cool. We all*

enjoyed the days when she got drunk and threw up and wore her bra over her shirt. It entertained us very much, and we thank her for that. Call her Erotica, for that is what she would want. Molly and Joe will be together, so deal with it!!! Boing!
By her best friend, Martha

Our edited version:
Molly was different. Sometimes she didn't look where she was going. We all want to thank her for her drama performances; she was great entertainment. Call her Mary Jane, for that is what she would want. She has a crush on someone whose name starts with a J.
By her best friend, Martha

Original:
Martha is truly libido gifted. She worships Marilyn Manson and other dangerous dudes. She is in her own cult with Molly and other cool and satanic people. When she grows up she wants to live in a van, and when she's old and senile she wants to open a hemp shop. She is going to marry the bookstore guy and have millions of affairs with really sexy men. She likes taking pictures of people with their underwear over their clothes. She likes to walk around the mall handcuffed to Molly, too.
By her best friend, Molly

Our edited version:
Martha is truly gifted. She worships Jose Carreras and other fine performers. She is close friends with Molly and other serious people. When she grows up she wants to live in a trailer park, and when she's a senior she wants to open a shop. She is going to marry a man who loves books. She is a good photographer and loves shopping in the mall with Molly.
By her best friend, Molly.

Bland was the best revenge, we thought.

One afternoon during that spring break, I rummaged through some dusty old boxes in the room next to my office. I have no recollection of what I hoped to find, but I did make an interesting discovery: thousands of photocopied sheets of yellowing paper with the school's name, address, phone number and an artist's sketch at the top. There was an obvious problem. The picture showed the school backwards, which explained why the sheets were not used. Had someone, a very tired someone, actually sent a letter or memo using that letterhead before the backwardness of the school was pointed out? Had it seemed a reflection of a certain time?

I remembered when a military officer marched into an inner city school where I worked, and haughtily informed the principal and office staff that our flag was flying upside down. *"Don't you know you are flying an international signal of distress?"* he had barked. Our principal had not missed a beat, and crisply replied that the flag was accurately representing us.

Who had run off a backwards school? Some poor principal trying to tackle Paper Mountain, I thought, as the copier had groaned through all those ignominious pages.

MEMO

To: Victoria School Administrators
From: Central Office

The process of developing yearly personal professional growth plans encompasses the concepts of life-long learning and promotes our district as truly a "learning organization." With the amount of change occurring in society and in the field of education the district needs to accept and promote risk-taking in order to facilitate change. Principals will often be operating in areas with no previous examples to guide them.

We know that real learning takes place when personal meaning is attached to the concept, so personal reflection becomes a necessary component. The process which involves data collection, personal reflection and discussion with others will result in continual learning and improvement.

Process

Principals shall on an annual basis undertake surveys of students, staff and parents, using the Criteria for Evaluation of Principals. The data, along with other information such as district surveys, student assessment and school plans will be used to develop a personal professional growth plan. The growth plan could be developed involving personal reflection, discussions with staff, the vice principal, other principals and shall involve the zone assistant superintendent.

Formal evaluation will occur in the first year and prior to renewal of term. Growth plans will be reviewed as part of the formal evaluation process.

Formal evaluation will be written in the form of commendations and recommendations and will include one of the three recommendations from the Assistant Superintendent:

1. Full renewal of term.
2. Reduced term related to concerns.
3. Non-renewal of term.

Journal Entry, April 3, 2003

*I think about the children in our schools and the media's coverage of the war in Iraq.*

*Many students will have left home this morning knowing that a huge city named Baghdad is surrounded. Our newspaper juxtaposed two pictures on its front page: a smiling nineteen year old American girl in fatigues, rescued from an Iraqi hospital; next to it, a picture of a grieving Iraqi father whose six children, wife and parents were killed at a checkpoint. Do these pictures convey hope and despair, good and evil, west versus east?*

*I wonder what final message the images give our children. And are they affected by them? Perhaps this war has become another action movie interspersed with commercials that flog material things promised to enhance rather than satisfy our western needs.*

*I wonder about discussions going on in classrooms and in staff rooms, and I wonder how principals are coping in their neutral zone.*

# 18   ON BALANCE

That first year at Fairfield I realized that principals seldom write letters to the editor or comment upon political windstorms. They are their Board's arm in the schools and have no real collective muscle. Anger with government, trustees or unions over decisions that affect them and their ability to do the best for their students must be stifled on the job. The resulting condition leaves many wondering about their emotional and physical health in the long term. For not only does the principal have to stifle disagreement about a mandate; he or she may even have to *promote* it and then evaluate its success.

During spring break in 1991 I began the self-evaluation necessary for the assistant superintendent to do his formal evaluation of me with the school community. I was constantly soul searching, so the process was not a difficult one. This process had, in fact, begun years before I accepted my position.

My own vice principal self-talk had occasionally been negative. I had no idea whether others did the same thing; we watched what we revealed about ourselves. When considering the step to principalship, I would frequently find excuses not to apply for a position:

> *You're probably too much of a perfectionist.*
> *You're simply too small. And you're female.*

*You're not strongly charismatic.*
*You are no expert in educational trends.*
*You have a shy streak and you hate public speaking.*
*You can never hide your feelings. Principals need to be*
*sphinx-like: calm and inscrutable.*

All of my excuses were voided, however, as staff colleagues insisted upon pointing out positive corollaries to what I saw as negative. And now that I was actually in the position and looking at my performance thus far, I tried not to revert to my earlier doubts.

After our superintendent visited the school that February, she sent a comprehensive letter summarizing her time with me. I read it over again. It included her impressions of the school and my work in it. She reiterated some comments regarding the enjoyment of my work and a description of the staff as "hard-working, strong and clearly focused on the welfare of the children in their care." We discussed the dynamics around the recent teachers' job action, exploring what it meant to them "in light of the evolution of teacher professionalism within a new context." She discussed her visits to classrooms that day, and then zeroed in on me:

*I observed that you, as Principal, related with the teachers*
*and students in a very easy and friendly manner. You affirmed*
*the work of several teachers very naturally within the context*
*of the classroom. This affirmation by you for the teachers is a*
*very important part of your work as Principal. It communicates to*
*the teachers that you understand their reality, support it and are*
*working to advance it in positive and productive ways.*

Devoutly conscientious, she would have sent a letter to each principal in Victoria after each school visit. I was aware of that, and yet her words meant a great deal to me, affirming and encouraging my own possible strengths.

I began to look at six months of work.

Judy Bertram Tomlinson

Who was I in relation to the students? That had always been a comfortable concept when I taught the same children for ten months. It was different now. I was the principal, *la directrice*, doler of discipline and encouragement, too, I hoped. At least one class of grade three students knew my name; I was certain of that when a teacher asked her primary children to print the name of their principal. The results were at least recognizable: Burtrum, Berchrum, Burchrum, burttrum, Burtram, Burturm, Burtrium, brchrim, Bertram, bertram, Bcheram, Burtroom, berchrum, Bertrem, brtram, Brchtunm, Brtrum, Burchram, Brcham, burcham. To some I was simply the voice on the morning announcements or the person who ran the assemblies. They scarcely knew me yet, I thought, unless they were in considerable and regular trouble or were in a class where I taught a little. Yet every action I took had to have their welfare paramount. Their maximized potential was my primary goal.

Continually operating with an organization's primary goal in mind is not always easy, as I was discovering. Theory of leadership courses I had taken for my master's degree examined organizations, the pathology of leadership and the philosophy behind it.

I went back to my texts. Christopher Hodgkinson, in *The Philosophy of Leadership*[1], wrote that the leader "must be indifferent to...the results of actions as they accrue to him personally.... His own ego has to cease to count, it has to be eliminated from the equation of organizational variables. It has to be transcended... by constant failure and constant effort."

He lists three "inhibitions" which should help to monitor and override the ego.

1. Not identifying emotionally to the point of loss of control with the ongoing flux of events, the ups and downs of vagaries of circumstance and chance...

2. A determination not to consider one's own ego, much less one's id, if the impulsions of that consideration

1 From Christopher Hodgkinson's *The Philosophy of Leadership*. Oxford, B. Blackwell, 1983. 213.

contradict one's organizational commitments in any way…

3. A general inhibition against *expressing* negative emotion…This is not to say that the leader will not feel negative affect, only that he will not normally express it. Nor is this to be confused with the popular psychology of "positive thinking." The leader may well be profoundly pessimistic about the turn of events but has a dramaturgical duty to express and inspire confidence and maintain commitment—so long as he can do this without trenching on the unauthentic or undermining his credibility.

Rereading Hodgkinson's last sentence, I was reminded of a rookie principal who regularly and publicly complimented members of his teaching staff, a gesture well received until someone pointed out that it was being done alphabetically. (At that point, the staff made a game of waiting for the next blessing from our fair-minded, earnest but transparent leader.) I was also aware, as I perused this again, of the utter incredulity my corporate friend would express: "You must submerge your *what*? How would you achieve anything at all?"

Override the ego. Be there for the general good, not your own. I re-examined my difficult situations thus far, looking carefully at my own motives in each one. Some problems were far from solved.

Finally, I began to list the work that I had continued for the school following its set goals, the work that had been started and the work that had been accomplished during the 1990/91 school year so far. That list became my self-evaluation and was handed in to the assistant superintendent. I did not include the extensive soul-searching I had done in relation to my suitability for the job. Here there was no indication that I had been wondering about the confidence of other principals who seemed to have answers to every dilemma that was presented. Did they always know what to do? Would I ever be as confident?

Although I had no real foreshadowing of the extent to which I would have to call upon humility, courage and intense focus on the organizational goal as I tackled emerging problems, my list's extensiveness was reassuring and even a little surprising to me. (It is included in its entirety for a quick skim and perhaps a stifled yawn.)

PRINCIPALSHIP
1990-91—Judy Bertram

Plant Management

- Weekly walk-about with custodian
- Office renovation
- Carpeting of primary classrooms
- On-going requests for servicing of drainage problem
- District rentals
- Encouragement of outside groups (i.e. Fairfield community)
- Fun Fair June 6—planning all sorts of community involvement
- Redesigning of computer lab to Primary One classroom
- Earthquake policy booklets

Business Management

- Budget:
  - Vice Principal coordinator
  - On-going consultation with staff
  - French money to French department
  - Hired secretary with business savvy—accounting done well and everyone accountable
  - Each teacher allocated $100 at beginning of year—plans to raise this in fall

- Organization for teachers' requests for expenditures for programs, e.g. musical instruments, specialized books, books, materials for special projects
- Binders—organized by secretary—clear budget process, open to staff
- Committees: Whole School Budget (w/o French money)
- French Budget Committee (report to whole staff).

Instructional Leadership

- School Improvement Planning in accordance with Year 2000 initiatives.
- Goals (Primary led by Judy; Intermediate led by Greg) Parents involved in response to Intermediate document.
- Parents Educational Committee set up. Regular, monthly meetings of each group; report to staff as a whole.
- Committee still has to be formed to look at 5-Year Plan, School Improvement Planning Process (SIPP) for next year.

Assessment and Evaluation

- File set up of collection of interesting and innovative reporting and assessment procedures by different schools' teachers. Open for perusal to anyone.
- Read and wrote encouraging comments on every child's report card
- Completed six evaluation reports (five teachers and vice-principal) and vice-principal did three. (Although nine reports a lot of work, it was worth it in a first year because we were in so many classrooms and dialogued with teachers about their work.)

- In-depth interviews with staff members regarding goals, how I can help them. (still on-going; intend to do all CUPE personnel as well)
- Suggested and facilitated opportunities for conferences for teachers and CUPE members.
- Constant encouragement for teachers to visit other schools. Have been successful with some, but need to keep at it.
- Professional Development Days: Cooperative Learning, District Team, Wellness Workshops, Cross/ Grade Sharing, Primary Ungraded, Using Computer for Assessment/Reporting.
- Staff meetings—try to have interesting articles on Year 2000 concepts with each agenda.

## Students

- Teaching: Grade 7 (peer counselors with other staff member), Grade 1 class (art and writing), Grade 3/4 (art)
- Pencil awards for birthdays, good work
- Recognition of excellence, wonderful art, good citizenship, etc. on P. A.
- Primary Games (Fridays)—run with peer counselors
- Discipline Contracts—signed by administration, teacher, student and parent to bring all parties together over issue.
- Continue with Intermediate Awards Assemblies which award all students over the year
- Primary Assemblies to showcase talent and invite participation

## Decision-Making and Communications

- Consultative Committee—every Monday 3:15

- Constant informal interviewing
- Approachability: goal is that all students/parents/staff feel comfortable with me and welcome in my office. (Have some problems fending them off!)
- Availability: before school, recess, lunch and immediately after school, teachers *and students* know that I am almost always available either in my office or on the grounds.
- Attend all parent meetings
- Monthly newsletters: principal's message, upcoming dates, calendar, staff names to articles, student work
- Parent Advisory Executive: meets with me before parent meetings and unscheduled meetings often— agenda for monthly meetings set in consultation with me.
- Interpersonal relations: hope a strong point! I insist on polite expression of ideas at committee meetings, staff meetings and all meetings where open expression is key.
- Working on school handbook with parent.

School Organization

- Careful consultation with teachers regarding placements of staff, students.
- New staff members "buddied-up"
- Hiring committee: principal, pertinent staff (i.e. working at same level), GVTA rep.
- In and out of classrooms as often as possible, teach in three, often involved in activities
- Read all report cards and write comments
- Involved in many parent/teacher meetings
- Regular, school-based team meetings
- Clear job description for Vice-Principal
- Appraisals of CUPE staff

Looking back, my hodge-podge of activities and accomplishments is glaringly unstreamlined, but it did give me pause to consider what had been done, not just by myself but by all of us in that community. Soon surveys to parents, students and staff would be sent to collect information and opinions of my performance. The assistant superintendent would meet with some students, parents and all the staff and then write a report on my work. Personal attributes would be examined: interpersonal skills; poise under pressure; listening, oral, and written communication; problem-solving skills; and so on. There was a myriad of other criteria under headings such as Mission, Beliefs and Goals; Culture; Management; Decision-Making and Community and Family Involvement.

Once I finished my list I put thoughts of the evaluation out of my mind. Although the process sounded daunting, there was too much to do to worry about the outcome. All I could give was my best; I would soon learn if it was good enough.

Vice principals were also expected to do some soul searching, and during the year they were to be evaluated by their principal and community, they were also expected to meet with a district review committee to determine if their contract would be renewed and for how long. Principals were to ask themselves the following questions as they worked through the process with their administrative partner:

1. What does the vice principal still need in order to prepare him or her for the principalship?
2. How have these needs been addressed?
3. What are the aspirations of the vice principal?
4. How has the vice principal demonstrated competence as an instructional leader?
5. How does the vice principal react in terms of making decisions in crisis situations?
6. Does the vice principal have a potential for the principalship?
7. Would you hire him or her?

8. Would you want your children to be in his or her school?

Greg was content to remain in his supportive role and was therefore not in the running for the principalship. He did love to improve and streamline processes, however, and he put together a package describing his accomplishments and goals, hoping that many questions could be bypassed in a subsequent meeting with central office that would be shorter and more to the point. The committee was impressed with his efforts, so much so that all vice principals were encouraged to take on this task. When one of his colleagues complained to him, Greg sent him this "misaddressed" item:

*Mike,*
*You mistakenly sent your contract renewal package to us. I know our school is the educational and sports center of Victoria but please send your documents to the Tolmie Bldg.*
*Greg*

MIKE'S CONTRACT RENEWAL PACKAGE
Contents:
1. Highlights of past three years: *Thanksgiving, Christmas, Spring Break, Good Friday, Easter Monday, July 1, Labor Day*
2. Job duties at Rowan School: *I come to school at 8:00 a.m. (approx.); I go home after school*
3. Career Path Document: *School---path---Home*
4. Principal's report: *Mr. G. comes to school in the morning. He goes home after school. The learning situation is satisfactory.*

That week I finished an evaluation of Greg's work as vice principal in his first year at Fairfield. He had done a remarkable job as part of a new team and one teacher enthused, "Greg is like the Duracell rabbit. He just keeps going!"

I knew that in ideal administrative teams the principal is able to trust the integrity of the vice principal implicitly, consult over any issue, delegate a clear, mutually acceptable job description for that role and then rely on it being carried out effectively. Real enjoyment, then, is shared over school successes. If the two complement each other's strengths, they have even more to offer their school community. The staff, in turn, should then be able to expect that their vice principal is "in the loop" and has the confidence and authority to operate as needed. "One man shows" are not nearly as effective in schools or in any other organization and they are not as rewarding for the formal leader. My report on Greg's work summarized our teamwork:

*Mr. O'Connor has done an* excellent *job as vice principal this year. He has carried out assigned duties well and has done far more than was asked of him. (For example, he single-handedly ran all the House Games and took on a very large class to help a teaching colleague.) During the difficult time of the teachers' job action, Mr. O'Connor handled students in the school, parent concerns and staff in an exemplary manner. His hard work has been appreciated by all.*

*In many ways, the administration of [Fairfield] School this year has been a team effort. Mr. O'Connor deserves a great deal of the credit for the relatively smooth operation of a large school in a difficult year. This principal could not have had better support.*

Given a good administrative partner and a skilled staff, a principal who is suited to the role should do well. And formal feedback from the school community and the school district staff should enhance ongoing efforts to continue to improve in that role.

Sometimes the most powerful support comes when it is least expected.

One late spring day I walked the playground in a daze, my mind nudging at an issue that had become overwhelming to me. I knew that a performance appraisal I was working on would have to end in an unsatisfactory report on a prominent employee; the results of my assessment were becoming obvious. I could not personally justify remaining in my position without following through with the process, in spite of a great deal of outside pressure to stop it. I knew the political ramifications that would follow my unsatisfactory report on this individual, and could only guess at the toll on my ability to do the rest of my job. I had been forced into this situation unnecessarily; this was an employee who was capable of doing better. I felt alone in a way I had not thought possible. If egos could be described in size, I thought, mine was a pea during that recess. I had been taught to transcend caring about that, had I not? I braced myself to return inside and put on my positive persona.

My distractedness may have been the reason a little girl disengaged from her friends and threw her arms around me. "You're a good principal," she told me, and, obviously expecting no response, she ran back to her recess activities. Her actions took seconds away from her play.

That little girl will be in her twenties now, and she will never know of the comfort and resolve she gave me that day, reminding me as she did of my principal mandate.

## Journal Entry, April, 2003

*After countless rumors, it has been announced that five Victoria schools are to be closed: three this June, two next year. One, in an affluent area, has only thirty-seven catchment students; the rest come from other school communities that have room for them. Parents from this school seem to complain the loudest about what they deem to be a lack of consultation. Teachers worry about their jobs and students must be anxious. Years of consultation would not alter the fact that this needs to be done, and probably should have been done three years ago given declining enrollments and provincial funding.*

*Knowing this, in a practical sense, does not ease the agonies. I watch the television coverage of the Board meeting. Trustees agonize and raise their hands to vote as each school's name is called. The camera then focuses on the tax-paying, affected public. Among the sign-toting indignant sit three of my former colleagues. One looks drained and older since I last saw her in June. Her school will close this year, and she has some years left before she is able to retire. The principal next to her is sitting with her eyes closed. Her school will close a year from now leaving her in a similar position. Of the two I would prefer the former's situation. I cannot imagine leading a school through its last year: no goals, no positive momentum, no building on successes. My third colleague is probably the most fortunate. His school will close this June and he will retire. Still, he has a worried, abstracted look.*

*With the final decision to close certain schools made public, the district budget process will go into high gear. Unless their schools are closing, principals will soon receive the anxiety-inducing message, "Your staffing is ready!"*

# 19    AGONIES

"Your staffing is ready."

People and paper come together like pressboard in that most stressful of times. Principals personally collect the staffing packages from central office and make an attempt at nonchalance as they greet colleagues and saunter back to their cars with the welfare of each school in large brown envelopes.

Once inside, I imagine most rip them open, as I always did from that first year on, to glance at the bottom line. Or bottom lines. If the full-time equivalent of teacher time is down, and/ or the special education dollar amount is down, there is trouble ahead.

At least a month prior to this ritual, the school's projections for enrollment for the following September are sent to the principal of each school. These are then carefully checked, grade by grade, against the numbers actually attending. Forty-five grade fours should equal close to that number in the grade five projections. Discrepancies are pointed out to those responsible for district planning, and, taking into account the kindergarten registrations thus far and the *traditional* numbers of students who are registered as late as September each year, a tentative organization of classes is developed with the necessary staff to service them.

The next stage involves the school district's interpretation of the annual provincial budget and the consultation portion of the decision making by the trustees. There have been reductions and angst since I was appointed in 1990, but the severity of the cuts and the proximity to student learning has increased.

By the time the principals collect their packages, they are well aware of the budget decisions. They have spent many hours in meetings with the superintendent, trustees and in mixed groups with all stakeholders. Any remotely doable solutions to mitigate cutbacks would have been acted upon by this point. Exactly how it will all translate into one's own school is usually not certain until the print is revealed.

Every number on those pages represents an individual who works in the building for students. An FTE (full-time equivalent) reduction may mean that a full-time teacher will leave for another school where 1.0 is available. It may mean awkward class combinations, such as two students in one grade learning with thirty in another: two grade fives with thirty grade sixes, for example. It may mean music and library are affected because preparation time for teachers is down and therefore so, too, is time allocated for the teacher *giving* those prep periods.

Walking back into the school with the package is an interesting experience. Many people know it is the day for the staffing process to begin and nervousness has usually made itself obvious, particularly among those teachers and support staff lowest in seniority. Questioning looks always followed me. If the staffing numbers are down and there are a few minutes of time in which no one needs immediate attention, the next most riveting sets of papers are the seniority lists. They need to be checked and rechecked, often with calls to Human Resources for further clarification. Union protocols are reread.

The staffing timeline frames the stress and the workload during that April period. Usually there is between a week and two weeks to finish what I once roughly estimated to be about seventy hours of work. This work included reading and absorbing the tomes for staffing and special education, doing a revised organization of classes based upon the new figures, giving each teacher the required prep time, keeping to the class size limits and consulting with individuals, small groups and the whole staff.

The special education budget's deployment is a huge task. From one lump sum, Learning Assistance, Resource Room and ESL (English as a Second Language) teaching salaries plus the support staff's special needs assistants' salaries must be calculated. These amounts are formulaic and little flexibility is available. If a single, funded special needs child leaves the school, assistant time for others may be affected as cutbacks have often forced students to share services. Setting up a timetable based upon a continual erosion of funds means increasing the assistants' load, sometimes to the point where student safety is marginalized. While principals can voice their concerns to colleagues and assistant superintendents, they must give optimistic and creative support to staff members often reeling under one year's personal workload.

During this time formal letters must be written when work has diminished or disappeared for a staff member, and there is a tremendous amount of precise paperwork which must be attended to by the deadline. Every nickel and every minute allotted has to be accounted for, each affecting a teacher, an assistant, their families and subsequent support for students. Retirements, leaves of absence or the addition of regular or special needs students occasionally help to retain staff, but there is never a year without some emotional turmoil. In my experience, the youngest teachers with the least amount of seniority are the most stoic. They have never known stability in their chosen profession and have embarked upon a teaching career expecting to be laid off and rehired a number of times before being able to settle in a school. Becoming an ongoing member of a working community, a teacher who can actually build up a relationship with students, parents and staff, is a luxury they look forward to. Sadly, some cannot wait for this to happen and look to other fields. Teachers who have returned to the profession or have begun it later in life find the low seniority status more difficult to cope with and are usually more vocal about being bumped around. Their financial status and emotional health may affect dependent family members and their well being, as well.

Heartbreaking scenarios evolve.

A special needs child of ten, who has bonded with an assistant for the first time, will lose the devotion, expertise and particular personality that person brought to the job and to the child. This assistant has turned the little boy around and given him a positive reason to look forward to his school day in a wheelchair. They love each other.

A teacher has suffered a nasty divorce and is supporting herself for the first time since her children have left home. Staff members have supported her, and, with their friendship, she has been feeling strong and has been doing a wonderful job with her students. She is laid off from the place where she functions as a healthy, appreciated member of a community; starting somewhere else is daunting for her.

In some cases the impact of a layoff is known only to the principal, who must support that person as much as humanly possible through the news itself and then through two more months of school.

Knowing less fortunate colleagues are heavily impacted by staffing announcements does not necessarily bring out the best in the more senior adults who work with them. Although her own hours are secure in her school, an assistant may rail about a minor change involving her job description. Teachers may display anger when a colleague's projected workload is seen to be easier: a kindergarten/grade one class, for example, with only ten students in the afternoon. A senior teacher may display the tantrum behavior of a child because it appears the make up of students in his class will be different than he has had in the past. A younger teacher with a split class may think she can bump a teacher with more seniority and a straight class from her position. These sorts of examples do not happen every year in every school, but when they do they always cause bad feeling and create tremendous work for the principal. He or she may have to spend an inordinate amount of time writing letters, pointing out contract language and discussing issues with union representatives and assistant superintendents. Most staff members who have behaved badly are sheepish after the fact.

Given ideal circumstances involving exactly the right amount of staffing and allocation dollars, a staff humming along as though on happy pills and a principal with an administrative team trained to look after details, would the staffing period be smooth and calm? Highly unlikely, for a number of reasons. The Daylight Savings syndrome has kicked in by this time of year, and students are getting less sleep. The weather is warmer, and the grade seven girls are shedding clothes. Hormones are popping, and all senior students are thinking about secondary school. They group in attitudes obviously dismissive of most formerly agreeable activities. Bees are out and there are the usual number of stings. Birds' nests are being built and raided, and crows cause incredible excitement. The photographer arrives to take the whole school picture and the district maintenance crew begins to cut the grass under classroom windows, driving some teachers loopy.

Spring concerts are often taking place during this period, and on many nights I sat working on numbers long after everyone had left. Journal entries that I made about this period over a number of years remind me:

*April IS the cruelest month…it was ever thus in this system! Long meeting over budget deliberations. Picked up staffing in a.m. and realized they have dropped us .5 on the French track. Won't work! The little musical will be splendiferous! One teacher wants to leave if no one retires and she cannot have her grade level. Kindergarten father raging because counselor made call to social services. Dear cat-loving primary teacher concerned about how bagged I appeared. She told me I looked tired and that I should "go home and stroke my pussy!" Marcia (grade 6) told our counselor that she was going to "HAVE" a boy as soon as she could…but would be armed with condoms and pepper spray in case she "didn't like it."*

*Picked up staffing—it's wonky, to be sure. Resource Room teacher a great help! Group arrived to do a skipping demonstration for the whole school; no one admitted to setting this up. French numbers are definitely wrong, what's new? Plus no preparation time for the person who gives it, again. Had meeting over Parent Involvement Policy. Dear little grade threes can't wait for the next chapter of <u>Ozma of Oz.</u> Had Hepatitis B shots for grade sixes—I welcomed author who was to read in the library as though she was one of the nurses. We registered four more kids—yeah! Major flood in the staffroom at end of the day...three of us rode around on a vacusuck, or whatever it's called.*

*Fax came in...staffing due this Friday, now! Told teacher she was excess to needs and she took it very well, which means that tomorrow could be difficult. Had to give three suspensions (great parents). Parent asking for kid to be repeated a grade but kid doing well, we think. Lots of time with each of divorced parents—real animosity there. Began long jump practices—nice to be outside for a bit. Met with special needs support staff. Not enough hours to go around. One gal has to make a decision quickly over whether or not to go into deployment and be assured of keeping at least the same number of hours she has now. Another offered a few of her own, but the air was blue. First night of concert...it was great. Came home and worked on numbers until midnight.*

*Long day! Kids reflecting the two full moons this month. Had to tell one teacher her time is way down for next year, and then another that she was being "bumped" out. She cried—felt so badly for her, and what a loss! I helped the school nurse with grade five body changes. Tommy brought me flowers again, what a sweetie! Our staffing numbers are WEIRD! Met with staff committee to go over them. Teacher distraught over leaving her kids for two months, another's home life collapsing around her. A mother in—terribly upset over abuse from fourteen-year-old after abuse from husband. Taught k's and grade one class. Great PAC meeting but couldn't answer all the staffing questions yet.*

Judy Bertram Tomlinson

Tensions do not ease because this phase of the staffing has been completed, although the weekend after the calculations are finished is usually celebratory, if only to experience a reprieve from emotions and number crunching. Staff names and corresponding grade levels or other work assignments have been sent into the impatient jaws of the district's financial and personnel machinery, but the actual students corresponding to those numbers (i.e. J. Blow, Div. 2, Grade 6, 30) have not been assigned. They are in the Student Information System, or SIS, and sit as living entities in a classroom now. But where will they sit next year, and with whom?

This would be relatively simple, if all students in one grade could be accommodated in one class. In the private system, seats are available for so many students and all in one grade are in one class. Or possibly in two classes. In the public system, teacher staffing is based on a formula that takes contract maximum class size into account. A principal may not, for example, have one grade seven class with thirty-five students and a grade six class with twenty-six, even if the individual teachers of those classes would prefer that configuration. Nor may there be twenty-five grade threes and twenty-five grade fours in two classes. In the latter situation, at least three of the grade threes would have to join the grade four class because of the class size limits.

The following represents years of streamlining communication to parents regarding the placement of their child in a class in September. It was eventually included in one of our parent handbooks and in the yearly calendar.

*Student Class Placement*

*By the end of April, schools have some idea of the numbers of students and staff for the following September. Tentative configurations of classes are organized based upon contractual class-size limits and the number of staff assigned to the school. Parents are invited to submit a written request based upon educational needs. These* requests should not indicate the preferences of <u>other</u> parents, without their signature. These should be submitted to the classroom teacher or to the principal before the end of May, when the staff begins to organize for the following year. Requests will be given serious consideration. However, the professionals who work with the students at the school will make the final decision based upon educational and social concerns. A great deal of time is spent on this task. Concerns around placements may be raised in a meeting with all pertinent staff.

Occasionally additional or fewer students in September may result in staff being added or removed. This necessitates the rearrangement of classes, and could happen, though rarely, well into September. Parental support will ease a student's concerns during this stressful time.

Classes are often organized before all teachers are assigned to a school. Some parents are then anxious about the uncertainty this presents and find it difficult to make a placement request. Some will be convinced that information is being withheld regarding Mr. No Name who will be teaching next year's grade four.

Not all parents respond to the request invitation. Some do not read the information that is sent home, and some trust the teachers to make the best decision regarding their child. A few have voiced the opinion that they will do better if they stay out of the process altogether. Of those who write requests, most express clear, simple but thoughtful suggestions for the staff to consider:

*If there is a straight grade four next year, I would appreciate it if Mary could be placed there. She has been in split classes for the past two years.*

*I understand Mrs. Purcel is likely to teach some combination with grade threes next year. She has taught all of our children and we would be delighted if she would have Johnny as well. The other kids did really well with her.*

*Peter needs more time to review. After talking to his teacher, I believe he would do best in the two/three class.*

*Sara and Jennifer work very well together, in school and after school. Would it be possible to place them together next year? Jennifer's mom is writing a note, too. You guys are great!*

*I know he's driving you all crazy. Poor Mr. Smith—I'm asking if Tim can be in his class again next year PLEASE! One more year with him and I know he'll be ready for anything. (Of course I guess Mr. S will have something to say about this. Tim's really sorry about drawing that picture.)*

To expedite things quickly as parent letters came in, I would print the student placement requests on blank class lists, then store the letters for future reference (or defense, if necessary) until the teachers met. Sometimes there would be letters that would be read, reread, and finally put in the "Beats Me" file:

*Regarding the placement of Tina (grade five) and Harry (grade three): I prefer straight classes. If this is not possible because they don't exist because this district is not sensible, I would prefer the upside of a down split. This is more challenging than the downside of an up split. Just because Harry wasn't that great in mad-minute math doesn't mean he won't do well in math in the upside. The same goes for Tina, who I know is gifted in spite of the testing and should never be on the downside. But if you were all sensible I wouldn't have to write this letter because all classes would be straight and I wouldn't have to worry about upsides and downsides. All this depends on who the teachers are of course and I might change my mind when I find that out.*

*I have heard that the grade threes will be split next year. They are in a class of 22 now, so I don't understand why they can't stay together. But I guess we have to live with it. Where should Maude go? If she is in the 3/4 she will probably be challenged more academically, and ready for intermediate. In the 2/3 she will be bored but fit in better because her friends will probably be there. The problem with the 3/4 is the teacher. Will the teacher understand Maude's moods? Will this teacher hug her and tell her she's the best at clay? I need to know these things. Thank you for considering my request.*

*Regarding Jason's class for next year:*
   *-no splits*
   *-no bullies*
   *-no teacher who takes time off*
   *-no field trips to the waterslides—he got sunburned*
   *-no homework*
   *-no pajama day—too embarrassing*
   *-no French—I hope they separate!*

Each year toward the end of May or beginning of June, I met with the teachers over the placement of each child for the coming year. With very few exceptions I was impressed with how well they knew their students and how carefully they had considered their best placements for the coming year. The receiving teachers did not always agree with these placements, however.

Teachers eyeball the students coming up and listen to reports regarding fatigue levels. They hear the wonderful, upbeat stories about student successes, but are often wary of being overloaded with those who require more than the usual attention. To an outsider, much of the rather tense dialogue might sound unprofessional:

"I'll take three of *those*, but I need four others to make a group."

"Well, where are my *leaders* in this arrangement?"

"You've given me too many problems!"

"Oh, all right, I'll have her!"

In actual fact, these teachers are being perfectly professional. They know, as no one else does, what constitutes a viable teaching/ learning situation. They also know themselves well enough to understand their own limits. If one of them took on more than her share last year and is now feeling burnt out because of it, she will probably express that. And in good school cultures this will be an acceptable practice that is carefully monitored by the school principal.

Things get dicey when a teacher balks, year after year, at taking a special needs student with an assistant. Many teachers welcome this scenario, but a few resist vehemently. There are a wide range of reasons put forward: they won't get along with that assistant, they won't get along with those parents, they resent the extra time necessary to plan, they don't believe in the philosophical basis for integration because "time is taken away from the other children." I believe the real reason lies much deeper, in some lack of self-esteem and/or shyness that contributes to their sensitivity regarding another adult in the classroom, one who is privy to all that goes on in there. This is one of the no-win situations for the principal. Staff resentment will naturally build if that teacher seems to be given special treatment. On the other hand, forcing the situation can be a disaster for all concerned.

Once class lists are tentatively ready for school opening, at which point they may have to be rearranged, they are locked away with the school secretary who will begin entering them into formal lists with student PIN numbers. Staffing and school organization pressures and anxieties should be over temporarily, except for the parents who persistently try to get teachers to spill the beans about the fall organization.

If there are classroom teaching positions open due to layoffs, however, the worst agony is yet to come: *The Dance Of The Lemons*. For me, it always began with the uncertainty of a gavotte, something like this:

"Hi, Judy. Jack here. I have someone for your grade seven opening."

"Who are you suggesting?"

"Not a suggestion, really. Has to be placed there."

"The name of your offering?"

"Oh jeez. Here we go. Joe Blow."

"I don't know Mr. Blow. How much experience does he have in elementary school?"

"I think part of a practicum was in grade seven."

"What was he doing last year?"

"Uhh, let's see." Paper rustles and Jack, my educational staffing dance partner, shows that he does not know if we are in step. "He was teaching physics last year for a couple of semesters at X School. Year before, uh, he did some math at Y. He was off for a while before that."

"Does he know this job is open?"

"Yeah, he knows it. Looking forward to working with younger kids there."

"Why?"

"Judy, *he needs to be placed*. He's a nice guy."

Much to Jack's chagrin, the beat is not going on, the music has stopped and he cannot move along to the next candidate in his bowl.

Calls to the secondary principals would confirm my suspicions: having Mr. Blow assigned to our school would prove to be a complete travesty for students, parents, teachers, and for the poor fellow himself. Joe does not realize, it turns out, that in elementary school teachers teach all subjects and stay with the same group all day. This was often overwhelming when it was pointed out to teachers who thought that the education of younger students would be easier for them.

The union's stance is that *a teacher is a teacher is a teacher*. Every professional knows this is ridiculous, even while sympathizing with those who need their livelihood. And if an unsatisfactory report is filed, the union cries foul: Mr. Blow was not in an assignment that was suited to him!

The worst agony comes when there is a placement after all efforts have failed to prevent it. The principal then tries desperately, during a few weeks in the summer, to forget what the coming year holds in store.

There are few journal entries about staffing in my first year at Fairfield. We were a school that was growing, the district was not yet declining in elementary enrollment, and budget cuts had not yet forced the decentralization of special education dollars to the schools.

In retrospect, in this, it was a green and golden time.

# CLASS COLONIST

F**ing Mad: Okay so yeah, we were sauntering by the boy's washroom when an unknown force pulled us in. And we saw that the washroom was under construction, what's with that? Hey are they getting like another room or something??? It sucks. That's it.

Annoying Stuff!!!!

Okay, so like I'm mad and stuff so are the other people (accomplices to operation Dumbo Drop). We accidentally fell into the boys washroom which wasn't pleasant. Their mirror is much bigger than the girls mirror, and they have urinals what if we wanted urinals (which we don't but some people might) it's like a matter of zipping. Plus there is no graffiti to entertain us I mean what's up with that. It's also a pretty blue colour our's is a blinding pink we might get radiation burns or something that's pretty much it but it also smelled really bad.

Note: This was the downstairs bathroom.

Devin might be missed for a couple of days. Devin went to the store 3 times so he could grab a bite to eat like a normal people and he got caught all three times. So he was not very sneaky, should he be punished for it? The sub thought so. Devin might be suspended for it. So you should say goodbye to him for more than one week. I don't think it's right but it is none of my business.

## The Store

I know that you probably think this is about how kids are sneaking to the store. It isn't. It's about how the people at the store treat us. I went in there one day and got some candy. First, he counted the candy, touching all of it, and that is really disgusting (thanks Steph and Carole). Then when I had paid he said "you done now?". When I said yes he said "Okay get out." Rude huh? Jenni and Leona went there and bought two bucks of candy. They totally handled the candy and when they were done they were told to get out.

## The Smell!!!

The Putrid smell has taken over the class of div. 1! Well, not quite, but close enough. We don't know what caused it, but it is definitely the worst in the Cloak room. (I think that's how you spell it. We don't know why.) I think it smells like someone let a cat do it's thing in there. Mr. G thinks it smells like sour milk. If anyone has read the book called the twinkie squad, they will understand what I mean. If not, they won't. Don't mind me. I'm in a silly mood.

# 20   CLEARING THE DUST

"We have a concern," our staff committee Chair intoned.

We have many, I thought to myself. It was the second week after school had resumed for the last term, and we had not met since before the holidays. The parent who had been charging sexism in the P.E. curriculum was now zeroing in on rugby, which was due to start shortly with the boys. Our strings teacher could not find staff to help transport students to the music festival and we desperately needed money for resources for the new primary class. There was to be yet another job action that would come with the usual hype and hyper. District principals were being told they were to be "reconceptualized" to meet the demands of the "paradigm shift" necessary for survival in a newly ambiguous system, and the Minister of Education was quoted as saying that the people of British Columbia needed to choose between education and health care. All sides were grinding their teeth and my own evaluation process was imminent.

Our Chair took the "concerns" envelope and held it upside down. It seemed to be empty, as nothing fell out in spite of a couple of vigorous shakes.

As the rest of the committee watched respectfully, my mind wandered again. The status of that envelope made sense to me, given the positive feedback I had been receiving about the school in general and the school tone in particular. Contemplating our accomplishments over the last seven months had given me a perspective that distanced and empowered, just a little. The result was some objectivity; perhaps my ego was learning to step aside.

"There's nothing in it," someone said.

"Correct," confirmed our Chair, looking back at us. She must use this technique with her class, I thought. It backfired.

"Good, I have work to do," Gill told us, getting up.

Great, I thought. I have some calls to make.

"There *is* a concern," the Chair admonished us, and we lowered our behinds reluctantly.

"But there's nothing in the envelope!" Jean snapped.

"Ex-act-ly," she enunciated. We stared at her. "No one is *expressing* concerns."

"Could it not be," pondered our librarian slowly, "that there is nothing in the envelope because things are going *well?*" He emphasized the last word a bit timidly, I thought.

She shook her head. "This shows a breakdown in *process!*"

"Maybe we need to remind the staff to get those concerns in to us. People may not have bothered because of the holiday." I wondered why I was helping this along. These meetings every Monday were becoming unproductive and I needed the time for other matters.

"Right," our Chair said. "I'd like to be on the agenda at the staff meeting. This needs to be raised."

We went over the complete agenda together and bolted.

There was another call from Mrs. Perry when I returned to my office. The woman was becoming rather Pankhurstian in her zealotry and was wearing on the staff who taught physical education to the senior students. I thought about her complaint again.

Our senior classes took part in what we believed to be a well-enjoyed physical education curriculum during that time of year. The boys were taken to a nearby playing field where they were taught the rudiments of rugby, a game considered satisfyingly rough and tumble for many at that stage of their development.

They were carefully weighed and had the opportunity to play competitively in a city-wide tournament at the end of the season. Coaching was very well done and the injuries were minimal.

While this was taking place, the girls learned the skills of field hockey. It was not so rough and tumble, but it was an opportunity to play a sport seldom taught in Victoria at that time. A huge bonus was that it was taught by Gill, who made it great fun and organized a tournament for the finale.

Mrs. Perry objected, vehemently. Her daughter, she felt, should have the right to play rugby with the boys, and anything less than that was pure sexism. We had had pleasant enough conversations over the phone regarding the activities; now she insisted that we meet face to face.

The following day after school, Mrs. Perry arrived and we went over it all one more time. From my point of view, the boys and the girls were equally blessed in these activities. My bottom line included the teachers' vehemence regarding the appropriateness of the sports as they were organized, versus the inappropriateness, as they saw it, of girls playing rugby, let alone mixed rugby. When I could not counter confidently with real jock knowledge, I knew I needed help and paged Gill to the office.

She arrived flushed and smiling from a field hockey session and nodded to our guest. She was well aware of the issues and waded right into the discussion. "Mrs. Perry, hello. Well, we've just had a *wonderful* field hockey game and the girls have really enjoyed themselves."

"My daughter wants to play rugby," she was told.

"Well, we have not organized our P.E. periods for that," Gill countered, "and we have always done it this way. And very successfully, I might add."

"I don't know how you measure success," Mrs. Perry said deliberately. "The fact is, my daughter feels that she is being discriminated against because she is female." Two dark red dots were manifesting themselves on Gill's cheek as she raised her chin a little. "Melissa understands that rugby is a sport many girls would avoid," Mrs. Perry went on, "so she is willing to play with the boys."

"And then I suppose you would suggest that we take on the odd boy for field hockey!" The red dots were spreading.

"Why not?"

"You know, there is a time and a place for boys and girls to do their own thing," our Brit said emphatically, probably thinking of some green, halcyon fields of England. And a simpler time.

"Not in our household!" Mrs. Perry snapped.

As I was leaning forward to attempt some mediation, Gill stood up. "Mrs. Perry, do you know what happens in a rugby scrum?" Mrs. Perry was not sure. "The boys grab, like this, through the crotch—." Gill performed an amazingly acrobatic maneuver on herself to the astonishment of both Mrs. Perry and myself. "Do you want your daughter to be groped, like *this*? And *this*? By *boys*?" She did it again.

That was enough for our parent. Where the threat of broken bones had fallen on deaf ears, pubescent groping was a terrifying prospect to ponder.

"I'll have a talk with Melissa tonight," she told us as she left.

The next morning Mrs. Perry phoned and very politely asked if I would have a talk with her daughter. She thought that might help to put the matter to rest, she explained, and she would be very grateful.

Melissa was a lovely and rather mature girl. We talked about the frustration females may experience in many areas, including sports. And I confided, a little, about some of the feelings I had about doing a job traditionally done by a male. It was not easy, I told her, and she nodded with all the wisdom of her thoughtful and wonder-filled twelve years.

That evening our parent group voted to give us one thousand dollars for the new primary class. It was just what was needed to supply the small kindergarten with some exciting learning aids. Parents were reminded of my upcoming evaluation and their anticipated involvement. They were excited about plans for a Fun Fair they were sponsoring, and joked about the possibility of lowering their principal into the dunk tank.

I had the same positive feelings in our staff meeting the next day. I went over the latest district information, including the formal cancellation of the Dual Entry for kindergarten. I informed the teachers of the money the parents' group was donating to the new class and went over the staffing process for the organization of the following year. They were reminded of my evaluation (they were to be interviewed individually) and good-natured bantering at my expense caused things to get out of hand for a while. Our senior French teacher, Roger, invited the staff to his final Café Française, a luncheon put on by his students and parents to raise money for the Quebec trip. Committee Chairs reported out and the teachers were reminded to get those *concerns* to the staff committee Chair. Greg reminded us that the track and field season was about to begin, and suggested a meeting of those who were interested in coaching. We finished with the calendar events for the final two and a half months. The Fun Fair was upon us and we needed to meet to begin the discussion around grade seven awards. Planning for our last professional development day was underway and more discussion time for that was organized. Final report cards timelines were noted, as well as other end of year activities.

I made a final appeal for the strings teacher. For some reason, no one was interested in accompanying over a hundred and sixty students from three schools on buses to the music festival, not even with a substitute teacher in their classroom and their own students performing. I cancelled a workshop I had planned for the following Monday and braced myself.

There were two buses. Our strings teacher was on one with his Gordon Head School students; I was on the other with ours and we were to pick up string players from a neighboring school. Mr. Lewis was very appreciative of my help, and told me that most students would be driven home by parents after the festival performance.

The Fairfield strings students were reasonably well behaved on that bus trip. They knew me by this time and, although some looked as though they were hyperventilating with excitement, they listened to the usual rules regarding the bus code of behavior. The bus driver smiled wanly as we clambered aboard, violin cases knocking against railings. As we pulled away, smug faces stared down at a class out for a jog on that warm afternoon.

The pick up of students at the neighboring school did not go as well. The adult waiting with the thirty or so young musicians seemed to have given over any attempt at controlling that school's pulsing, curbside mob. When the doors were opened they pushed each other on board with alarming force, causing the driver and myself to bellow, "Hey, slow down!" in unison. The rest of the trip to the festival is now a blur, although I do remember trying to play the principal with little strangers who had no idea who I was and were not interested, anyway.

All three schools did eventually arrive, get arranged into a combined orchestra and perform rather well. The adjudicator praised their musicality and focus, the latter unfortunately lost long before his comments were complete.

Just as Mr. Lewis had predicted, many parents who had attended the performance were able to drive their budding musicians back to their schools. He went on the one bus with the remaining Gordon Head students and I climbed aboard the other with about twenty from the neighboring school. All Fairfield students had rides in parents' cars.

The return trip is also a bit of a blur now, although I know it was much, much worse than the drive there had been. Added to the initial excitement of being out of school together and the adrenaline from the performance, was the sudden release of tension. These kids were wild. Spitballs flew back and forth. They sang off key and made rude gestures to other vehicles. There were yelps as necks were pinched and eyes were covered with foreign, sweaty hands. Windows were opened and bodies leaned out. Seats were exchanged. Our driver stopped the bus twice and threatened to make them walk. I threatened more than that, and each time they sobered up for a few blocks and then went haywire again.

One violinist was particularly crazy on that trip. Short and stocky with straight black hair and a very large mouth, she was by far the loudest and most obnoxious that day. Gladys (I learned her name early in our adventure) was out for a really good time. She was not going to waste one minute of serious partying on that bus, and who did I think I was, threatening to have her de-stringed forever? As if all the singing, pinching, leaning out of the bus and exchanging seats was not enough, Gladys took to heaving herself up and down on her seat and on the lap of the girl next to her. She then returned a punch she had received.

In spite of the racket, the driver's groan of relief was clearly audible as his bus pulled up in front of their school. I squeezed down the steps first, hoping for some semblance of order in dismounting, but those students left the bus strangely quiet, probably quite winded, and quickly disappeared. I neglected to see whether they went into their school or went off to their homes, because I was distracted by two events happening simultaneously just then.

The bus was rapidly disappearing down the street without a farewell from the driver, who, I would like to think, must have forgotten I had originated from the other school. And Gladys was down on all fours on the boulevard grass throwing up.

When her system seemed to have collected itself, she sat up and I wiped her face. She was too weak to walk, she told me, so I set off to get help after reminding her to stay put in the shade.

It took some time to get into her school. Every door was locked, and in spite of my rattlings and bangings no one responded. After circling the building I spotted the custodian emptying trash into a dumpster. He let me in through his entrance. "We lock up after school for security purposes," he told me. I bit my tongue and barreled up a flight of stairs toward the general office. Students had obviously gone for the day and only a few adults were visible in the halls.

Judy Bertram Tomlinson

The secretary looked up, startled. I must have seemed crazed: hot, tired, and frustrated, I am sure I radiated pure venom. "I need to see Jim," I told her, breathing heavily. She hesitated, as though weighing her responsibility to screen true crazies from her principal against my obvious, unstoppable intention to confront him. She opened the door to his office.

My colleague was enjoying what was very likely a well-deserved break. His feet were up on his desk, his hands were behind his head and his office was cool and peaceful.

I babbled. "One of your students needs help. *Now!* Been sick— front of school." He called to his secretary and she said she would have someone check on the child. "I have been with one hundred and sixty strings students all afternoon. Played well. Awful the rest of the time. *Yours out of control! Never do it again!*"

Being the kind man he is, he probably drove me back to Fairfield, although I have no memory of that and I do remember that I had what felt like blisters on my heels as I walked into our staff committee meeting. It was Monday.

"Ah, she's *finally* arrived," our Chair announced. "We *do* have a concern today," she continued, and smiled at me while unfolding a slip of paper. Surreptitiously, I forced my shoes off under my chair and my feet screamed relief.

"It seems someone has noticed that the trophy cabinet needs dusting."

We all waited a while to hear if there was more.

"The trophy cabinet needs dusting," I parroted, quietly. I could still hear some of the bus bedlam ringing in my ears. It faded away and I focused on the concern at hand. The words began to make sense, in a strange sort of way. "THE TROPHY CABINET NEEDS DUSTING?" I croaked. The staff committee members were looking at me intently. Our librarian's mouth twitched. "Who on earth would send that in as a concern to a group of busy…" I looked around the table, knowing full well that meetings next year would be once a month.

Back upstairs, I left a message on the staff bulletin board: *Would the person who expressed concern regarding the dusty trophy cabinet please bring the matter up with our custodian. Thank you. Your consultative committee.* According to our custodian an hour later, no one had approached him about the dust in the cabinet, but he had seen the message on the board and cleaned it up smartly.

"How was your day?" my husband asked, reading an expression that struck him as "off."

"Never to be repeated," I assured him.

On the following Sunday my journal reports that I worked in school from 11:00 to 4:00, and that night I wrote that I would be glad when the following week was over.

Our assistant superintendent was there early the next morning to begin the formal evaluation process. At recess he poked his head into my office and told me that the individual interviews with the teachers were going very well. I have noted that I thought it was kind of him to give me feedback so early, and that there was a support staff meeting with him at 10:30 the next day.

Sometime during the week he met with the grade seven students. He arrived chuckling after that one. "Wonderful kids, Judy. They like you."

"Good," I said, thinking of some of the discipline scenarios that had unfolded. They *were* great kids.

"And I don't want you to take this the wrong way, because they really do like you…" I was prepared for anything. "A couple suggested that you could have been a little taller." We laughed.

The parents who met as a group were enthusiastic, apparently. They told our assistant superintendent that they did not always get their own way with me, but that they felt they were being listened to and were thankful for that.

The process went on during an otherwise busy but uneventful week and Friday he met with me again. Apparently things had gone very well. In spite of size, sex and an open countenance it was just possible that I was suited to my job.

As it turned out, teachers' job action that had been threatened earlier involved an afternoon "study session" and caused little upheaval. This time no one asked me to explain or condone.

Administrators had their "reconceptualization" workshop, and I noted that it was very well done, although I no longer remember how it was we were to be transformed, if that is the word.

I do remember, vividly, watching track and field practices during noon periods at that time. Young bodies raced, jumped and hurled the shot-put and themselves through the air to the encouraging comments of our teachers. There were no playground upsets; even the primary students who formed part of the audience with me seemed to be enthralled as much by the interaction of the teachers and the intermediate students as they were by the athletic prowess we were watching on their lovely, sun-splashed playground.

# THE RUNNERS

We're hopeless at racing
Me and my friend.
I'm slow at the start
She's slow at the end.
She has the stitch
I get sore feet,
And neither one of us
Cares to compete.

But cooperation's
A different case
You should see us
In the three-legged race!

Grade seven students (Fairfield)

# 21   ECSTASIES

They may be so fleeting that they are appreciated only upon reflection: a smile of understanding from a child learning something new, or a hidden wave at waist level, signifying recognition from a troubled one passing me in a hallway. The intensity on a young face as every nuance of teaching is captured or the bounce in the step of a youngster whose spirits have lifted: these moments affected me in a way that would enthrall and transport my spirit. I could instigate the sensation by reading a book I loved to a class, causing small jaws to go slack as my audience became totally engrossed. And I could look forward to the sensation each year when paper organization became human and the quiet of students in classes signaled learning had begun.

"*Ça va?*" I would ask French Immersion kindergarten students after a week or so in September.

"*Oui!*" The response was always a little smug and very proud; this learning business was fun.

I first experienced this kind of feeling in my principal role during the second week at Fairfield. One of the band students arrived at my office door and asked if I would go out to their portable so they could play for me. "We're pretty good," he said hopefully on the way over.

"We have something we'd like you to hear," the band teacher said, and raised her baton.

Naturally, I have no memory of what they played, nor am I sure that I recognized the piece at the time. I do know that I clapped very enthusiastically as the cacophony died down and that they all positively beamed as I marveled at their ability to play together so early in the school year. As I walked back into the school, I suddenly realized that my opinion was considered important. There was great responsibility connected to that, but it was heady stuff. Heady and humbling. My work as a cheerleader had begun in earnest.

Schools have a serious mandate: supporting the actualization of each student's potential. Some years seem harder than others while working toward this ideal, and any negativity can be hard to shake off during the summer break.

At the end of a particularly difficult year for many, a teacher came up with a way for each of us to shed the stress we had accumulated over the previous ten months. Jean had just one rocket left from the group his students had fired over the school neighborhood that spring. The climax of their science project became ours, and during the June staff party each of us was given a piece of paper on which to write experiences we needed to shed. All the paper was tucked into the rocket when it blasted off over Victoria's Inner Harbour, taking our negative memories with it. We laughed, cheered and began our summer lighter in spirit.

Staff bonding allows for collective fun and celebration. Good stories, repeated often, are enjoyed many years later and are a way to reconnect and relive experiences together.

A Fairfield teacher asked, anxiously, to meet with me one day. She was uncharacteristically tense. "Judy, I don't know what to do and I just have to talk to someone!" She sat down and put her head in her hands. Into her early forties, Karen had never seemed less than a happy, well-adjusted person, fazed by nothing in her profession.

"What's happened?" I asked, preparing myself for something truly awful.

"I'm *pregnant!*" she sobbed, not looking up at me.

"At the same time as your daughter!" Karen nodded and wiped her eyes. She was about to be a grandmother for the first time. What timing! "What does your husband think?" I asked her, expecting that he would have mixed emotions at this stage.

"I haven't told him yet," she cried, looking more and more distracted. She seemed to be talking to herself now, and, looking down, she added, "We don't believe in abortion. But I just got back to working full time and it doesn't seem fair!"

I was flummoxed. No helpful advice came to mind and I could not imagine being in her situation. All I had to give her was my attention, which was being distracted a little by some sound outside the open office window.

"Sorry, Karen," I apologized as I got up to shut it. "You're absolutely *certain*, are you? Maybe you're having a symptom of early menopause."

"I'm quite certain. I've been to my doctor!" She was red in the face now, and I suspected it was from the heat that was rapidly building around us. It was April. "I would prefer the window open," she told me. "Wide open."

I cranked it out as far as it would go. There was singing outside, and there seemed to be an awful lot of people on the basketball courts. "Sorry, Karen. Sounds like someone's having a birthday. Now, when do you plan to tell Jim?"

"*Oh, for heaven's sake, Judy!*" She jumped up, took me by the shoulders and pushed my face toward the window. The whole school body was assembled outside. They were singing "Happy Birthday" and waving up to my window. It *was* my birthday and I had been drawn into Karen's condition so entirely that it took me quite a while to believe anything she told me for a long time after that.

We know that laughter relieves negativity and raises the endorphins. It cuts through too much seriousness and promotes positive school cultures. It needs to happen in classrooms more than it does, and the ability to appreciate humor—in irony and even in slapstick—is a lifelong blessing. Sharing it helps understanding and promotes bonding. It infuses energy.

Thinking back to my own first day as a junior high school student, I realize it began as a tense time. After elementary school, the new building seemed huge with its thousand students, and the necessity of changing rooms and teachers every hour was exciting but daunting. We had done a run-through of our timetables the morning before; now things were to begin in earnest.

We assembled in our homeroom. Mrs. Kerr was the teacher who greeted us first thing and took attendance; she was also to be our English teacher. She seemed pleasant and friendly enough, but none of us were taking anything for granted. Too much was unknown and we were wary. Five or ten minutes after we had our roll call, we were listening to some serious pedagogical musings on the importance of being punctual and I was sure that every teacher was going over a list of expectations at the same time. Tardiness was not to be tolerated here; this school had very high standards.

Just at that moment a yawning boy walked into our classroom and stopped in front of us. He stared and we stared back. His hair showed which side he had been sleeping on, his eyes were half lidded and his mouth remained in an arrested yawn. He looked at the spot where his empty desk should have been. I was in it. Slowly, he turned and looked at Mrs. Kerr, obviously trying to remember if she was yesterday's teacher. It dawned that she was not and, dumbfounded, he was rooted to the spot. As if on cue he had materialized as a dopey visual aid.

"Room 41?" he managed, as his mouth became operative.

"Next door," our teacher told him and pointed the way.

He left and we erupted. The best part was that our teacher grinned and giggled about the incident for days. Everyone relaxed, including Mrs. Kerr, who was teaching junior high for the first time. She was human and we loved her.

There is nothing like the sound of laughter from classrooms and staff rooms and I always wished there was more. That first year at Fairfield we ordered an erasable board for the staff room so that messages could be exchanged. A second board was ordered shortly after the first, not because of the serious messages to deliver, although we did use them for that purpose, too. We needed space for teasing, plays on words and general titillations.

For example, the Freedom Of Information and Protection Of Privacy Act was serious business, and the staff had to know all of its contents and ramifications. "What is FOIPOP?" was written on the board long after the finer points of the act had been labored over and apparently forgotten. There were some responses during that morning:

1.  It's who the gifts are for on Father's Day.
2.  It's fake pop—i.e. "foiled pop."
3.  An area code in Rwanda
4.  Financial Overview For Investing In Property Or People.
5.  For Ordinary Idiots Passing Out Peanuts.

"I need a sharp pointy thing," written by a primary teacher, was the starting point for two boards of responses that amazed the external accreditation team evaluating the school during that week. And later, when she added, rather petulantly, "I really DO need this badly," we were off and running again, erasing and composing. It would not have occurred to any of us that the seriousness of our mandate should have been equated with propriety in our staff room, or that we should have kept our messages serious for that week. The high-spiritedness of our staff culture was praised by the team. Those educators knew that our students were benefiting from our positive energy.

Sometimes staffing went extremely well, and there was the perfect match of a teacher or an assistant to a particular job. Securing talented people involved stamina and luck, and when it happened I rejoiced with everyone involved. Those appointments were events that were celebrated by everyone affected, and the whole spirit of the school was elevated.

That first year at Fairfield committees met to examine aspects of the school that needed attention: discipline, technology, library and others. Over time, as all community groups were represented, the level of discussion was elevated and stimulating. With parents involved, there was a growing excitement about what our community could become. Goals were set, policies drafted, and the positive high was well earned, especially when improvements began to show because of the contributions from *every* part of our community.

Over the years, in two schools, evidence of hard work came in concrete feedback through formal survey comments by parents:

*Our last parent-teacher evaluation (grade 2) was led and facilitated by the students themselves. They and their teacher did a great job! It was great to see the pride in the students, the leadership skills displayed and a wonderful opportunity to view my child "at work." I applaud all the hard work, creativity and time spent to make this parent-teacher-student "talk" so successful.*

*Staff are an incredible mix of great abilities; teachers strive for high ideals which is transferred enthusiasm to the students. Parents are very involved and supportive—no task is too large to be considered. By putting these two factors together you have an awesome combination...I am now the biggest advocate of the public school system.*

*The greatest strength for this school is its continued compassion for its diversity of students. It continues to set down and maintains clear boundaries and guidelines for all students to carry out that which encourages fairness and respect.*

*Greatest strength is communication; the desire by staff (and parents) to create a rich, healthy learning and growing environment for our children, the sense of community, the willingness to examine issues that arise from all angles.*

*I believe this school is goal-oriented, determined to reach its goals, and this reflects among the students. It fully supports non-bullying, two different languages, special needs students and encourages children to participate as a team. All of these are life skills which they will need throughout their lives. I am very delighted to have my child in this school.*

Whole school feedback was not always ecstatic and therefore did not produce the corresponding sensation. However, it could conjure fascinating images:

*Move principal's desk to the playing field!*

*I think that children need to be outside more often. Knowing that broccoli is actually flowering buds, worms clean and enrich the soil and that food we eat comes from the earth originally, may benefit some. These days, kids are inside at home (in front of the t.v. or videos). So, to counteract, schools should be in the fresh air so they learn to respect our planet!*

But student achievement is the greatest high for educators. I had beginning readers in my office as often as possible and experienced joy whether the student's progress was plodding or rapid: the system was not only working, these youngsters were thrilled with words and their own accelerating discovery of the power of print. Over time, nothing could top that for me: little necks bent, glossy hair falling forward, the occasional plump forefinger guiding the way and the big grin at the end, after which the proud student would strut away to heaps of praise. Reading report cards and noting individual progressions through grade levels was gratifying when breakthroughs occurred. I could see how a special relationship with a particular teacher was affecting a student and notice how the calming of a troubled household worked magic in learning. Curriculum fairs were overpowering examples of fine collective work by students and teachers.

I have leaned against gymnasium walls and been transported with choirs practicing for concerts, and I have been taken completely out of myself at exciting sports events where principals with enviable reserve sat or stood stoically while their school's athletes battled for a trophy.

The most memorable sports event for me was what some of us called the Year 2000 basketball championship. The game happened long before that year. I was at Fairfield, and Laurie, the first teacher we had interviewed for the staff, was the coach. She had been working with a group of boys who loved the game and were very responsive to her coaching. Her approach exemplified the Year 2000 ideals: students learning at their own pace, being supportive of each other, working cooperatively and learning from positive reinforcement. We made it to the city finals and played against a school known for its athletic accomplishments. Their coach had worked very hard with boys who were highly skilled and aggressive.

"Nice play, Jordan!" Laurie called, gently.

"Get that ball MOVING! What's the matter with you?" the other coach yelled.

"Good rebound," Laurie beamed at her team. "Nice try, Joe! Never mind."

"Paul! WHO ARE YOU CHECKING? WAKE UP!"

"Set it up, guys," our player called, calmly, as he worked his way carefully down the court. He passed the ball to a teammate who scored the winning goal for Fairfield. We were city champs.

Working with a whole school community to pull off a superb event is exciting and rewarding for many reasons, not the least being that students need to be part of the planning and execution of excellence. Canadian Citizenship ceremonies were such events, and after witnessing one in a former school, I promoted them at Fairfield and Rowan, my last school. These events involved consultation with the citizenship court, letters inviting special dignitaries, the formation of a choir, parking arrangements and refreshments organized by parent groups. Programs had to be designed, chairs ordered and the neighbors notified of the many extra cars expected around the school area. Artwork was displayed, map studies revealed countries from where the special guests had emigrated, and most adults and students took part in the general decorating and other preparations. Teachers prepared their classes for the understanding of the profound importance of the upcoming event to the people most affected: the new citizens. A choir practiced songs such as "This Is Our Land."

Many of these new citizens had tears in their eyes afterward, overwhelmed with their new status, the purity of the choir voices, the fresh young faces of students welcoming them so wholeheartedly, and the hundreds of Canadian flags.

"Here come the *new Canadians*!" an excited youngster said to the girl beside him. These people walked a proud path to our library reception, down halls lined with primary students who cheered and gave out letters of welcome. It was a swill of color: the black of the judge's robes, the red of the mountie's uniform and our flag preeminent.

"This is our land, O Canada," our choirs sang. At those times I always thought that a public school was the perfect place to host that ceremony, because it represented all of our society and it represented our future.

"Principals have no power," a friend said to me, shortly after my appointment. She was probably reflecting upon the many changes that were occurring, changes that did strip facets of position power from that role. Privately, I disagreed. I knew the position had power to affect schools in profoundly positive ways when the people in them were well supported in what they needed to do.

Staff evaluation comments were gratifying that first year, and there were a couple that I mulled over for some time. One teacher wrote, "I sense that the 'needy' staff are drawn to her like moths to a light…and I appreciated her suggestion that we try to solve our problems by talking to one another first…she would be available if we needed help after that process." Our vice principal suggested "…pulling up the drawbridge when necessary—perhaps too many people are given too many audiences."

They were both correct, and I was never very good at pulling up that drawbridge. However, in time most staff recognized that I tended to glaze over when I had had enough. Besides, *being there* for them, when it made a difference, was one of the ecstasies.

# CLASS COLONIST

Bad news. Jason is leaving to go to Royal Oak. Hopefully he'll like it and have a good time but a lot of people will miss him. We might be having a going away party today for him but since today is his last day there might not be enough time. In any case have a good time Jason!

## To Smoke Or Not

Smoking is a touchy thing to most people, that's if they smoke. They say it calms them and tastes good. I think it tastes disgusting and makes me cough, but I guess that if people want to die young then that's their problem.

## To The Guys

I think you guys in this class are a tad immature. I think you should be a little more open about your feelings and ask some girls out. Look at other schools classes. They have been dating since grade six. Face it, we are a little behind. We girls have tried to start a dating thing. But you guys are just not committed. This means that if we start dating there is going to be no teasing. So guys don't be shy! Ask!!!

## To The Girls

We guys think you girls are slightly immature. If you want to go out with us why don't you ask us. Because if we don't ask you that probably means we don't want to go out with you. There is no rule that you have to go out with the people in your class. So girls don't be shy. ASK!!! (This shows your own immaturity, Matt!!)

## Why Do We Hate?

As a daily observation, girls in our class have a tendancy to like the opposite sex more on a personal level, not a bad thing, they just like boys more for who they are. And as for boys, well, they just hang out with each other, maybe they like girls, but they certainly don't make the effort to get to know the girls. They don't seem to respect the girls as much as the girls respect the boys. I'm not saying that all boys are dogs and all girls are little angels sent from heaven, but in some cases this is exactly what is happening. So in the future, I guess, try to be nicer, and respect the opposite sex more, PLEASE!

## Mrs. Bertram

Mrs. Bertram is a terrific gal,
Who's always happy to be your pal
She is so nice
just like sugar and spice.

There isn't anybody whom she loathes.
She always wears beautiful clothes
She's not for sale; don't give me your bids.
She's really involved with all the kids.

She always has a smile on her face,
and is happy to help in a troubled case.
Even Superwoman can't compare
to this woman with the dark brown hair.

She's always up with the latest trends
Everyone's eager to be her friend.
Her sense of humor is a sensation.
We're glad she chose principaling as her occupation.

She spends her lunch playing basketball in the
gym protecting the kids from breaking a limb.
To the primary kids she often reads.
Dear Mrs. Bertram has done so many good deeds.

She never looks tired, weary, or mad.
This is what makes us all very sad,
for we have to go as soon as she comes…
off to a new school and miss all the fun.

So to Mrs. Bertram we say goodbye.
This is getting hard, I'll try not to cry.
To all the students sitting out there,
Be careful with her, remember to take care.

Mrs. Bertram, we'll really miss you,
And remember forever that we love you, too!

*Graduating grade sevens*

Journal Entry
March 14, 1997

*I know it's time to transfer to another school. I've been here (at Fairfield) for seven years. There are good reasons we're encouraged to transfer every five years or so...new broom concept, etc. But that would have been too soon!*

*I feel such a match for this school, and saying good-bye will be <u>awful</u>. I'll try not to show it...be dignified and positive. HA!*

*I'll have one more school, one more principalship before I retire. If every cell really does change every seven years, then I should be a whole new person. Inscrutable? Time for other things? Maybe a new image?*

*Why do things have to change?*

## CLASS COLONIST

We are going to be in FIVE (5 – count them!) different schools next year! Most of us can't wait but some of us are just a bit sad. We may never be all together again, which could be a good thing. But we now we are all going to be happy, rich and famous! Right?

Dear Staff Committee,

- *Due to the fact that* [another teacher's] *classroom becomes available.*
- *Due to the fact that I work on a regular basis with* [teacher's name] *class exchange*
- *Due to the fact that I have seniority over the other interested parties (vultures)*

*I hereby request a change of location from room #16 to room #18 second floor. I'll be ready to move as soon as I get the green light.*

*Resident of Room 316*
*No phone number*

# 22   SHEDDING

As a school year draws to its closure, there is an odd, dismantled feeling about the place called school. Hall boards shed displays that go home in student backpacks, leaving dead spaces where so much visual energy had been. Hallways look cluttered: the lost and found is spread out in the faint hope that students or parents will spot something lost months before. Tables and chairs are piled near the gymnasium where final events will take place. And the office area is cluttered with student files that will be sent off to receiving schools, report cards that need to be read and copied, responses to ceremony invitations, and strange items left on the playground from evening revelers.

The staff room, a pristine respite area on school opening, is now in disarray. Remnants of Bingo Night, spring fairs and professional development publications are piled on window ledges. HELP YOURSELF! signs on tables and trolleys implore people to remove items from piles teachers cannot bear to throw away. The erasable board has so many messages they run into one another causing a crazy, incoherent confusion of words. Only the countdown numbers stand out: 10, 9, 8 days to go! Empty chocolate boxes and encrusted cake plates give notice that dietary resolve is temporarily breaking down. Even fussy eaters need a sugar fix.

People are dismantled, too. Clothes are shed as the hot weather arrives—often too many of them, if they belong to grade seven girls. Teachers have that buzzed, distracted look if they have not yet finished their report cards and a smug, slightly distanced one if they are done. Most adults by this time are operating on sheer nervous energy; if not, they are highly suspect. The kids are busting to be out of the place and the staff members can barely constrain them in this last term. It is a taxing time when students know it is almost over, particularly if it is the end of elementary for them. The grade sevens present a strange mixture of sentimentality and bravado, young child and cocky adult. Teachers complain that social and academic skills have reverted to the previous fall.

"It's beautiful out there!" the tanned young mothers chirp to the office staff who smile wanly back and blink at the intensity of the sunshine blazing through their windows.

Emotions are close to the surface now. This may not be the time to bring up the fact that you believe Meredith should have had more lines in the Christmas concert, or that, as his mother, you are concerned about Harry's relationship with his best friend in the class. It is certainly not the time to look for resolution to peer discord; by September, rested and eager to begin again, staff and students will be like new. Just now they are bagged. On top of report cards and other paperwork, awards assemblies, graduation ceremonies, parent appreciation teas, concerts, end of year outings and all the feelings and activities connected to layoffs and transfers, the staff may have at least one person retiring.

Our school district honors all of its retirees in one ceremony in June of each year. Principals accompany departing staff members on this occasion and the order of events is predictable. Each person is presented with a bell that sits on an engraved plaque, and then shakes hands with the superintendent and chairperson of the Board while a picture is taken. The district's choir, squeaky clean and smiling a collective white strip smile, sings about rainbows and other good things. Custodians, secretaries, teachers, administrators and others sip tea, munch, and are thanked for their wonderful service. Then they are asked, dozens and dozens of them, to climb onto risers and ring their bells for a group picture. Having watched colleagues enduring the bell ringing over many years, I finally became convinced that some of them were having out-of-body experiences at that point in the afternoon.

Much more personal are the retirement activities in schools. Fairfield had few retirements or personnel turnovers during the seven years I was there; it had a relatively young staff. Rowan, my second and final school, turned over two-thirds of its staff in several years, and many of these people retired during that time. In the spring of 1999, the school district offered a monetary incentive for teachers able to retire. It was not a whopping amount, but for those people ready to go it provided some impetus.

Five Rowan teachers decided to retire, and a more disparate group could not be imagined. One of them immediately acquiesced to having a "do," the others demurred until worked upon by staff who were understandably flummoxed about doing something special for only one or some of their departing colleagues. Some of those retiring colleagues then worked upon me. I was to see that there would be no "monkey business," no "silly skits" or terrible stories. They had examples of past practice, they assured me, and they would not be part of events that were anything like some they had witnessed over the years.

"They don't want skits," I told the teacher who organized those fun activities.

"I told her you don't want skits," I reassured one of the retirees. Later that day our skits director, who had not taken my word for it, was lambasted at the staff room sink when she tried some hopeful persuasion. The organization of that celebration was uniquely stressful, partly due to the apparent unwillingness of some of the committee to listen to what the retirees actually *wanted*, and partly due to the differences in the personalities of the retirees themselves. To the relief of many of us, it ended up being a dignified, small but elegant affair, and an important confession was made during it.

For years the drawers in the staff room had been repositories for junk: rusty nails, tissues, car parts, old bill envelopes and much worse. The staff had always blamed a former vice principal, a brilliant prankster who continued to visit regularly. On those days someone always had a drawer full, confirming suspicions.

When Gary, a teacher who had been at Rowan for many years, came to receive his gift, he put on his reading glasses and proceeded with a remarkable, touching speech. He had always been a quiet, sensitive fellow, one who was seldom in the spotlight except during concerts when he played guitar with his "Out To Lunch Bunch."

"Now I have a confession to make," he told us. He put his glasses and his papers down and stared out at his audience. For decades, he had been slipping that junk into the staff room drawers, biding his time, listening to the complaints, never being caught. It had obviously given him great personal satisfaction to pull it off so perfectly for so long.

*All* the retirees expressed satisfaction the next day, and we went on with the year-end madness.

As principals are ultimately responsible, and as most are on a kind of automatic pilot once these final events take place, it is fortunate that careful planning usually ensures they unfold without a hitch.

We did have one memorable embarrassment at Fairfield during a grade seven awards luncheon. Things began perfectly. Our students were typically unrecognizable because of their attention to grooming; the parents were beaming as they were escorted to their seats, and trophies and plaques were impressively arranged on stage with the presenters. In the kitchen area, to the right of the gymnasium proper, Pauline and her parent, student and staff helpers bustled with luncheon preparations. Each graduating student was introduced by myself or Greg at two microphones: the pair then entered by the front doors and stopped in front of the audience before heading (wobbling if in high heels) to the back of the gym and then to their own parents' table. All safely ensconced, we sang "O Canada", and the major awards were presented.

I had just had the fleeting thought that things were progressing smoothly when I noticed Pauline looking up at the stage to catch my eye. Our stalwart overseer was looking a bit frazzled. I raised my eyebrows and she shook her head. A couple of awards later, a note was passed onto the stage: *Lasagna hasn't arrived!* This was, at that point, something of a catastrophe. The menu consisted of tea, coffee or juice, crusty rolls, Caesar salad, lasagna and strawberry shortcake. I knew the salad and dessert were ready, but the lasagna, which had been ordered from an Italian restaurant, needed to be cut and placed on plates—a job that required considerable time. It was 11:45 and we were on a tight timeline. After lunch, all seventy grade sevens would be recognized individually with certificates and affectionate reminiscences by their teachers. There was just enough time, after that, to give out their report cards and dismiss by 3:00.

I began to perspire and I knew from the color of Pauline's face that she was in distress. I presented the next award, then noticed a bustle at one of the entrances where our animated assistant was accepting trays and shaking her head vigorously. The next note was slightly hopeful: *They have delivered 50. Problem with ovens. Going to phone.* The last award was being announced as the final note came my way: *Ovens broken down. They send apologies.* One hundred and fifty people were not going to have their main course. They had paid very little for this luncheon, a meal subsidized by our parent group, but that was not the point. The point was that this was a very special occasion for these students and their parents. Many had taken time off work to attend and all were *hungry.* Would they remember this time in their lives by their lack of lasagna?

With a nauseous dread building behind my professional facade, I congratulated the winners of our major awards and announced that it was time for lunch. Unfortunately, I said, the restaurant responsible for the lasagna had been unable to fill all our orders due to the fact that its ovens were not working properly. We would be happy to refund the $2.00 per person for that part of the meal. There was a soft, collective groan and lunch proceeded.

Filing out past me, most parents seemed very happy about the event and sympathetic regarding our predicament.

"It was a lovely ceremony, and we had plenty to eat!" one assured me.

"Too bad that restaurant let you down!"

"Great event! I'm phoning that place myself, though!"

Only one parent phoned for reimbursement, which made most of us feel better. Pauline, however, took some consoling.

One year we had a bit of a jolt to our collective nervous system shortly after a perfect final assembly and dismissal on the last day of school. The fire alarm screamed as I was saying a farewell to the last of our visitors and our students who were leaving laden with school supplies, artwork and report cards. Other schools had reported students ringing fire alarms on the last day: what better prank to pull when running home for a two month break or leaving elementary altogether? This had never happened at Fairfield, but we all knew there was an active student grapevine.

Two of our teachers caught the culprit across the street after chasing him into the neighborhood drug store. He was left in the outer office while a former parent who worked for the Victoria Fire Department changed into formal parade gear and arrived in my office looking formidably resplendent. He gave me a wink and then made Jason aware of how miserable he would be if he tried that again.

A year later, the prevention of that happening was added to my list of year-end jobs. First I met with Jason. He assured me that he would not ring any kind of bell again, ever, at which point I reminded him that it was only the fire alarm we were referring to, and that a second offense would necessitate calling the police. He swallowed hard. He *did* know of a plot this year, but he was not part of it.

"It's a case of outwitting them," I told the assembled group of custodians, assistants and a few parents.

By 2:45 an adult stood at each point around the school where fire alarms were mounted. These people almost blended into the throngs who were milling about the hallways and stairwells. I stood on the steps just outside a grade seven classroom, saying goodbye to parents and students. Suddenly, two boys careened out of the room, grinning wildly and looking straight ahead at the alarm mounted on the wall across from their room. "Have a good summer!" I called over to them.

Their sudden stop reminded me of the old cartoon with Beep-beep the Roadrunner. I imagined clouds of dust floating up around them as one rather stupefied dear blinked at me. "Why are you *here*, Mrs. Bertram?"

"I wanted to see you off," I responded with great affection.

The boys left, but when our little army reassembled in the staff room, we found they had re-entered the school at several points only to find various members of that community equally eager to say their final, tender good-byes before waving them off. We had all waited for twenty-five minutes at our posts, until it was obvious that the pull of the holidays had become the greater attraction.

June tears are usually the result of tiredness or peer differences, although there is no doubt that many students experience stress and a sense of loss toward the end of a school year. Even with the prospect of a homework-free summer, many will be leaving teachers they have bonded with and friends who may or may not be in their class in the fall. Awards ceremonies, end-of-year trips and peer behaviors may not be positive and relaxing for them. They are learning that nothing remains exactly the same in their lives.

One final assembly was more than a bit tense. This group of grade sevens had been difficult: pseudo-sophisticated and rather belligerent with each other and with staff. Individually, they were likable and typical adolescents. But more time was spent sorting them out than all four hundred other students. Even the rehearsal for the assembly was fraught with recriminations from their teachers and from each other.

"*Don't* talk when I'm talking!"

"Look *this* way!"

"Stop pushing, asshole!"

"Stop swearing!"

"You *don't* sit there!"

The finale of that last June assembly at Rowan was a traditional slide show set to music. Our music teacher captured the sevens in informal groupings around the school and took photographs that revealed feelings around friendships and their coming of age. They were moving on, and on this occasion we could not wait for that to happen. The lights went out, the music began and faces appeared on the screen: young faces with heads together, draped over playground apparatus, answering office phones, carrying pizza boxes, monitoring primary classrooms. Although taken within a short period of time, Len had captured the essence of their final year. They looked adorable. I leaned against a wall, sagging a bit with relief.

The slideshow was about half over when there was a loud, "WAAAAAAAAH!" I came to and contemplated crawling across the room in the dark. This was the last straw; someone was acting up during the final few minutes. Before I could stumble over to the offending noise, it began in another spot and then another. Soon the music was drowned out completely by student wailing, parent muttering and the nervous tittering of the younger audience. The slide show mercifully ended and I turned on the lights, looking for signs of guilt.

To the astonishment of all the audience, many of those "cool" and confident young people were sobbing uncontrollably while their classmates patted their backs. Some, particularly the boys who considered themselves the most cool-and-to-be-emulated, were swallowing and putting their faces in their hands. I opened the big double doors to let them file out and they walked past, some hugging me and all looking flushed and rather frightened of their own and their peers' emotions.

Anyone working in schools knows there are more tears in June. Like the staff, these kids are tuckered out. They are also sensitive to what is happening around them, to changes becoming all too apparent in their previously predictable school world.

A year after retiring, I delved into the pages of my student "memory books" for clues. These books were put together for me by the staff, and each student had done a page. I poured over the eight-year spread of school years and all the ways they had expressed a farewell. This time I found much more than the previous June when, excited and tired, I had flipped quickly through them.

*Mrs. Bertram, we will miss you*, a grade one boy had printed with a picture of myself, green-faced, standing in the library surrounded by a reassuring collection of number facts he wanted me to know he knew: 8+8=16, 10+10=20, 14-7=7. I appeared in other grade one pictures looking crazed or glamorous, depending upon the artist, and I had numerous, kindly adjectives such as "unique directrice," "notre amie," and "speciale."

A grade two girl who had a lot of problems and could be fairly violent wrote, *You were a great principal! Because you helped me when I was a bully*. I thought of all the meetings over this child, when we had no sense that any of our actions were having an effect upon her. She had never, to my knowledge, admitted she was in the wrong.

Occasionally, in their effort to be kind and flattering, they pulled out all the stops. One wrote, *I don't want you to go because I'll miss you so. You are the greatest principal. And I also think you are kind, nice and tall*. The "cool" ones expressed themselves that way: *You are cool/You are neat/And you dance to the beat*. And in a surge of words the author knew was appropriate, the order was sometimes a little askew: *Thank you for being our principal, you were great, I will miss you a lot. Hope you have good luck and your cups of memory, never forgetful and kindness be filled, with your heart full of joy*. I did know what that child meant.

On one, two small hands had obviously been traced and then filled in with bright orange felt marker. The fingers end in bilious green nails, and a happy sun looks down upon the words, *I never held your hand before but I know you're very gentle.*

There is a picture of the school during the previous year's earthquake. I am standing with a "MRS. B." sign over my head and the word "cool" in a cloud over that. SCREAM, PANIC, RUN, issue from windows and below is the message, *Thank you for playing it cool during the earthquake.*

Some included more memories:

> *You helped us when we were sad*
> *And disciplined us when we were bad*
> *You cared about us, too*
> *That's why we will miss you!*
> *You were there when we were down*
> *And you never had a frown.*
> *You were there when we were young*
> *And watched us when we sung.*
> *That is why we will miss you!*
> *You are a star,*
> *That's who you are!*
> *That's why we will miss you!*

One really tough little character had trouble with the form of his poem, but it is rather powerful, nonetheless. An awful black and white photograph of my head is pasted on a sun, with the following underneath:

> *Mrs. Bertram is as laughing gas and as a comedian*
> *Judy is as a good person as a honest person that understands*
> *She is as a person that would care or take a bolet even for a*
> *person*
> *She is GREAT!*

One page tells me to *Follow The Yellow Brick Road It Could Make Your Dreams Come True!* And, underneath: *Remember when you used to read this to us in the library? It was five years ago! You never finished it because it was the end of the year and you were too busy. I'll miss you...*

There were lovely, sophisticated pages by senior students, some with clever computer graphics. *To be a principal you need a computer, a phone, some coffee, a chair and a briefcase. But to be a good and respected one you need a good heart. Thank you Mrs. Bertram for being our principal we'll miss you a lot.* The first five items are shown on one side of an equal sign, then a woman plus a heart, an equal sign and all of that equaling, in her eyes, a good principal.

Three pages by grade three boys made me wonder if they were tapping into a part of my psyche that I had tried very hard to suppress. For much as I loved them, and as pleased as I was that they had appreciated my work, I was ready to give over my responsibilities with them.

The first of these pages had the message, *We will miss you very much! Have a good retirement!* A huge Canadian flag flies outside the school and lots of little stick kids stand along the drop off area with tears pouring down their faces. It is the sight of myself, driving past them, that is noteworthy here. I am in a purple car that is loaded down with gifts. The trunk gapes open and they are piled on the roof. I look straight ahead, oblivious, it would seem, to those poor little creatures, and I am grinning with the obvious anticipation of my freedom.

On another I lie under a beach umbrella in a black bikini, a truly demonic grin on my face. This rather startling expression is reflected in the sun's face as well as the grill of my car, which is parked behind me. We are all wearing sunglasses.

*Ahhh, no kids!* I am saying, as I stretch out on yet another lounge chair by a serene-looking ocean. *Enjoy!* the artist advises below.

So what does a principal *do*, given the rather disembodied and emotional state of people at this time of year? The principal could be, and very likely is, the most exhausted of the lot, simply due to the amount of responsibility carried and the need to be "on" at all times. What does a principal do when staff and students are sad, anxious, tired and/or stressed? Lighten the atmosphere whenever possible with a positive comment, good news or humor. See that the organizational facts and figures are as accurate as possible, even if it does take the whole of a weekend. Be the person who takes responsibility all of the time—whether things are going well or not. Be open to listening and then be prepared to make decisions and own them.

I recently read the transcript of an interview with Brian Little, the popular Canadian Harvard psychology professor. He described the "pseudo-extrovert," and I recognized my personality type:

> [they are] apparently extroverted and outgoing. They tend to be optimistic in their personal behavior—they stand for comfortable communication, have lots of eye contact, lots of body contact. They are fast paced...I think many of our daily functions and the things we feel passionate about, our roles in life, the projects we commit ourselves to, demand that we act in that extroverted fashion. And yet, in many cases, this is a guise, a subtle acting out of a role that sometimes compromises what I call our first natures, which are physiologically based. A pseudo-extrovert isn't being phony when she's acting in this fashion—it's often in the service of something about which she feels very passionate, such as teaching. She's animated behind the podium, yet often you can tell through very subtle cues that she has been playing out a role...Now I take advantage of a place called the washroom...cubicle nine if it's a nine cubicle washroom.[2]

I recognized my personality type and thought about how I had tried the cubicle haven getaway, often unsuccessfully. But as time

2 From Peter Gzowski's *The Morningside Years*. Toronto: McClelland & Stewart, 1997.

Judy Bertram Tomlinson

went on I gave off subtle and not so subtle cues of over stimulation, particularly, as Gail first pointed out, a kind of "glazing over" of the eyes when I had had too much. Fortunately, most people never saw that, which is a good thing. For in order to be supported, a school staff needs the person in that principal role to remain even-tempered, optimistic, energetic and well organized, even if it is the end of the year. They are not interested in how demanding their principal's role is during June or any other time, nor should they be. If the person in that role is moaning—for whatever reason—he or she is not fulfilling the obligations to that community.

In June of my first year at Fairfield, I was fulfilling the obligations of my job by sheer will power and adrenaline. My journal pages that month consist mostly of appointment dates; the brief notes do not always conjure memories, but a few are vivid.

The last staff meeting included updates on staffing, year-end dismissal procedures, report cards and the teachers' checklist of paperwork to be completed. The staff thanked those members of the staff committee, including the chairperson, for their service, and elected new people for our future *once a month or more often if necessary* meetings. I met with new kindergarten parents and realized how much simpler the following year would be without the dual entry of youngsters in January. We had our Fun Fair, and I noted the comment, "Oh look, Mrs. Bertram isn't dressed!" On Sunday, June 9, I wrote that I had worked all weekend and felt "sort of anxious thinking about the week to come—how can I do it all?" Then I added, as though giving myself one of my own cheerleading pumps, "I realize I can and will—just fine!"

Final concerts went well, although I noted that a fuse burned out one evening. I have a vague recollection of Greg scrambling around, one more time, to replace it. His memory is likely much sharper. The Parent Appreciation Tea went well, end of year photographs were taken, an office assistant was "bumped" from our school by a person in another school, and there was not enough food for the library volunteers' tea. One teacher was upset about his class makeup for September, and it was suggested that a certain parent would be "out for blood" because she did not have either of her daughters in placements she had requested. I noted a meeting at the Board Office with the superintendent: "Don't get involved in asking teachers to compromise the contract," she warned us.

Our final assemblies went off beautifully, and after the last, when the students and parents had gone and "contact" time was over, I shut my office door and peeled off my nylons. I hung my power-dressing jacket on a hanger and went into the staff room feeling naked but relieved. "We've done it!" I wrote later.

The following day, there was a meeting with someone regarding our portables, a parent saw me about a new French placement, and others wanted to discuss sundry things for the fall. I presented Dan, our departing teacher, with his gift, and noted it was a sad leave-taking. I have a photograph taken during this presentation, and the staff members in the picture look wistful. Dan was the teacher who was putting out the "Welcome, Judy" sign over the office door when I first arrived after my appointment. That act was typical of his kindness to his colleagues, his students and their parents. He had moved far out of town and after a lot of agonized pondering, decided to work in a school closer to home. He was a positive part of the puzzle that made up Fairfield.

"Everyone's expendable," is often heard when staffing changes threaten the status quo. There is some truth here, but there is also a kind of tremulous bravado in the remark. For as everyone on a school staff knows, each person has the *potential* to contribute positively to a school culture; what is certain is that each of them *will* affect it.

That June, some members of the school community were voicing a kind of disconnectedness in their comments:

"How relevant is this Year 2000 stuff?"

"That teacher doesn't have his kids pick their stuff up off the floor—I can't clean in there!"

"Our custodian never cleans desktops!"

"The library doesn't have enough books that we like, Mrs. Bertram."

"How can we get the teachers interested in a Knowledge Fair?"

"Parents are objecting to the homework we assign in French Immersion."

"I want a say in my child's placement!"

"Parents shouldn't have a say in their child's placement!"

In spite of some internal blocking and external pressures, I knew, as I watched our staff interact with each other and with students and parents, that there was the potential for an extraordinarily cohesive and effective school community. And I wondered how much time and hard work would be required before we were all pulling together for our students.

We were closer than any of us could have imagined, I suspected, as I submitted my "growth plan" to Central Office.

PRINCIPAL'S PERSONAL GROWTH PLAN
(June, 1991)
- Goal: All groups of stakeholders in the school community will be represented in relevant decision making.
- Indicator of success: Increased responsibility by all stakeholders.

Committees:

Discipline: *Students + Parents + Teachers + Support Staff + Administration = Policy*

Awards: *Students + Parents + Teachers + Support Staff + Administration = Policy*

Long-term Planning: *Students + Parents + Teachers + Support Staff + Administration = Policy*

*Judy Bertram, Principal*

# 23   BOOKEND

June 2001: In bed on the night of that awful meeting with our district's trustees, I lay waiting for my system to settle. My husband and our cat were fast asleep, both emitting soft, satisfied and peaceful snores. The distraction of my digestive system was compelling, but not enough to override my mental gymnastics. For I could not decide whether I was more embarrassed over my *faux pas* or angry at an elected official's treatment of an audience of people who had dedicated themselves to the education of young people. *So teachers weren't teaching, principals weren't leading, students weren't learning?* Was that what he said? Did he actually believe it or was he grandstanding? And surely that was beside the point: we had put up with it.

I could retire, I thought; I was not really powerless. The school year was almost over and not taking on the next year was an option. But then there was so much I knew I had to do, and there were great people to do it with.

As I calmed a little I wondered if I had brushed my teeth or washed my face. I tried to remember what appointments I had on the following morning and thought, with a prick of alarm, that there might be a conflict with two of them. I briefly considered scanning my leather organizer and then wondered what the weather would be like in the morning. I could wear something a little casual, if there was no need to power dress. Then I supposed it could all wait until morning, and began to fall asleep.

Just before that happened I sat bolt upright and turned on my light. *I had not written in my journal.*


The 2001/2002 school year, the following year, was my last. It was my twelfth year as principal, and I knew, as I drove to work that August, that I would very likely never open a school again. I had put many years into our system and there was a bit of a sea change happening. My clothes were flowing more, my energy was waning and my diplomacy was dipping. In retrospect, perhaps it was more like a Phoenix rising: there was definitely another—or former—persona beginning to emerge and assert herself.

In other ways I had not changed. I still cared profoundly about the kind of job we were doing for our children. I cared about how the school as a whole performed, and I tried very hard to support the staff with openness, humor, honesty and empathy. I still showed how I felt when I would rather have been unreadable, and I still pushed myself to the limit. Even if this was to be my last year, I told myself I would not give up on kids or *coast* through the next ten and a half months.

I knew my career was ending, but I had no foreshadowing of the extraordinary similarities the bookend years of my principalship would have. Much had changed, after all. After seven years at Fairfield I had moved to a new school community and the education system as a whole had adopted a very different set of priorities. The Year 2000 philosophy had given way to an emphasis on testable outcomes; Paper Mountain had grown in spite of technology; most administrators could not understand the language of the district technology reports when they were presented, and some aspects of central office no longer wore a very human face. We were "decentralized"; even initial teacher "interviews" were done by machine. On the upside, Gail, our wonderful Fairfield secretary, had transferred to Rowan when there was an opening and our vice principal, Vic, was warm and supportive.

I put my briefcase down and looked around my office with satisfaction: my granddaughter's face beamed from my desk, my two daughters looked at me in graduation garb and a beautiful painting by my sister took my breath away, as always. A sketch of a school where I had been vice principal and one from our talented Fairfield custodian were on the walls where I had hung them. A cartoon from a staff member showed a woman being shaken from slumber: "What do you mean, you don't want to go to school Judy, you have to! You're the principal!" My stress rocks sat on the circular meeting table with the lizard a little Fairfield boy had given me, and the lovely interior courtyard looked fresh and new outside my office window. All surfaces were tidy and clean. I threw my purse onto the table and looked in the mirror.

A tan helps, I thought, and though I was not wearing a suit I knew it was a good thing I had done my summer exercising. Most of the time had been spent on schoolwork. We were due to go through the accreditation process during a year when the teachers' union had advised teachers against taking part, and for those who did there was a finite amount of time they could meet to share their opinions when called to do so. It was an exceedingly bad time for this assessment to be on a school's agenda. I dreaded the additional workload in this climate, but I also wanted the school community to recognize and celebrate its successes. The initial data from student performance was excellent, and the next five years' goals would need to be in place if there was to be a new principal the following September. As accreditation was a provincial process that evaluated the school at all levels, and particularly the pertinence of the goals that were set, it was exceedingly important that we do well whatever the political climate. Hence my days of preparatory work otherwise done by school personnel began.

That last school year began with the ordinary, the bizarre, the usual and the unexpected.

I complimented the custodians on the sparkling school and heard one of them rant about the delivery of a parcel to the wrong location. They had spent an inordinate amount of time looking for it.

"By the way, Judy, there's a box of huge bones in the freezer," one told me. "Daycare freezer. Right on top of kids' stuff."

"Human?" I managed.

"Don't know yet. Sure big. Want to see them?" I did not, just yet. Possibly after lunch, I told him.

Four new children were registered that morning and several teachers chatted about their summers. I phoned the photocopier emergency number; it was not performing with the enthusiasm that would soon be needed. I put the first day welcoming signs up around the school and carried the carton of district mail into my office. Leaving the slow mail on the table, I turned on my computer and scanned the principal to principal messages, and then the district's. There was the usual reminder of the superintendent's meeting with all the district leaders. I met with our special needs coordinator over assistant time and talked to a parent who must have seen my car outside. Halfway through his concerns about the cost of school supplies, the phone rang and a woman with a strange accent insisted, rudely, on being informed of a plethora of facts regarding the school. I inhaled, very slowly, to prevent saying what I longed to say, and at the count of five I heard wild laughter and a retired friend's voice. The parent had left.

Later, before I locked my office, I checked our numbers one more time. There was a good chance we would lose .5 of a teaching position. I could not face the bones.

The first week in session was as hectic as always. We did have to cut the .5, but Janet, the teacher concerned, was going to stay and work part time. A parent brought me flowers to thank me for a June incident, and we moved the English track into their permanent classes. The only glitch I saw in my performance that week was that my emerging persona uttered an unmentionable word when the fire alarm was triggered by a faulty boiler just as the students were rearranging themselves. "In *all* our years together, I've *never* heard you say anything *like* that! In fact, when we first worked together, I thought you were a bit, well, you know, *proper.*" Gail, our usually empathetic secretary, looked gleeful.

*Monday, Sept. 10: Could be Friday! Not a moment to breathe, but all positive. All kids are in place. There's a good feeling in the school!*

*Sept. ll: Unimaginably horrible day. U.S. under terrorist attack. Kids want to know <u>why</u>, and will it happen to <u>them</u>?*

*Sept. 12: Most staff had headaches—glued to television news reports. Staff meeting was long, but productive. Bones put in freezer by Brian will make a lot of moose soup.*

*Sept. 17: Union rep came to school to rev up troops for a 34% wage increase and strike. Seems some troops mutinied….Am feeling a bit sad and emotional and think I need this job to be over.*

*Sept. 19: Barbecue and Open House—parents told a teacher I looked "thin" and "little." Well, I am! [Parent] commented that I had "crazies" working there. Took a while before I realized he was referring to the teachers' wage demand!*

*Sept. 21: Teaching staff shown a "Solidarity" video. Had a horrible moment when I thought more staff would be pulled. Will hold my breath until the end of the month.*

*Sept. 25: Lost great young, part-time teacher to a full-time, continuing position. She had to grab it. What a shame.*

As October began, the teachers, support staff and parents on the school's internal accreditation team worked on the process in spite of the 91.4% vote by teachers in favor of job action. These people were extraordinary, and I was able to finish collating the survey and report card data that was required. I consulted then drafted a letter making a case to save our beautiful courtyard if proposed upgrading took place to our building, and I wrote my final Growth Plan. Most goals were simple and finite:

- To lead the school community through a meaningful accreditation process, with thorough involvement and the establishment of a clear direction for the next five years.
- To oversee the preparations for our building upgrade, which includes consultation with parents, staff and students.
- To prepare for a change in the principalship of Rowan.

Toward the end of the month I privately informed the assistant superintendent that I intended to retire. It would have been much easier to wait until spring to do that, and it would have given me some more time to ponder, but I was ready. And with preparations underway for the district's reconfiguration of schools and many principals looking for moves, my early announcement was helpful. The most difficult part of the accreditation report was now done, and the committee rewrote the school's mission statement for staff perusal. The usual October activities culminated in the annual craft fair, and while people shopped that Saturday I cleared a lot of Paper Mountain. It was a fun event, as always, but the uncertainty of impending job action and 9-11 fallout were palpable.

"Let there be peace on earth," our choir sang in what I thought was the most moving Remembrance Day assembly ever. I was not alone; many people had tears in their eyes. "...and let it begin with me..." I looked at some of our more troubled students. Randy, a tiny grade three boy, had been moved to foster care. He was becoming unmanageable. Two new girls in early intermediate were already creating a sensation. Overly large and lacking in social skills, Candy and Marge had teamed up by default and had frequent rows. Our counselor was working with them. There were many more needy among the majority of well-cared for, well-adjusted children that made up that wonderful school, I thought.

"…let this be my solemn vow…" Future labor leaders, provincial and world leaders? There was such potential here.

Job action had started, an "unstrike" during which teachers would teach during their regular hours of assignment. But they were not to meet with parents or students outside of their teaching time, and they were not to meet with their principals except in emergency situations. Regular staff meetings and the extraordinary meetings around accreditation were not to happen, and teachers were not to do paperwork, the most profound example being report cards.

The ramifications of the "unstrike" became evident as the days went on. I could not call the staff together to announce my retirement when it was officially time to do that, so I contacted our union rep and she did it for me. One teacher wondered if I had decided to retire because they "weren't talking to me enough." She looked sad, and I assured her that my decision had nothing to do with their job action. "I don't have another year in me," I said. It was an honest response and it worked during the coming days with staff, parents and students.

"Just stay one more year. Next year won't be like this one!"

"Please don't go until John finishes grade seven!"

"We've taken a survey. We don't want you to retire." Many students simply asked *why*.

When I was told that I was too young to retire, I would say, "No, I'm not," which always precipitated intense and disconcerting physical scrutiny. I could have prevented this by telling them my age, but some stubborn reluctance about giving everything away, born years before at the Fairfield science fair, always prevented me.

"How did you manage *that*?" one father asked. It was not at all clear to me whether I was being chastised or given a compliment.

There was even some gender discrimination. "I've only had her for three months," a new grade three boy complained to his teacher, "and we'll probably get a *boy*!" I fleetingly wished he'd added "tall." It was an awful time to make the announcement; it was too early in any year, let alone this one. There was so much uncertainty in the air.

"I hear you're *hiring*!" a young father smiled ruefully at me. His kindergarten daughter knew he had been laid off his government job as so many of our parents had, and she told him my news with great excitement.

Classroom teaching and learning continued without the usual build-up to report cards and parent-teacher interviews. Pizza days and other activities that required some teacher help were cancelled, and the news media was full of it. Our local television station carried an interview with some of our students and myself as we were assembling Christmas hampers for the needy. It was an activity the union had said it did not support that year, and it could have made a great story. I think the cheerful attitude in our school around this activity was a bit of a disappointment to the attending television reporter.

At the beginning of December I attended the funeral of a much loved Rowan parent, and a few days later was in the audience for a beautiful Muslim/Jewish /Christian service which emphasized the common traditions of creating light in the middle of darkness. In school, our Christmas concerts were held in the daytime to much smaller audiences than usual, and many staff members went home for the break less tired but unseasonably somber. There had been one delicious reprieve: our favorite "retired" vice principal had put on a one-man craft show to cheer us up, complete with reindeer droppings, fluff from Santa's navel and a hilarious school advent calendar.

In January, phase two of the strike cancelled extra-curricular sports, and ski trips planned by many schools were off. My journal describes that time:

*Jan 11: Student walkouts over the strike at one elementary school here and one on the mainland.*

*Jan 14: Our kids are itching to walk out over teacher job action. Parents are beginning to complain. They've been so good so far, guess it was bound to start.*

*Jan 15: Kids are difficult! Vic and I are run off our feet. Parent in office, wanting to know what we are going to do for the Queen's 50thbirthday. Had the Lieutenant Governor, bagpiper and Monarchist League speakers all lined up. Tried to explain why this might be a bit dicey if not impossible to organize, given the climate.*

*Jan 16: Superintendent says when the provincial budget comes down we won't recognize this school district. Thousands of government workers laid off...feels like everything is in a flux, like a slow-moving earthquake. Met with three reps from grade seven and tried to focus them on the possibility of some kind of trip later in the spring.... They desperately wanted to ski, but think they're feeling a bit better. Four kids staged "walk outs," except they never arrived in the first place and had the misfortune to be in the vice principal's class, so had to make up time—and work—after school.*

*Jan 17: Premier says that job action will be over by Friday. Two more kids "walked out," one with a note saying, "George has our permission to walk the teachers." After dealing with images involving leashes, I told them that George didn't have <u>ours</u>, and his parents returned him.*

*Jan 21: M had rearranged the staff room on the weekend, and J and G rearranged it back again...No new word on job action, but am organizing and turfing.*

*Jan 22: Fun reading with kids. Am clearing out more and more stuff...at 3:10, within a couple of minutes, a father grabbed me by the shoulder and told me I should phone the police about a woman parked in the handicapped spot...on my way to see her was* subsequently grabbed on the same shoulder by a woman who said she needed to know where I bought my slacks….

Jan 23: Vic's penis-pulling primary kids into another incident involving peeing into a juice box. Sara brought a live chicken in after school and said she sleeps with it…wondered if someone in the neighborhood was missing some poultry…Phoned the superintendent's office with some "good" news regarding a grant we were to receive, their secretary passed the first part on to them and they thought I wasn't retiring.

Jan 24: Teachers to walk on Monday. Turns out the chicken was taken from a neighbor's yard (I'd been told it had a name, a mate who was dead, was trained, etc. Fact that child was covered in straw should have been a clue.) Unstrike over, sort of.

Jan 25: Ready for no teachers on Monday. They have been given 7.5% over three years. Bart finished his apology letter for theft—took a week to do it, but it sounds sincere. Great fun in grade one class. One more day, then one five month marathon. Can't complain, must count blessings and pitch in.

Jan 27: (Sunday). We've had little direction from central office as to how we carry on Tuesday—hope there aren't too many kids tomorrow! And if there are, will they like "Treasure Island"?

Jan 28: (Monday) Fifteen kids. The day care people helped out, bless them. Thousands of teachers rallied today. I talked to our external accreditation Chair, and he agrees that it would be LUDICROUS to go ahead with it in this climate. Feels as if my life is suspended.

Jan 29: A few teachers were really ranting. Our spirits are just low, and there's a strange quiet.

Jan 30: Felt some anxiety over the apparent need to push ahead with accreditation. Told by assistant superintendent to pin the response sheets up in the staff room. Know that won't work here. Phoned Calvin, my Fairfield colleague and accreditation expert. "We'll get you through with a smile on your face." Bless him…felt calmer. Kids were WILD and BCTF talking about returning to Phase One of the job action!

Jan 31: Last day of January! Started at 7:30 with a good meeting with the superintendent, staff great, though kids difficult during breaks.

Feb 1: Male teacher rearranged staff room furniture again, to Gail's dismay. He said another male was "livid" that he wasn't sitting in the same spot…think stress is getting to them! Our wonderful district survey collator retired at Christmas and the department is terminated. No word to us; would have liked to have sent a card, at least. BCTF making more threats. Went to my closet and stared at my summer clothes. Want to get this job done!

Feb 4: Met with teachers over reports and good meeting with accreditation committee.

Feb 5: In grade five class at noon. Kids wanted the name of the new principal. I had to explain that he WAS NOT the premier, even though he had the same name. Staff room furniture is still being rearranged.

Feb 6: Female staff members in lunch room early and sat around MALE table that had been dragged to its original spot again. Guys didn't show; think they were tipped off. Day ended well with PAC doing the accreditation surveys this evening. Really nice tone to the meeting. Emails flying through cyberspace…principals are DOWN.

Feb 12: 7:30 meeting…8 million to be cut from the budget! Everything was put on the table…parent asked me to explain district decisions.

*Talked to our external Chair—he doesn't know if his own staff will go ahead with their accreditation.*

*Feb 13: A highlight! Staff did a great job of the satisfaction surveys… so satisfied, in the end, there could be a problem setting goals!*

*Feb 14: Busy Valentine's Day! Excellent parent satisfaction survey meeting. Vic's penis pullers stomping on a lunch outside. Dad thought "no party" punishment too much. Two primary French immersion teachers showed a cartoon about a mermaid and discovered the little sea creature's nipples were prominent. Pulled the plug and told their classes that "Mme Bertram needs the VCR!" Lots of fun finger painting in chocolate with grade five kids.*

*Feb 20: Read two sets of reports and was able to tie up a lot of bits and pieces. Outside with the kids in the sunshine and it felt like spring. Blinking like a groundhog.…*

For weeks, Gail and I worked on the accreditation document whenever we could find the time. I was also reading over the first report cards of the school year as they came in to me and doing the usual work in that most unusual time. On the twenty-first, I noted the union stance that teachers should not cover for another teacher unless hired as a T.O.C. or ordered to do so, and I added that it was not my style to "order." However, we had a sad incident over that stance. Just before the bell rang at 1:00 one day, Gail asked a few teachers in the lunchroom if they would look into Vic's class to let his students know he would be along shortly. He was attending to an injured student on the playground and I was dealing with some in another part of the school. She was told of their union directive, and she, Vic *and* our union rep felt let down.

On the twenty-second, with my colleague Calvin, I rewrote our first goal, to make it more student-focused. I was pleased that two of our students were finally going to have psychiatric assessments, and I noted that Bingo Night was lots of fun. The highlight of that day was during the lunch period as I watched Canada win the semi-finals in hockey, along with sixty kids in the library.

I found my first wild spring flower and pasted it in my journal that weekend. I took my winter suits downstairs and noted that I would never have to concentrate on a power dressing winter wardrobe again.

On the twenty-seventh, Candy and Marge were apparently in a huge altercation of some kind. The girls were brought into my office by our assistant, Kay. Flushed, she explained that the fight started when the girls were trying to see who was the "slimmest" by squeezing through a narrow gap between two library tables. I found out that a retirement "do" was being planned for me, and wrote that I thought there should be "nothing for me in a year like this." One of my colleagues helped her husband clear out his government office desk, and more parents expressed fear over government job losses.

*Mar 5: Spring weather! Gail and I worked on "accrud" all morning. Am worried about her back and neck. More accrud in the afternoon. $8 million to be cut from school district. NOTHING THIS YEAR SINCE SEPT.11 HAS BEEN "AS USUAL!"...Mother of three year old phoned, shopping for schools for 2004. Demanded assurances that all would be well in our school at that time!*

.

*Mar 6: Tired. Took great mental energy to get through most of the document! Gail's back going out by the end of it. Felt awful, and she's so good about it. Should have hired someone to do all that typing. Mother brought in nice loaf to thank me for attending the psychiatrist's meeting.*

*Mar. 7: Superintendent announced that we are in a new world. Awful meeting: doom and gloom. Met with staff committee to go over all the accreditation and the staff meeting. PAC very appreciative of all the work that had gone into it and liked the goals. Feel "up" now!*

*Mar 8: Thick snowfall and kids wild, though rather nice tone in the school in spite of it. I keep slogging through the accreditation stuff as though it's a ruddy thesis!*

I vowed that I would finish the document for accreditation that weekend, I would organize the next staff meeting, and I would try to do something "for my soul." Nothing is written to assure me of the latter.

And the next week was more of the same. I noted in my journal that we had a "really productive" staff meeting, and the accreditation goals were formally passed. "I was informed that the union would overlook the oversize class that isn't one—what does that mean?—and do I care?" I added. The following day the part of Paper Mountain that related to accreditation was redundant and was heaved, and I noted mixed feelings about the clearing of my office. On the fifteenth of March the head of the union was in, "ranting" according to some, and informing our teachers that people with eight years seniority could be laid off. Apparently he told them to make paper airplanes of the district surveys. "Sort of a nice day, other than that," I wrote. "Kids boogied in the gym, sold donuts, etc…office is clear of excess trivia…this is the calm before a tempestuous last term, I think…must rest up this spring break!"

*Mar 22: After snow all spring break, new season's here! Worked outside, felt good, and now tomorrow…last gasp…hang in there kid!*

*Mar 23: Got out District surveys…put accreditation goals up and around…Bart playing hookey again…felt the most relaxed today I have ever felt about my job! Treasure each moment connecting with our kids. Sad: former colleague, special ed director, passed away. What a loss of integrity and humor—knew how to diffuse anxiety and stress in us: unique gift.*

*Mar 27: Randy crazy...there is an almost tender and nostalgic feeling among staff now...not much pettiness.*

*Mar 28: 7:30 meeting over budget proposals for cuts. Mostly very well done (further from classroom than anticipated), except for what will affect daytime custodians.*

*Mar 29: Queen Mother died, end of an era. Terrible fighting: Israelis surrounding Arafat's compound.*

April began, and our students seemed calmer. On the morning that all the accreditation documents were couriered off in their boxes, and just as some of us were admiring the calm appearance of the office and the clear pathway to my door, a new delivery of boxes arrived to take their place, cluttering the floor. They were the provincial FSA tests and surveys, and I am a little ashamed to say that I furtively kicked one of them. I had everything ready for the external team, however, and that was some consolation.

*Apr 4: Gloomy budget meeting. Went to hospital again, to discuss two kids. Calm in school.*

*Apr 9: Spent a long time with our librarian over her letter of request for placement next year. Looks now that elementary library may not be chopped altogether...if we don't get those extra French kids someone may have to go. Am weary. Our English grade 6's on t.v. expressed themselves beautifully regarding the Queen Mother's funeral...THINK I CAN HEAR FROGS!!! IS THAT A SIGN OF SPRING?*

*Apr 10: April zone meeting cancelled. Several little boys exposing themselves after CARE program. Vic dealing with the little dears.*

On the evening of the seventeenth of April, a colleague phoned. She had been at the Board office for a meeting on the day when people there had been let go as a result of budget cuts.

Our assistant superintendent, the director of special education, people connected to staffing, all curriculum staff, human resources staff, the whole of the print shop, one assistant superintendent's secretary and other CUPE employees were gone. Many others, apparently, were waiting to hear what their own position would be. These were people who had worked hard for our district, some for many years. It was difficult enough to imagine their knowledge gone, let alone their expertise. Worse yet, the layoffs seemed to have been done callously. Apparently they were to leave immediately, some supervised by their own secretaries as they boxed up their belongings.

Numbed down and in some shock, many principals attended the following evening's public meeting with the trustees. It was the last opportunity for those trustees to hear from employees and parents before making the rest of their cuts. The meeting was held in my old junior high school. Students brought their string instruments into the same auditorium where I had played violin in that school's orchestra over forty years before. I looked around the room that held memories of my adolescence: assemblies, concerts, dances and fund-raising activities. I had attended hundreds of meetings in this room. During my first year as principal, our newly appointed superintendent had stood at the door to shake hands with each of us, amazing everyone with her personal approach and ability to remember the name of each and every administrator attending. This evening, the large room filled with people from various district departments and schools. The trustees took their places along the front, microphones ready at tables in front of them. The few central office administrators remaining and in attendance were ashen-faced.

A prominent music teacher spoke eloquently about those programs and their benefits to students in other areas of learning. The head of Maintenance read a letter from a special needs child at Rowan. "Thank you for making the computer desk for me. It works great!" A custodian from an inner city school made a case for the importance of those workers; he had found hypodermic needles and used condoms in the children's sandpit. He pointed out that the custodian knew the building best, and was needed in emergencies like an earthquake. There were stories about children turning blue without adequate assistance time allotted to them. Alternative school representatives made their own pitches, one sobbing into the microphone. Another group brought knitting and I thought of the French Revolution.

Some parents emphasized what they saw as the need for the trustees to fight the government.

"I want YOU to protest those budget cuts! Refuse to do these cuts! You have been elected; you have been chosen, you need to draw the line in sand!"

"...fed up with the system facing cuts again...you're the trustees...you should have the moral authority NOT to consider cutting again...leave special ed funding alone—INCREASE it!"

"Stand at the top of the mountain: say NO!"

"Keep the trust—let the government know the cuts are too deep!"

"Let them come and find you! You don't come and be THEIR agent!"

There were eloquent quotes from the past, including "The test of the morality of a society is what it does for its children," and "An appeaser is one who feeds the crocodile hoping it will eat him last." The latter was apparently from Churchill; I did not hear who should have credit for the former.

Near the end a member of the VCPAC (district-wide parents group) told the trustees that she "appreciated the cuts to central administration." However, she believed they should have been done earlier and the process should have been more transparent. Sitting there, I had the distinct feeling that she might have enjoyed being part of the purge. "Flatten the hierarchy!" she continued. "Reconsider reconfiguration!" Her lips pursed. "School planning councils are coming," she warned everyone. How very sad, I thought. I began my career, like many of my colleagues, working to bring parents and staff members together, and now that sounds like a threat.

Judy Bertram Tomlinson

The microphone was passed from tired trustee to tired trustee. Our notorious one, the trustee who, a year before, had claimed that principals weren't leading and teachers weren't teaching, finally had his audience. He did his usual rail, ending with a general scolding. "They should have cut 50%, not 30% of central administration!" If possible, the few of those people left in that room were even paler as the meeting adjourned.

"Are you a member of the press?" I was asked, eagerly, by one someone in the audience as I put my pen and notebook away.

*Apr 19: All the accreditation pressure is gone—everything else is so awful. Had two French Immersion teachers in for meeting. One may have to go, but at least all the cards were on the table and they seemed to appreciate that.*

*Apr 21: Talked to a few of the district's "laid off" people. A couple of them very upset—one angry secretary said they were told to "supervise" their people packing up...district people still in shock, but it hasn't sunk in at the school level.*

*Apr 25: Our external Chair phoned from Saanich. Had heard news of all the people let go and was concerned about our morale. I'm past worrying about the accreditation, and know I can't make it right for all those people. Must talk to our counselor about her CARE program...second kid flashing his "privacy" publicly!*

On Sunday I watched a memorial service in honor of four Canadian soldiers killed by "friendly" fire in Afghanistan, and then went into school with the rest of the internal committee to meet the external team members who had come to do their accreditation assessment. They seemed a friendly group of people and put us at ease immediately.

The week the latter was to be doing its work in our school was the same week the staffing process was to be underway, a process that remains a time-consuming, full-time job in itself. I knew it would be an almost overwhelmingly busy time and reminded myself of the constant reminders from our staffing workshops: get plenty of sleep, eat well, exercise and keep breathing.

The first day began for me with a 7:30 meeting with our superintendent. In response to a colleague's inquiry, he said the district cuts had been done in such a manner due to legal counsel. There was no more discussion about it, despite what many of us were feeling, and the agenda was long. Meanwhile, at school, Vic introduced the external team to the staff. Very quickly, the team demonstrated to everyone that they were respectful of the staffing process that would be happening simultaneously, and they unobtrusively went about their examination of our school. That night I wrote, "the team seems to like our school a lot...Tomorrow is the last day of April and soon my new life will begin...let me be well enough to enjoy it! I will think profound thoughts. And very mundane ones, like keeping my gums healthy."

Thursday morning, May 1, the accreditation team met with all of us. *"Celebrate your successes!"* the staff and parents were told. They wholeheartedly praised all aspects of the school with speeches, poetry and a beautiful banner. I studied the faces of the staff I knew so well and hoped this affirmation of their work and their students' accomplishments was having a meaningful affect. And I looked, occasionally, at the door, half expecting our assistant superintendent to join us. She had been so interested in the progress of this school.

For the remainder of the year we were, with few exceptions, under a bell jar, basking in what had been accomplished and what was possible in the future. The umbilical cord that connected us to the district, to the province and to the outside world, to unions and associations, seemed not so much severed as unplugged. We still had our troubled children, of course. Gail finally put Randy in the courtyard one day only to discover that he was enjoying trying to start a picnic table on fire with a little magnifying glass. But the worst of student unrest had passed with the sunny weather, field trips and a happier staff. All the usual end-of-year activities went perfectly, and the staff hosted a spectacular event for me, attended by people from all the schools where I had worked.

"You're going to cry!" the retirement organizers had told me, over and over. "It will be impossible not to!" I was assured. But I did not cry, although many others said they did, affected by the wonderful musical presentations, speeches and slide show of my life. It was not that I had not been deeply affected. It was simply that seeing so many people I had enjoyed over thirty years was both extremely fun and distracting. Besides, I had spent years keeping my emotions in the neutral zone.

At the end of that week, grade six students from both the English and French tracks put on a display of their last term Social Studies projects. These were studies of countries around the world and included passports, food samples, well-displayed research, flags maps, diagrams of population densities, industries, tourism and all the other aspects these young people found interesting. The range in the quality of work and their pride in what they had displayed reflected the public system perfectly, I thought. I lost myself in the enjoyment of taste testing, reading and commenting upon aspects of their projects.

I had just complimented Sam, a boy with a disorder in the autistic spectrum, when he looked up into my eyes and spoke, both rare things for him to do. "Mrs. Bertram," he said. A bit startled, I looked into *his* eyes and realized that we had never made eye contact. "You've been a very good principal here, and we're going to miss you."

"Thanks, Sam," I whispered.

I propelled myself out of the gym, ignoring people calling to me, and dashed through the office, shutting the door onto my own space. I leaned against it and cried, hard. I cried because I could not make the school "shake" for all of them and I cried because what I had loved was over. I cried because I was glad to be finished and because I was tired.

The twenty-minute lunch period passed and I heard students dismiss for the outdoors. I had been left blessedly alone for all that time. There was a sound on the other side of the door that was still holding me upright, but no one knocked. Eventually, a note was passed under it, directly between my feet.

*Judy,*
*Candy and Marge have fallen in the recycle bin! Can't lift themselves*
*out. Pat's gone out to help. Thought you should know.*

I raced out to catch up with our patient and dependable custodian. He had been looking uncharacteristically tired himself, and the status of *his* position the following year was still up in the air as the budget talks dragged on. It was not over yet, this job of sorting out and supporting.

I looked up at the gentle giant who worked tirelessly for our school. "Tell me honestly, Pat. Did you think of simply shutting the lid and calling for pick up?"

"Sure did," he laughed.

Grinning, we walked out together into the dazzling exuberance of that final school day.

# AFTERWORD

Immediately after I retired, I had some moments of utter glee over my new freedom. I took up t'ai chi, did volunteer work and began piano lessons. I went to retirees' gatherings and travelled. I spoke at school events and wrote the first draft of this book while my work ethic's adrenalin was still pumping and my "magic propeller" was still whirling.

The sun did not always shine as gleefully as it does in the grade three student drawing, however. Two of my family required caregiving and subsequently passed away. Letting my emotional dust settle has been a long process, but finishing the work on *What's Shaking The School* has given me great satisfaction, and not in the least because of the need to reconnect with former friends.

Further, it appears that the reconfiguration of Victoria schools has been a successful venture. The more impractical initiatives of the Year 2000 thrust in education have gone by the way, while many fine educators have enriched their teaching strategies and deepened their understanding of individual learning styles. Students have learned to examine their own performances more critically, and while the necessary paper testing is very much in evidence, so,

Judy Bertram Tomlinson

too, are other ways to assess pupil outcomes. Teachers have more manageable class sizes than they did in 1990.

In spite of good feelings about those years in my chosen profession, and in spite of the lovely expanse of free time that now stretches intriguingly, I have finally realized that while school communities and trustees go through their painful, public grappling with the forces that shake our schools, "retirement" becomes a relative term.

# In Memoriam

Remembering Students, Parents, and Colleagues
No Longer With Us

Richard Ashworth
Ken Bertram
Lorenzo Cadoni
Ernie de Madeiros
Stephanie Doney
Vic Escudé
Mike Fisher
Milla Gubbles
Dr. Dan Koenig
Gwen Koenig
Linda Herrington
Linda Massé
Liam Matthews
Laurie Pimlott
Eric Thompson
Lois Tippett
Elaine Wilkinson
Laurie Wright